Narrating Infertility in Spain

Campos Ibéricos:
Bucknell Studies in Iberian Literatures and Cultures

Series editors:
Isabel Cuñado, Bucknell University
Jason McCloskey, Bucknell University

Campos Ibéricos is a series of monographs and edited volumes that focuses on the literary and cultural traditions of Spain in all of its rich historical, social, and linguistic diversity. The series provides a space for interdisciplinary and theoretical scholarship exploring the intersections of literature, culture, the arts, and media from medieval to contemporary Iberia. Studies on all authors, texts, and cultural phenomena are welcome and works on understudied writers and genres are specially sought.

Recent titles in the series:

Narrating Infertility in Spain
Catherine Bourland Ross

Making Modern Spain: Religion, Secularization, and Cultural Production
Azariah Alfante

Space, Drama, and Empire: Mapping the Past in Lope de Vega's Comedia
Javier Lorenzo

Dystopias of Infamy: Insult and Collective Identity in Early Modern Spain
Javier Irigoyen-García

Founders of the Future: The Science and Industry of Spanish Modernization
Óscar Iván Useche

Shipwreck in the Early Modern Hispanic World
Carrie L. Ruiz and Elena Rodríguez-Guridi, eds.

Calila: The Later Novels of Carmen Martín Gaite
Joan L. Brown

Indiscreet Fantasies: Iberian Queer Cinema
Andrés Lema-Hincapié and Conxita Domènech, eds.

Between Market and Myth: The Spanish Artist Novel in the Post-Transition, 1992–2014
Katie J. Vater

For more information about the series, please visit bucknelluniversitypress.org.

Narrating Infertility in Spain

Catherine Bourland Ross

Bucknell University Press
Lewisburg, Pennsylvania

978-1-68448-574-1 (cloth)
978-1-68448-573-4 (paper)
978-1-68448-575-8 (epub)

Cataloging-in-publication data is available from the Library of Congress.

LCCN 2025012673

A British Cataloging-in-Publication record for this book is available from the British Library.

♾ The paper used in this publication meets the requirements of the American National Standard for Information Sciences—Permanence of Paper for Printed Library Materials, ANSI Z39.48-1992.

bucknelluniversitypress.org

Distributed worldwide by Rutgers University Press

For anyone who has struggled with infertility

Contents

Preface

I discovered that I was infertile when I was twenty-eight. The doctor came into the room, told me something about a blood test that he had run, and stated that I would only be able to have children through assisted reproductive technologies. This information was a shock. Although I wanted children in the abstract, I had never considered that I could not have them if I decided to. All of my life, I had been encouraged to reach my goals, told that with hard work I could achieve whatever I wanted—a PhD, a tenure-track job, a long-term relationship with a man I love. I never considered life without children, but then everyone I knew had children and told me (or insinuated) that a woman without children was unfulfilled and incomplete. Being told that bearing children would be unlikely if not impossible—as well as very expensive—seemed like both a warning and a challenge. Surely I could do anything I put my mind to? There is much more to this story, years of expensive interventions, too much to tell here, but my own experiences caused me to think about infertility from an academic, not just personal, perspective.

Many years later, when I began to read works like the ones I analyze here, my heart rang with a connection to the struggles, comments, emotions, and worries that these female authors recounted. *Yes!* I thought. *That was me!* These challenges are not just mine but those of every woman who deals with infertility. I fell in love with the topic and began to read anything I could find about infertility. That distilled into this project. I hope that when you read it, you will discover something that speaks to you.

This book has been a long-term commitment. From the time my first book came out with Bucknell, I wondered if I would be inspired to write another. During the pandemic, I discovered the Asociación de Literatura y Cultura Española SXXI (ALCE SXXI), a group of scholars that focuses on literature and film from Spain in the twenty-first century. This group, and especially the subgroup of motherhood studies organized by Olga Albarrán Caselles and Marina Bettaglio, that I joined virtually for two years until we were able to meet in person served as a springboard for ideas about infertility that I had been thinking about and playing with. A special thanks to all those who listened to me, gave feedback, and suggested ideas and works that I should consider.

For me, writing is a group event. Thanks to all of my colleagues and friends who have worked with me, both virtually and in person, over the past five years while I have written, rewritten, questioned, and struggled with this work. A special thanks to Novia Pagone, Sandra Schumm, Emily Sydnor, Julia Barnes, Melissa Byrnes, Mary Grace Neville, and Laura Senio Blair—but there are so many more supportive colleagues and friends. A previous version of chapter 1 was published in the book *Refiguring Motherhood Beyond Biology* (2023) with a coauthor, Bailey Barlow. I would like to thank her for giving me permission to use a revised version of that chapter in this book. *Refiguring Motherhood Beyond Biology* is available in an open-access format.

This work wouldn't have happened without the financial support of Southwestern University. My sabbatical time allowed me to finish the book, and the university research funds allowed me access to libraries, books, and other resources. During much of the time I was writing this book, I was also supported by the Wilhelmina Cullen Robertson endowed position. I would also like to recognize the Sam Taylor Foundation for their generous support of my research and scholarship.

Thank you for picking up this book. I hope you find something useful in its pages.

Narrating Infertility in Spain

Introduction

In March 2023, Spanish TikTok star Julia Menú García gave birth to twin girls after fourteen years of trying to conceive. Menú currently has 24.8 million followers on TikTok, the highest following in Spain after the singer Rosalía. Although she started posting funny videos as a hobby, she began to post about her journey through fertility treatments, which increased the number of followers. She says that, for her, making these videos where she talked about the fertility treatments she received has been "como una terapia" [like therapy]. She continues, "El apoyo que he estado recibiendo me ha dado todavía más fuerza para luchar" [The support that I have been receiving has given me more strength to fight].[1] From showing the hormone injections her husband gave her, to the negative pregnancy test results, to the positive test results, to the loss of her first pregnancy, Menú has shared both the ups and downs of fertility treatments after being diagnosed as infertile. Her perspective on her pregnancy is one of disbelief: "Aún no me lo creo. Me miro al espejo y digo: '¿Esta barriga es mía?' He soñado tantísimo con este momento. Estoy orgullosa de mí, de no haber tirado nunca la toalla. Pero psicológicamente yo he sufrido mucho y eso no me deja disfrutar de la gestación como debería" [I still don't believe it. I look at myself in the mirror and say: 'This is my belly?' I have dreamed so much about this moment. I am proud of myself, of never having thrown in the towel. But psychologically I have suffered a lot, and that does not let me enjoy my pregnancy as I should].[2] Menú and others like her have begun to talk openly about their struggles with infertility, an issue that continues to become more visible in Spain. While this book does not specifically deal with social media and its impact, the example from TikTok serves to show how narratives about infertility in Spain have large audiences and wide viewership.

No one expects to be infertile. For most of our lives, since menstruation began, women have avoided or feared pregnancy. All of us were born from a woman who was, obviously, fertile, so we assume that when we choose to become pregnant, we will. And most of us hope that if we choose not to become pregnant, we have a choice in that too. According to feminist critics Loretta Ross and Rickie Solinger, when we speak of reproductive choice, what we should say is reproductive justice, which is made up of three main principles: "the right not to have a child," "the right to have a child," and "the right to parent children in safe and healthy environments."[3] Women should not only have the right to choose whether or not to have a child; they should also be able to support that child. All three of these principles seem simple and reasonable; however, patriarchal and neoliberal societal structures negate women's rights to seek reproductive justice.[4] Reproductive justice includes the right to access assisted reproductive technologies.

According to the International Federation of Obstetrics and Gynecology, infertility is the inability to conceive a child after a year or more of unprotected intercourse or the inability to carry a pregnancy to term. That definition, however, does not take into account the varying physical and emotional impacts of the inability to conceive or carry a child to term. Margarete Sandelowski, in her article "Failures of Volition: Female Agency and Infertility in Historical Perspective," delves further into the ways infertility can be interpreted:

> Infertility has been variously described as a syndrome of multiple origin, a consequence or manifestation of disease rather than a disease entity itself, a biological impairment, a psychosomatic disorder, a condition characterizing a couple rather than an individual, a failure to conform to cultural prescriptions to reproduce, and a failure to fulfill the personal desire to beget a child.[5]

Sandelowski's statement draws attention to the variability in how infertility can be defined to include those who do not follow the cultural imperative of reproduction, how infertility impacts those who experience it, and how society interprets this inability to reproduce. In her book *With Child in Mind: Studies of the Personal Encounter with Infertility*, Sandelowski also tells us that "the line between reproductive capacity and incapacity, between health and disease, and between normality and deviance has always been unclear in the matter of infertility, varying with individual reproductive choices, social circumstances, and cultural norms."[6] Within the cultural context of Spain, women have been expected to embrace motherhood. Women who cannot or choose not to have children feel pressured to reproduce in order to avoid judgment from those around them. These binarisms (mother versus nonmother, health versus disease, etc.) set the stage for the texts examined in this book.

When the Spanish birth rate dropped to its lowest point in 1998 at 1.1 births per woman, people began to question why Spaniards had so few children.[7] This long-term, very low fertility was accompanied by a boom in publishing books about motherhood. Marina Bettaglio tells us that since the early 2000s,

Spain has seen an "emergence of new narrative forms, ranging from blogs to diaries to comics, that express their authors' ambivalent feelings" about motherhood.[8] Bettaglio includes the writers Lucía Etxebarría, Care Santos, Isabel García-Zarza, Yolanda Sáenz de Tejada, Inmaculada Gilaberte, Gabriela Wiener, and Gemma Sesar in her list as examples of women who have published about motherhood.[9] As cultural products that reflect a moment in time, these books dealt with motherhood and the cultural norm of mothering. Very few, with the exception of Wiener, questioned why women become mothers or mentioned the prevalence of infertility in Spain. Even though women's struggles with motherhood are now more visible, so far there is not a book that studies infertility from the viewpoint of female-authored literature from Spain. *Narrating Infertility in Spain* examines the perspective of infertility, both primary infertility as defined above and secondary infertility and structural infertility, as narrated in female-authored texts published since 2008.[10] This book introduces and analyzes how women deal with their infertility through discussions of adoption, assisted reproduction, egg and sperm donation, and the decision not to become a mother due to economic or social instability.

The purpose of this book is to position the issue of women's fertility in Spain within the cultural context of the post-2008 Great Recession, using recent female-authored literature about women who are seeking ways to overcome their inability to have children or accept their decision not to have children. I examine five books, all published since 2008, that narrate different aspects of infertility: Silvia Nanclares's *Quién quiere ser madre* [Who Wants to Be a Mother] (2017), *Tengo los óvulos contados* [My Eggs Are Numbered] by Raquel Sánchez-Silva (2017), Samanta Villar's *Madre hay más que una* [There Is More Than One Mother] (2017), Laura Freixas's *A mí no me iba a pasar* [That Would Never Happen to Me] (2019), and *Maternofobia: Retrato de una generación enfrentada a la maternidad* [Maternophobia: Portrait of a Generation Faced with Maternity] by Diana López Varela (2019). All of the texts discussed are self-narratives, meaning that they are written in the first person, a style that is typical in motherhood narratives. Each of the authors presented here is also a vocal feminist activist either through journalism or television (Nanclares, Villar, and Sánchez-Silva) or through literary works and theater (Freixas and López Varela). These writers and their successes illustrate the importance of the topic of infertility at this time.

We need to examine a system of reproduction that both pressures people to have children and penalizes them for doing so. While the medicalization of infertility creates one framework for understanding childlessness, structural barriers to parenthood—whether economic, environmental, societal, or relational—create structural infertility, which is distinct from but intertwined with biological infertility. This concept bridges medical and sociocultural understandings of childlessness, acknowledging both the involuntary nature of biological infertility and the constrained "choices" that lead to postponed or foregone motherhood. Paradoxically, the same capitalist system that creates these barriers then profits from commercialized fertility treatments and international adoption, making access to parenthood increasingly dependent on purchasing power rather than genuine reproductive autonomy. In this book, I analyze this complex dynamic through four main concepts: the commodification of assisted reproduction, the grief and stigma attached to both involuntary and voluntary childlessness, the fallacy of reproductive choice under neoliberalism, and the class privilege inherent in international adoption. While this book considers diverse family formations, it does so with a limited heteronormative framework based on the texts I found and the scope of this study. This work also builds upon recent feminist movements, such as the 8M strikes in Spain, which have highlighted how reproductive labor and barriers to parenthood are deeply political issues requiring collective action.[11] Through this intersectional analysis, I demonstrate how patriarchal and capitalist structures have transformed reproduction from a matter of bodily autonomy into one of market access.

Spain faces a difficult situation in terms of fertility, with more women postponing pregnancy, which leads to fewer children, and more women choosing not to have children. According to the "Encuesta de fecundidad: Año 2018" [Survey of Fertility: Year 2018], 87 percent of women between the ages of eighteen and fifty-five would like to have children, and three out of four would like to have two or more children.[12] These statistics show that even though women might not be able to have children, the desire to be a mother still exists for the majority of women in Spain. According to Teresa Jurado, a sociologist at Universidad Nacional de Educación a Distancia [National University of Distance Education], Spain's low fertility rate is involuntary. She explains what this means:

> Hay gente que quiere y no puede. Y tenemos que conseguir que quien quiera, pueda. Sin meternos en su vida. En libertad. Respetando sus derechos. Sin pasos atrás. Hay que promover la fecundidad y, al mismo tiempo, la igualdad de género. Esa es la clave. Porque en el caso contrario, las mujeres asumen que, para ser libres, tienen que renunciar a su maternidad.[13]
>
> [There are people who want to but cannot. And we have to ensure that anyone who wants to can. Without getting into their life. Freely. Respecting their rights. No steps back. We must promote fertility and, at the same time, gender equality. That is the key. Because otherwise, women assume that in order to be free, they have to give up their maternity.]

The statistics show that Spain has what is called a lowest-low fertility rate (1.3 children per woman in 2018), which is substantially lower than the replacement rate (2.2 children per woman), and it has been this way for three decades.[14] After this much time of low fertility, Mariona Lozano, from the Centro de Estudios Demográficos [Center for Demographic Studies] (CED), explains that the problem "es responsabilidad de la sociedad, no de las mujeres" [is the responsibility of society, not of the women].[15] While it may be the case that low fertility rates need to be addressed at a societal level, the personal experiences of women who cannot become pregnant or who choose not to be mothers cannot be overlooked.

Paired with this low birth rate—which means that women, whatever the reason may be, have fewer or no children—Spain faces a distinct situation that some have termed "structural infertility," defined as low fertility due to social, political, and economic reasons.[16] For this reason, I discuss education, politics, and cultural norms, both current and historical, in order to situate the concept of infertility and its effect on the national birth rate. Spain is unlike other European countries in that it had a dictatorship for most of the twentieth century, followed by a rapid transition to democracy, which makes Spain's story of fertility worthy of study. From 1939 to 1975, Spain lived under the dictatorship of Francisco Franco, a general who, after the Spanish Civil War (1936–1939), came into power. Under his leadership, Spain was forced to return to a more traditional style of life in contrast to the liberal changes that defined the Second Republic (1931–1936), previous to Franco's rule.[17] For the purpose of this introduction, I show how the Franco regime (1939–1975), the transition to democracy, and the more recent social, political, and economic events have impacted women's fertility in Spain. Although the legacy of the Franco period continues to impact Spain today, most of the authors analyzed here were born after Franco's death in 1975. However, three aspects of the Franco dictatorship and his National Catholic ideology stand out for their lasting repercussions on women: the pronatalist political policies implemented by the Franco government, the support of the Catholic Church, and the propaganda infused into the educational system.

The Franco regime, like other European authoritarian regimes such as those found in Italy and Germany, implemented pronatalist policies to increase the autochthonous population decimated by war. Historian Pilar Folguera, in her article "El franquismo: El retorno a las esfera privada (1939–1975)" [Francoism: The Return to the Private Sphere (1939–1975)], enumerates some of these policies: "Aumento de la nupcialidad, aumento de los matrimonios jóvenes, lucha contra la esterilidad voluntaria y lucha contra el aborto criminal" [Increase in marriage, increase in the marriage of young people, fight against voluntary infertility, and fight against criminal abortion].[18] On the one hand, these strategies worked to realize new cultural norms, but there was also the need to support families if women were to have multiple children. From the perspective of the government, large families were desired. Aurora Morcillo states that "women's national duty at this juncture [the 1940s] was to produce as many children as possible for the fatherland. The female political persona was defined by biological destiny: motherhood."[19] The Ley del 18 julio de 1938 [Law of 18 July 1938], first applied to nationalist areas during the Spanish Civil War, established a nationwide family subsidy in 1939 to provide "un auxilio económico en relación con el número de hijos o asimilados a ellos que tengan a su cargo y vivan en su hogar" [economic aid related to the number of children or dependents that are under their charge or live in their home].[20] The emphasis here is on women and their position within the family: Women serve as procreators, producing children whom they then care for while the father works outside the home to support them financially. As an addition to the above law, there was the Order of 27 December 1938, which affirms that the purpose of the law is to ensure that "la mujer dedique su atención al hogar y se separe de los puestos de trabajo" [women dedicate themselves to the home and separate themselves from jobs].[21] A woman, at that time, was expected only to work inside the home taking care of multiple children as well as her husband, not to seek remunerated work outside of the home. As Morcillo explains, "In the new Francoist Spain, women's bodies were turned into the vessels needed in national reconstruction. Women were given a national purpose; as mothers, they would have to devote themselves to their natural task, procreate for the patria in body and soul."[22] This domestic structure, while not unusual in the time period, was reinforced by the dictates of the Catholic Church, which supported the Franco regime.

The Catholic Church during this time helped reinforce Franco's pronatalist policies, as Catholic doctrine concurred with the beliefs of the regime. More than concurring, the church actively supported the idea of an "estado totalitario cristiano" [totalitarian Christian state].[23] The church echoed the concept of the need for women to bear children and stay home with them, suggesting that this is the natural order of the family, with the husband as "el bastón de mando" [the baton, or ultimate authority] and the wife as "el cetro del amor" [the scepter of love].[24] The church also imparted its ideals for both men and women as part of a marriage. Morcillo shows how these gendered concepts date back centuries, summarizing Benito Jerónimo Feijóo y Montenegro's 1726 treatise *Defensa de la mujer* [Defense of the Woman], in which he details that "male qualities were robustness, perseverance, and prudence, and female qualities beauty, docility, and simplicity."[25] For these reasons, matrimony must be made up of both a man and a woman who must perform their God-given roles within the marriage. Of course, procreation was a significant issue for the church as well. Along with the idea that sexual intercourse was acceptable only for its procreating possibilities, the church's stance on birth control kept women from being able to limit pregnancies. The Comisión Episcopal de Ortodoxia y Moralidad [Episcopal Commission of Orthodoxy and Morality], in their "Normas de decencia cristiana" [Norms of Christian decency], states,

> La fecundidad es una de las glorias del matrimonio cristiano, que lo orienta hacia su fin principal y hace a los esposos merecer bien de Dios y de la Patria. El anticoncepcionismo, de cualquier forma que sea, es un pecado grave. El

> Estado debe apoyar con todo su poder la fecundidad del matrimonio y reprimir cualquier propaganda contra ella.[26]

> [Fertility is one of the glories of a Christian marriage, which orients it toward its ultimate goal and lets the spouses well deserve the good of God and Country. Anticonceptionism, in any form it may take, is a serious sin. The State should support with all its power the fertility of a marriage and suppress all propaganda against it.]

Both the state and the church exalted the primacy of children in marriage. Children were seen as a gift from God, and the state supported that outcome both through its policies (antiabortion, anti–birth control) and through its messaging. Franco rewarded those who followed his orders through his Premios Nacionales de Natalidad [National Natality Prizes] (see figure 1). These awards were granted yearly to families who had the most children born, families who had the most living children, and families who had the most children with them in their home. Using its society-wide influence, the church supported the Franco regime's desire to encourage women to have multiple children. Along with the exhortation to procreate for God and country, the Catholic Church also increased its participation in the Spanish educational system.

To make sure these pronatalist propagandistic messages impacted the entire population of Spain, the church and the state worked together to inculcate citizens through the educational system. One of the major changes brought about by the Franco dictatorship was the implementation of new state-sponsored required elementary education, whose curriculum was guided by the Catholic Church. Morcillo offers that, in the new curriculum prescribed by the Law of Secondary Education of 1953, "the study of domestic matters was essential to women's proper training as part of their patriotic duty to the fatherland. Girls' instruction included a synthesis of the political indoctrination, physical education, and home economics [enseñanzas del hogar]."[27] Young girls were trained in family and social norms, physical education, sewing, and music and then later added cooking, home economics, and infant care.[28] However, these ideals needed to be instilled in all women, no matter their age. Thus began the Sección Femenina [Women's Section] (SF), the Falangist women's educational system. Founded by Pilar Primo de Rivera in 1934, the SF was a political organization for women that worked to embed a "traditionalist image of the 'Spanish Woman'—a loving wife whose life was sacrifice-bound, a devout Catholic."[29] The principal objective of the SF was to train women "to become perfect wives and mothers through the six-month mandatory Social Service to the state."[30] From its organization to the classes taught, its purpose was to encourage women to subordinate themselves to the requirements of marriage and motherhood, "siempre en una posición de

Figure 1. Oriol de Riba and his wife pose with their sixteen children after receiving the first national prize for natality, Barcelona, 1968. EFE/rba.

subordinación al varón y al esposo" [always in a position of subordination to the man and husband].[31] These teachings reinforced the lessons learned from the pulpit as well as the laws in place to keep women pregnant and at home. While there are various positive aspects of the SF, such as "la creación de bibliotecas, de cátedras ambulantes y la recuperación de danzas populares" [the creation of libraries and traveling schools and the recuperation of local dances], the SF also intended to "reforzar la concepción patriarcal y jerárquica de la familia y garantizar la aplicación de la política natalista del régimen" [reinforce the patriarchal and hierarchical concept of the family and guarantee the application of the natalist policies of the regime].[32] The organization lasted until 1977, two years after the death of Franco. While the number of women indoctrinated by these teachings is unknown, it is likely that generations of Spanish women lived and learned under these conditions.[33] It was only in the 1960s, when Franco's grip on Spain lessened and the nation began to reenter international politics, that these messages and concepts began to change.

The 1960s in Spain marked a period of dramatic change both politically and culturally. While Spaniards still lived under an authoritarian dictator, Franco understood the importance of modernizing, and he and his advisers began to make changes, such as the implementation of the Ley de Derechos Políticos,

Profesionales y Laborales de la mujer 22 julio de 1961 [Law of Women's Political, Professional, and Labor Rights 22 July 1961], which recognized the same rights for women and men with the exception of the armed forces.[34] While this law marked the beginning of change for women, the stipulation that required women to get permission from their husbands to work (and allowed the husband to be paid for his wife's work) stayed in place until it was revoked by the Ley de Relaciones Laborales [Law of Labor Relations] in 1976.[35] The liberalization of the Catholic Church from the Second Vatican Council allowed for new interpretations of women and their position in society.[36] These social changes coincide with a decrease in birth rate during these years, one that continues to be low.[37] Morcillo notes that although the birth control pill did not become legal in Spain until 1978, it arrived in Spain in 1963 and began to make an impact on the birth rate.[38] According to a 1974 study by the Fundación Fomento de Estudios Sociales y Sociología Aplicada [Foundation for the Promotion of Applied Social and Sociological Studies] (FOESSA) in Spain, the use of the birth control pill in Spain was already widespread before its legalization.[39] These nods toward modernization during Franco's regime became profound differences in post-Franco Spanish society.

In post-Franco Spain, change came quickly. During the early years of the transition to democracy, 1975–1982, politicians worked to write a new constitution and embark on a journey toward European integration.[40] Teresa Vilarós, in her book *El mono del desencanto: Una crítica cultural de la transición española (1973–1993)* [The Monkey of Disenchantment: A Cultural Critique of the Spanish Transition (1973–1993)], considers that Spain finished its transition after the signing of the Maastricht treaty in 1993, which officially formed the foundation of the European Union.[41] Along with the transition to democracy and its entrance into a new European political and economic system, Spain legalized birth control in 1978, divorce in 1981, and abortion in 1985, making way for women to control their own reproductive choices. These new freedoms allowed women to control natality and, according to Elena Vásquez, caused a rapid drop in birth rate, from 2.8 in 1975 to 1.15 in 1995.[42]

Spain is not alone in its declining birth rate, however. A sustained decline has been a common trend across countries in the European Union since the 1960s. Fertility statistics provided by Eurostat show that in 2022, the total fertility rate for Europe was 1.46 live births per woman, with France being the highest at 1.79, Malta the lowest at 1.08, and Spain the second lowest at 1.16.[43] Overall, 3.88 million children were born in Europe in 2022, the lowest number since 1961 (figure 2). Spain, Malta, and Italy have historically identified as primarily Catholic countries, a similarity that makes their low fertility rates notable. Spain's political and economic changes since 2008 differentiate it from other European countries because of Spain's slow movement toward substantive maternity and paternity leave policies.[44] Spain, though, stands out for the difference between how many

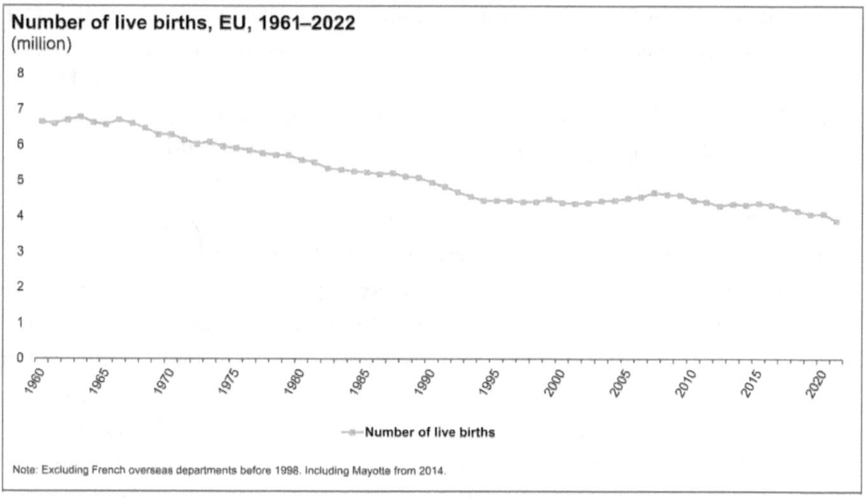

Figure 2. Number of live births in the European Union, 1961–2022. Eurostat.

children women actually have and how many children they would like to have. In an article in *El País*, Teresa Castro states, "El retraso es una tendencia en toda Europa. La diferencia es que en otros países el lapso entre el primer y el segundo hijo es menor. Nosotros tardamos más en llegar al segundo, si es que se llega" [Delay is a trend throughout Europe. The difference is that in other countries, the period between the first and second child is shorter. It takes us longer to reach the second, if it is reached at all].[45] Another article claims that both men and women in Spain would like to have more children, with 2.52 being the number of children desired.[46] These numbers suggest that low fertility rates do not correspond to a lesser identification between women and motherhood; rather, in general, the majority of women in Spain continue to desire motherhood even if structural barriers exist to prohibit them from achieving that desire. While high fertility rates might suggest a stronger association between women and motherhood, this correlation is not always true, since multiple other factors influence fertility rates.

In addition to following European fertility trends, in 1992, Spain became culturally integrated into European society, with the 1992 Olympics celebrated in Barcelona, Madrid recognized as the European Capital of Culture, and the World Fair held in Seville.[47] While the country gained recognition as a stable European democracy, the people living in Spain were still less than twenty years from the death of Franco. Vilarós describes the time period of the early 1990s as marked by "un exceso económico y libidinal" [an economic and libidinal excess] filled with "incertidumbre económica" [economic uncertainty].[48] During this same period, women's access to education soared. From the 1990s to today, "women have overtaken men in educational attainment," a fact that impacts gender relations and marriage patterns.[49] When discussing women's fertility in Spain, Josune Aguinaga adds that women's education impacts fertility, stating, "El salto con relación a la educación es mucho más importante que ninguno de los otros cambios comentados" [The jump related to education is much more important than any of the other changes mentioned].[50] Aguinaga's research shows that "la fecundidad analizada juntamente con el trabajo remunerado de la mujer muestra fuertes relaciones" [fertility analyzed together with women's remunerated work shows a strong relationship].[51] Factors such as education, economic status, and access to birth control clearly affect the way women perceive fertility.

The economic pressures on families in Spain only continued to increase during the first decade of the twenty-first century. The Great Recession, which struck the world's financial systems in 2008, caused the 2008–2014 Spanish financial crisis.[52] But even before the economic crisis that saw 27 percent of Spain facing unemployment, women viewed maternity as causing inequality.[53] Vásquez recounts that the women interviewed for her study acknowledged that motherhood would heighten their experience of inequality even while these same women considered motherhood "insustituible" [irreplaceable].[54] Vásquez claims that "de hecho, quizás el elemento que explique las bajas tasas de fecundidad en España sea justamente esta incoherencia: la igualdad laboral y educativa no se ha correspondido con un incremento de la igualdad en la esfera doméstica" [in fact, perhaps the element that explains the low rates of fertility in Spain is exactly this incoherence: Educational and labor equality have not corresponded to an increase in equality in the domestic sphere].[55] This inequality between the sexes regarding care work strikes a chord with women across the country who share that they spend more time on household chores than men. According to a 2015 survey from the Instituto Nacional de Estadística, 31 percent of women spend three or more hours a day cooking and cleaning, while only 11 percent of men do the same.[56] This invisible and unpaid work is one cause of women's decision not to have children. In her book *Neoliberalismo sexual: El mito de la libre elección* [Sexual Neoliberalism: The Myth of Free Choice], Ana de Miguel explains that "las decisiones que toman las mujeres sobre sus vidas personales, como cargar con las responsabilidades domésticas, no son fruto de su libre elección y de sus negociaciones como pareja sino de un sistema de poder, es decir, político, que no les deja más opción" [the decisions that women make about their personal lives, like taking on domestic responsibilities, are not the fruit of free will or of negotiations with their partner but rather a system of power, which is to say, political, that does not allow them any option].[57] The argument that women choose whether or not to take care of the house, care for children, or care for elderly relatives is not valid, argues de Miguel, since there is no choice in these matters. These gendered roles of women as caretakers date back to the indoctrination of women through the SF during Franco. These familial responsibilities inordinately continue to fall to women as part of their invisible, unpaid, gendered labor.

The issue of the invisibilization of care work is a principal concern for Spanish feminist politicians and thinkers alike. Marina Garcés, in her article "Comprensión y reparación: Por una filosofía del cuidado y el daño" [Understanding and Reparation: For a Philosophy of Care and Harm], defines care work as "todos aquellos trabajos asociados con la reproducción social" [all of those jobs associated with social reproduction], especially those chores that have been relegated to the domestic environment and are, for the most part, unpaid and unrecognized.[58] In *Tiempo de cuidados* [Time for Caring], Victoria Camps explains the importance of care work:

> Cuidar implica desplegar una serie de actitudes que van más allá de realizar unas tareas concretas de vigilancia, asistencia, ayuda o control; el cuidado implica afecto, acompañamiento, cercanía, respeto, empatía con la persona a la que hay que cuidar. Una relación que debe ocultar la asimetría que por definición la constituye.[59]
>
> [Caring involves displaying a series of attitudes that go beyond carrying out specific tasks of surveillance, assistance, help, or control; care implies affection, accompaniment, closeness, respect, empathy with the person who must be cared for. A relationship that must hide the asymmetry that by definition constitutes it.]

Camps points out that care work is both labor and an affective responsibility. Even as she claims that women are not genetically specifically gifted as carers, she shows that women, in general, bear the responsibility of this work.[60]

In a special issue of the political magazine *Viento sur* (South Wind) from February 2018 that focused on the feminist economics of care work, Sandra Ezquerra calls for change. Her position asks for the recognition of the work women do inside the home and shows how these extra tasks cause discrimination in the workforce. By identifying care work as essentially feminine, "se traduce en un aumento de la carga global del trabajo de las mujeres—se incorporan en el mercado laboral y a la vez continúan siendo responsables del trabajo del hogar y del cuidado—, en una reproducción de la división sexual del trabajo existente" [it translates into an increase of the global load of work for women—they are incorporated into the workforce and at the same time continue to be responsible for house work and care work—in a reproduction of the existing sexual division of labor].[61] As an example of the impact of care work on women, the author tells us that the salary gap for women in Catalonia is 26 percent.[62] Ezquerra uses her voice to explain one aspect of why women may not have children in Spain: the inequality between men and women in the domestic sphere. But Patricia Merino Murga, in her article in *Viento sur*, warns us that this is not the only reason for women to be hesitant to become mothers: "No es la brecha salarial lo que explica la bajísima fertilidad de las españolas, ni tampoco la escasez de los permisos para padres. Lo que hace inviable la procreación en España es un modelo de conciliación negador de la maternidad" [It is not the salary gap that explains the low fertility of Spanish women, nor is it the scarcity of parental leave. What makes procreation unviable in Spain is a conciliation model that denies maternity].[63] Merino Murga makes the point that women struggle with issues such as "negación de la biología y los deseos, renuncia, aplazamiento y comercialización de la maternidad, problemas de fertilidad" [denial of biology and desires, resignation, delay and commercialization of motherhood, fertility problems] along with political and economic policies that make maternity complicated.[64] Neither the work of mothering nor the lived experience of motherhood can be simply defined or improved.

Motherhood has long been equated with womanhood, a woman's natural job in the world, predating Franco's support of this concept. However, as women have become increasingly involved in the workplace, motherhood has changed. In her book *Maternidad, igualdad y fraternidad: Las madres como sujeto político en las sociedades poslaborales* [Motherhood, Equality and Fraternity: Mothers as Political Subjects in Postlabor Societies], Patricia Merino Murga explores the changes facing Spanish mothers in the twenty-first century. Along with her previous comments about the lack of balance between work life and home life, Merino Murga points out that patriarchal motherhood does not allow women to enjoy being mothers. She states that "la maternidad priva efectivamente a las madres de la libertad, entendida esta como la capacidad de disponer de una misma y del tiempo de vida propio. La disyuntiva: o libertad o maternidad" [maternity indeed deprives mothers of freedom, being understood as the capacity to have time for oneself and one's own life. The dilemma: freedom or motherhood].[65] While Merino Murga does not have an answer to this quandary, she presents one option: "O bien transformar la sociedad para que la maternidad deje de ser un hándicap, o profundizar en su invisibilización, expropiación e instrumentalización" [Either transform society so that maternity is no longer a handicap or dig deeply into its invisibilization, expropriation, and instrumentalization].[66] In order for maternity to be more appealing to women, the work of mothering must be supported, recognized, shared, and remunerated at not only a societal level but also an interpersonal level.

While economic and political policies affect fertility, gender equality can also play a major role in when or if women decide to have children. The European Institute for Gender Equality uses a tool to measure the progress of gender equality that "gives more visibility to areas that need improvement and ultimately supports policy makers to design more effective gender equality measures." When we compare the gender equality index in Spain with other low birth rate countries such as Malta and Italy, we see that Spain has one of the highest scores, at 76.4—just under Sweden, the Netherlands, and Denmark—while Italy earns 68.2 and Malta 67.8, both falling below the EU average of 70.2 (see figure 3). It would seem, then, that Spain would

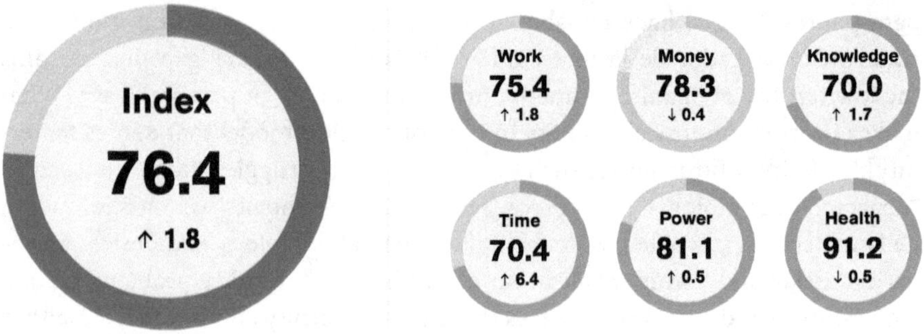

Figure 3. Gender Equality Index results for Spain, 2023. © European Institute for Gender Equality.

provide a more comfortable and equitable space for women to have children. However, when we look at the results provided by the tool, women are 20 percent "more likely to do housework or cook every day, compared to men" and earn 30 percent less than men. In addition, 50 percent of women in Spain have experienced sexual harassment.[67] Therefore, while Spain's gender equality situation continues to improve based on the indices measured by the European Union, women still experience gender-based setbacks in both social and economic situations.

These statistics intimate changing societal norms; however, the item of discussion, women's low fertility rate, continues, which affects society at all levels and therefore is of utmost importance. Spain's increase in immigration, especially from 2000 to 2007, affected the overall birth rate slightly, as "immigrants show higher levels of fertility than the native-born"; however, "fertility among immigrants is also low and seems to rapidly converge with the native-born level."[68] While these statistics illustrate that Spain experiences low numbers of babies born across the board, "statistics for 2011 [. . .] indicate that nearly one out of four newborns in Spain (23.1%) had at least one foreign-born parent."[69] Women born and raised in Spain still confront the specter of Franco's gender policies. Esther Vivas, in her book *Mamá desobediente* [Disobedient Mom], points this out when she mentions the changes between generations of women in Spain: "Somos hijas de una generación que luchó, y mucho, por hacer de la maternidad una elección; nosotras creíamos que teníamos la batalla ganada, pero no éramos conscientes de los condicionantes sociales, económicos y ambientales que nos lo dificultarían" [We are daughters of a generation that fought, a lot, to make maternity a choice; we women believed that we had won the battle, but we were not aware of the social, economic, and environmental conditions that would make it difficult for us].[70] She recognizes the need for change in how maternity is lived in Spain and expands her perspective to include all parents, showing that motherhood can be defined as "el ejercicio de cuidar independientemente de que lo haga la madre o el padre; un trabajo de cuidados imprescindible para el sostén y la reproducción de la vida, pero menospreciado en una sociedad capitalista, mercantilizada e individualista como la actual" [the exercise of caring regardless of whether it is done by a mother or a father; essential care work for the support and the reproduction of life, but undervalued in a capitalistic, commercialized, and individualistic society like ours].[71] What does this mean for the younger generation of women who are deciding whether or not they want to (or can afford to) become mothers? Vivas tells us that there are young Spanish women who see motherhood not as "un destino ineludible, que se replantean el significado de la maternidad en clave emancipadora y de experiencia que merece la pena ser vivida" [an unavoidable destiny; they reevaluate the meaning of motherhood as an emancipatory key and an experience worth living].[72] However, for many Spanish women, maternity no longer seems accessible.

Children are a long-term investment. Pregnancy lasts nine months, but having a child lasts a lifetime. Women in Spain find it "difficult or impossible to arrive at the level of stability that they feel is necessary for motherhood" for a long list of reasons: job inequality, lack of affordable housing, and lack of public policies to support families and mothers, just to name a few. These barriers make up what Bruna Álvarez and Diana Marre term *structural infertility*.[73] With a delay in childbearing due to structural infertility, along with the question of the burden of childcare, the concern arises: When women are ready to have children, will they be able to? *El vientre vacío* [The Empty Womb] by Noemí López Trujillo addresses that question. Through interviews with friends, posts on social media, and quotes from other books and newspaper articles, López Trujillo explores the situation of fertility in Spain from the perspective of a thirty-year-old Spaniard who embodies the problems of her generation: "Sin casa, sin curro, sin pensión, sin miedo" [No home, no work, no retirement, no fear].[74] She adds, "Y sin hijos" [And no children].[75] From her perspective, and that of those she cites in her book, delaying childbearing is not only an economic issue, though that is a major problem, but also an issue of housing and long-term work contracts (not just freelance work), not to mention the difficulty of maintaining a committed relationship. Her fear is that once she is in a situation where she wants to become a mother, she will not be able to.[76]

López Trujillo expounds upon the many reasons women in Spain wait to have children or decide not to have children at all. She tells multiple stories of friends who try to get pregnant and cannot, friends who are waiting, those who have spent thousands of euros on assisted reproduction technology (ART), those who realize that they will never be in an economic situation where having children is viable—the list goes on. From her social media platforms, she is plagued by ads for freezing her eggs or for in vitro fertilization (IVF). She mentions one ad that particularly stands out to her from the IVI Clinic that says, "Tu bebé recién nacido o te devolvemos el dinero" [Your newborn baby or we refund your money].[77] This slogan encompasses the capitalistic perspective on childbearing, the idea that anything can be monetized, which is how de Miguel defines the concept of sexual neoliberalism.[78] López Trujillo states that "la inacción del Estado nos ha empujado no solo a comprar el tiempo de descuento como una inversión en bolsa donde cada minuto se revaloriza porque a cada minuto tus óvulos pierdan calidad" [the inaction of the state has pushed us to buy discounted time as a stock market investment where every minute is worth more because every minute, your eggs lose quality].[79] The connection between women's fertility and the state calls to mind the statement by Silvia Federici, who during a tour for her 2014 book *Revolución en punto cero* [*Revolution at Point Zero*] claims that "el cuerpo de la mujer es la última frontera del capitalismo. Quieren conquistar el cuerpo de la mujer porque el capitalismo depende de él" [women's bodies are the last frontier of capitalism. They want to conquer women's bodies because capitalism depends on them] to produce workers.[80] The uterus, according to Federici, is seen as a factory for making workers.[81] De Miguel claims that Spain's economic and social situation calls for an "auténtica huelga de natalidad" [authentic strike on natality].[82] López Trujillo's question is, What happens when women do not or cannot procreate? She explores the answer of selling women the possibility of motherhood through ART.

Spain has, from the U.S. perspective, a generous state-sponsored family leave (twenty paid weeks) and state-supported fertility treatments for women under forty who are diagnosed with fertility problems.[83] Women can access up to three rounds of IVF and four rounds of artificial insemination through the state-sponsored medical system. While Spanish socialized medicine does provide women under forty with access to fertility care, these public clinics generally have long waitlists, typically anywhere from eighteen to twenty-four months.[84] Therefore, many Spaniards opt to use private clinics and pay out of pocket for their fertility treatments. There are 307 fertility clinics in Spain. As a comparison, the United States (with a population almost eight times that of Spain) has approximately 450 fertility clinics.[85] Of these 307 Spanish clinics, 96 are public and only treat women under forty years of age. The other 211 clinics are private, where a round of IVF costs about €3,500– €5,500 plus the price of prescription drugs, which can cost up to €1,000 more.[86] The option of using ART to attain a pregnancy appears in the first four novels analyzed in this book. All of the novels include stories about women's interactions with the medical system in Spain, illustrating that health care represents yet another institutional force that can either hinder or support women who are infertile.

Spain's profound social changes since the end of the dictatorship in 1975 have affected women's fertility in several ways. First, as we have seen, expanded legal rights to abortion, birth control, and divorce allowed women to take control of their fertility quickly since the 1970s. In 2005, Spain became the third country in the world to legalize homosexual marriages, also allowing gay couples to adopt.[87] In 2015, Spain began to allow married lesbian couples to include both names on a child's birth certificate.[88] These deep changes in Spanish society and lifestyle mirror how much Spain has changed since the transition to democracy. Fewer Spaniards choose to get married, corresponding perhaps to a lack of identification with a faith practice, since recent studies (2023) show that only 36.4 percent of young Spaniards between the ages of eighteen and thirty-four consider themselves as either practicing or nonpracticing Catholics, a steep decline since 1998.[89] In 2023, 49 percent of births occurred outside of marriage in Spain, a rate much higher than its European counterparts.[90] This increase in nontraditional families, mono-parental families, and delay in childbearing, along with the economic factors discussed earlier, indicate that the state of fertility in Spain merits closer investigation.

Narrating Infertility in Spain begins the conversation about how cultural products of the time period reflect these changes in fertility. Each of the works analyzed here approaches infertility in Spain from a different perspective. All published since 2008, these books have in common a female narrator, a realistic plotline, and an autobiographical (though at times fictional) tone. Each chapter of this book analyzes one work through a different critical lens, which allows the reader to understand various ways of interpreting and understanding infertility. In chapter 1, "Infertility as Business," Silvia Nanclares's novel *Quién quiere ser madre* introduces us to the precarity of work in Spain and its effect on fertility and access to fertility treatments. In chapter 2, "Infertility as Stigma," I turn to *Tengo los óvulos contados* by Raquel Sánchez-Silva, whose fictional story of a doctor in a fertility clinic covers issues from egg donation, to sperm donation, to unexpected pregnancies, to the intricacies of the Spanish system of ART. In chapter 3, "Infertility as Crisis," I look at Samanta Villar's book *Madre hay más que una* as she chronicles her struggle with infertility and her use of donor eggs to achieve her pregnancy. Chapter 4, "Infertility as Classist," analyzes *A mí no me iba a pasar* by Laura Freixas and the option of international adoption in order to fulfill the desire to have children. Chapter 5, "Infertility as Choice," focuses on the book *Maternofobia* by Diana López Varela, who faces structural infertility and narrates her decision to have an abortion and be child-free.

In her 2017 novel *Quién quiere ser madre*, Silvia Nanclares narrates the story of Silvia, a forty-year-old woman who uses various assisted reproduction methods to try to attain a pregnancy. The novel both elucidates Spain's system in support of fertility treatments as well as questions the glorification of biological motherhood. In her more recent articles on the theme, Nanclares wonders if these reproductive techniques are a betrayal of feminism. By commercializing the female body, by selling products in order to fulfill her maternal desire, are we not continuing to reinforce gendered norms of motherhood and to praise the maternal body as the most womanly? As a writer, editor, and cultural activist, Nanclares's perspective on infertility looks collectively at women, both mothers and child-free women, in order to better understand the social impact of infertility. Nanclares questions the commercialization of motherhood, bringing the subject of the maternal from personal to political. Using the feminist concept of embodiment, chapter 1 examines how Nanclares represents the infertile body as a dysfunctional body and how the fertility industry in Spain preys on women's perceptions of the pregnant body as normal and the nonpregnant body as deviant. As women continue to search for motherhood with ever more invasive procedures, the politically supported medicalization of the female body creates a loss of a sense of self and a lack of coherence regarding what it means to be a woman.

Chapter 2 focuses on the 2017 novel by author Raquel Sánchez-Silva, *Tengo los óvulos contados*. Her book tells the story of Dr. Miranda Ortega, a gynecologist who specializes in assisted reproduction in Spain. Through the stories of her patients, the doctor recounts her experiences of treating infertility in Spain, expanding on the psychological, economic, and social impacts of the quest to become pregnant. The author states that the purpose of this novel is to send "un mensaje claro que rompa el tabú social que rodea la reproducción asistida y, además, ayude a muchas mujeres y hombres a tomar decisiones basadas en una información rigurosa y no en los rumores" [a clear message that breaks the social taboo that surrounds assisted reproduction and also helps many women and men make a decision based on rigorous information and not on rumors].[91] In this chapter, I discuss the social stigma of infertility and how Sánchez-Silva's novel creates a space in which to debate the stigmatization of childlessness and the commodification of the assisted reproduction market in Spain.

Samanta Villar, a journalist, wrote her book *Madre hay más que una* (2017) about her experience with fertility treatments and her eventual pregnancy with twins through egg donation. After becoming pregnant, she filmed the experience of her pregnancy and the birth of her children on the television program *9 meses con Samanta* [9 Months with Samanta]. Both the book and the program not only cover her own experience with fertility treatments but also bring in other aspects of family life, such as polyamorous families, sperm donation, and surrogacy. Within the framework of assisted reproduction, chapter 3 explores so-called donation and the commercialization of women's bodies (both donors and recipients). Drawing on Villar's book as one perspective of this concept, I examine various feminist standpoints on gamete donation and analyze how these reproductive services are marketed to women who want to become pregnant.

Chapter 4 analyzes *A mí no me iba a pasar* and the issue of international adoption. The chapter investigates this practice as an alternative means of family formation. In her autobiography, Laura Freixas recounts her experience of bringing a son born in Russia into her family. Employing the work of theorists on international adoption, this chapter uses Freixas's narrative to examine the concept of transnational adoption as rescue versus kidnapping. Freixas sees her adoptive process as both harrowing and joyful, complicating the theoretical perspective analyzed. However, the classist nature of international child placement, based on financial costs and the expertise needed to navigate the system, stands out in her account.

Chapter 5 explores the book *Maternofobia: Retrato de una generación enfrentada a la maternidad*, a nonfiction work by journalist and scriptwriter Diana López Varela. The author presents the difficulties of a life without children, and I rely on the term *structural infertility* to expand the definition of infertility to include nonbiological infertility. In her discussion of the social pressures to become a mother, of the marketing of reproductive technology, and of the essentialist idea of woman = mother, López Varela breaks the silence about women who decide not to become mothers due to economic, political, romantic, and timing-based factors. Although the patriarchal structure of gender roles in Spain reinforces the primacy of motherhood for women, López Varela works to deconstruct the binary of woman/mother and find new ways to define what it means to be a woman, even as she faces backlash for her decision. I examine the concept of choice as it connects to reproductive decision-making to analyze how this text represents the unattainability of pregnancy under structural infertility.

The book concludes by suggesting that motherhood in Spain is in crisis. Questions of economic inequality, access to paid systems of medicine, and privilege connect the works analyzed in this book. From the disproportionate number of women who delay childbearing, to the number of births using ART, to Spain's high number of adopted children, women have to embody and live their lives as women and mothers differently—or not at all. As the conclusion illustrates, some women see their inability to have children as structural, not based on choice. Young women in Spain saw their mothers struggle with a lack of equality both in the workplace and in home life, strict gender roles, and a dearth of options for education and professions. While these issues have improved for the most part, these concerns still affect women and their decisions to have children, postpone childbearing, or not have children at all.

CHAPTER 1

Infertility as Business

QUIÉN QUIERE SER MADRE BY SILVIA NANCLARES

While Franco's pronatalist policies stressed that the most basic role of women was to be mothers, the sharp decline in birth rate after his death that has continued into the present appears to express women's rejection of motherhood as essential. The Spanish feminist movement worked to legitimize the decision not to become a mother as a means for emancipation, but even with this emphasis on nonmotherhood, Spanish women see mothering less as a duty and more as a "desire whose nonfulfillment incites guilt and extreme distress."[1] In order to capitalize on these feelings, the fertility industry has been successful at marketing itself as a way to achieve motherhood. This chapter examines the commercial aspect of infertility, or the selling and marketing of fertility treatments to women who cannot conceive naturally, through the analysis of the 2017 novel *Quién quiere ser madre* [Who Wants to Be a Mother] by Silvia Nanclares in order to show how the market preys on women's desires to be normal (mothers), not deviant (nonmothers).[2]

Silvia Nanclares (b. 1975, Madrid) is a Spanish writer, editor, and activist, and *Quién quiere ser madre*, her first novel, is an autobiographical narrative that recounts a fictionalized version of the author's experiences with fertility treatments and assisted reproduction.[3] In an interview with *Pikara* magazine, Nanclares said that she wrote her book to fill a gap she saw in the topics covered in published fiction.[4] The lack of books that addressed infertility and assisted reproduction contributed to her sense of loneliness during the experience. She wrote *Quién quiere ser madre* to begin to open that dialogue for herself and other women experiencing similar challenges.[5] Olga Albarrán Caselles, in her book *(Pro)creación* (2022), suggests that Nanclares's text

> señala la ausencia de voces en el campo cultural que, sin idealizar a los hijos e hijas como complemento necesario y esencial en la vida de la mujer ni fuente

> inagotable de amor puro e incondicional, desafíen críticamente la institución de la maternidad para que ésta pueda convertirse en espacio creativo de igualdad libertaria.[6]
>
> [signals the absence of voices in the cultural field that, without idealizing children as a necessary and essential accompaniment of a woman or as an endless source of pure and unconditional love, critically challenges the institution of maternity so that it can become a creative space for libertarian equality.]

María Reyes Ferrer, in her article about reproductive justice and Nanclares's book, describes the novel as one that "breaks the taboos surrounding motherhood and infertility, bringing to light a problem of a public nature which is struggling to abandon the private sphere."[7] Nanclares refuses the categorization of women into mothers and nonmothers in an interview, stating, "Las maternidades son muy complejas, cruzadas por condiciones materiales, emocionales e incluso filosóficas. Entonces, ¿por qué nos tienen que catalogar como madres y no madres?" [Maternities are complex, combining material, emotional, and even philosophical aspects. Then why do we have to catalog ourselves as mothers or nonmothers?].[8] Nanclares's complex, feminist perspective on assisted reproduction and the challenges of becoming pregnant illustrates that women encounter difficulties in their interaction with the assisted reproduction market. While motherhood may not be a necessity, many women still want to become mothers. The narrator of this novel, Silvia, is one of those women who decides to embark upon a quest to become a mother despite the biological challenges presented by her age. The book, set in Madrid, Spain, chronicles her challenges as she, alongside a group of women friends, seeks to become pregnant.

Nanclares's novel elucidates Spain's system in support of fertility treatments and questions why Spanish culture privileges motherhood. As mentioned previously, Spain offers state-sponsored family leave for women who have a full-time work contract and offers state-supported fertility treatments for women under forty, which makes such treatments fairly accessible.[9] By showing the protagonist's struggles to accept her state as a nonmother, Nanclares's narration emphasizes Spain's cultural portrayal of the nonmaternal female body as biologically and socially deviant. The cultural context of Spanish fertility along with the theoretical perspective of the nonmothering body as deviant allow for an interpretation of how the protagonist comes to reject the mother/woman binarism and to give up the effort to have a biological child due to her experience with the medicalization of women's bodies and the commercialization of infertility.

The cultural shifts that Spain has experienced since Franco's death affect fertility, partially due to the postponement of childbearing. Under the Franco dictatorship (1939–1975), Spain's total fertility rate (TFR) was one of the highest in Europe, at 2.8 children per woman. By 1996, it was 1.17, one of the lowest in the world.[10] In the 2015 survey by the Instituto Nacional de Estadística (INE), Spain's TFR was 1.23. By the end of 2015, the mean maternal age at birth of the first child in Spain was 31.9 years, well above the EU average of 28.8 years.[11] Diana Marre, Beatriz San Román, and Diana Guerra suggest that economic conditions contribute to Spain's low fertility rate.[12] The authors explain that Spain changed quickly from an authoritarian, conservative, Catholic country under the Franco dictatorship to a liberal, democratic country with some of the least-restrictive assisted reproduction laws.[13] They also suggest that the "trend of fertility postponement has occurred at the same time that parenting has become increasingly intensive," which results in smaller families and higher rates of infertility.[14] According to Sharon Hays, intensive mothering centers on the needs of children, who should be cared for primarily by the mother, with "methods that are informed by experts, labor-intensive, and costly."[15] Due to both the cost of and the time involved with intensive mothering, women might choose to have fewer children.[16] Marre, San Román, and Guerra's article on the work of reproduction focuses on the connection between women and infertility, specifically how the burden of childcare delays motherhood even while the desire to have children has increased in pronatalist Spain.[17]

The cost for women continues to be high, as either path, bearing children or not, impacts a woman's value. A woman who is not a mother is subversive, making us question the status quo of motherhood, whether or not motherhood does define womanhood. Anthropologist Elixabete Imaz in her book *Convertirse en madre: Etnografía del tiempo de gestación* [To Become a Mother: Ethnography of Gestation Time] finds that women who are not mothers are considered "en definitiva, una anomalía" [definitely an anomaly].[18] In Nanclares's novel, the protagonist, Silvia, at first interprets the nonmother not as subversive but as unfulfilled or incomplete before coming to terms with her infertility. Nanclares's work illustrates how a diagnosis of infertility affects a woman's interpretation of herself and her societal role.

In order to analyze how infertility is represented in Nanclares's narrative, I first look at the history of the term *infertile*. According to Robin Jensen in her book *Infertility: Tracing the History of a Transformative Term*, the term *fertile* to describe women capable of having children came into use in 1868.[19] Other terms used for women who were not capable of this were *sterile* and *barren*, which Jensen explains have different connotations: sterility can "be fixed by medical intervention," while "barren bodies were a sign of one's moral failures."[20] Sterility removed some of the blame from women who could not become pregnant, while barrenness was seen as the woman's fault based on her choices. Reframing women's reproductive capacity as a question of fertility instead of sterility or barrenness became the most common concept for discussing women's inability to procreate. In her novel, Nanclares views infertility as a story to be shared since recognizing the "cantidad de historias ocultas que hay en torno al deseo de ser madre o de ser padres, de lo silenciosamente que se vive este estado intermedio" [the quantity of hidden stories that there are around the desire to be a mother or to be parents, of how silently one lives this intermediary state].[21] She finds that every time she brings up her experiences, "hay tantas historias" [there are so many stories] of people who have lost children, who desire to have children, who have fears and worries.[22] She calls the topic of fertility "una bomba de relojería" [a time bomb].[23] Nanclares contemplates the concept of the nonmothering body in Spain in order to understand and undo how Spanish cultural norms and expectations view motherhood as normal and nonmotherhood as deviant.[24]

The experience of infertility is gendered, as motherhood is central to the social understanding of womanhood. Although infertility can be seen as a condition that affects a couple, most commonly we see that infertility is a woman's problem, because a woman's identity is so closely tied to being a mother. Kelly Oliver's article "Motherhood, Sexuality, and Pregnant Embodiment: Twenty-Five Years of Gestation" presents a summary of feminist thought on the connection between women and mothers, explaining that "pregnancy, childbirth, and child-rearing have traditionally been the ways that women could gain recognition, such as it is, from a patriarchal culture that values them only insofar as they reproduce future citizens."[25] While Oliver speaks from a historical perspective, she recognizes the close ties that exist today in how women interpret themselves within the concept of women as mothers or nonmothers. Gayle Letherby expands on this idea, explaining that "motherhood is valued rhetorically (even though it has little material and social status) [and] non-motherhood is defined as lesser."[26] Therefore, women who are unable to become mothers struggle with defining themselves within these societal norms.[27]

The pressure to achieve motherhood, especially through the birth of a biological child, causes women to search out medical options for achieving their goals. Spanish feminist theorist Esther Vivas, in her book *Mamá desobediente*, when talking about the decision to start treatment for infertility, states that

> someterse a un tratamiento de reproducción asistida no es fácil: cómo gestionas el proceso, lo cuentas o no, de qué modo lo enfrentas. [. . .] El dolor, el malestar emocional, el sentimiento de fracaso, la incertidumbre. Por no mencionar la pérdida de control sobre el propio cuerpo y la hipermedicalización que significan las técnicas de reproducción asistida, así como las contradicciones que implica ser partícipe del negocio de la infertilidad.[28]
>
> [subjecting yourself to an assisted reproduction treatment is not easy: how you handle the process, whether you tell about it or not, how you face it (. . .) The pain, the emotional unease, the feeling of failure, the uncertainty. Not to mention the loss of control over your own body and the hypermedicalization that

these assisted reproduction techniques mean, along with the contradictions that being part of the infertility business imply.]

Vivas clearly situates the experience of infertility within the constructs of commercialization and also mentions the emotional cost of participating in fertility treatments. She talks about a new generation of Spanish women "que se replantean el significado de la maternidad en clave emancipadora y de experiencia que merece la pena ser vivida" [who reconsider the meaning of maternity as emancipatory and an experience that is worth living].[29] In this analysis of Nanclares's novel, we see how these factors affect women in Spain in their journey to become pregnant and how the protagonist decides that the cost—both monetary and emotional—is too high. These conflicts between wanting a child and not wanting to participate in the process of fertility treatments illustrate the loss of a sense of self and the discontinuity in what it means to be a woman when faced with the decision to remain childless.

Women perceive the biological failure of infertility as personal. In the article "The Continuity and Discontinuity of the Embodied Self in Infertility," Laura Hurd Clarke, Anne Martin-Matthews, and Ralph Matthews investigate "the relationship between an infertile person's sense of self and the perception of the female body as a dysfunctional machine."[30] They focus on how "women tend to experience infertility as a devastating stigma that jeopardizes their sense of self of being 'complete' women," while "men perceive infertility as a threat to their masculinity and sexual potency."[31] The way that women perceive their infertility leads to an embodiment of this failure, as women come to see "the infertile body as a malfunctioning machine" that instills a "perception of loss of control over the body."[32] Women see their bodies as failing them because many of these women "have been socialized with the assumptions that they are in control of their lives, that their successes and failures are the result of their abilities rather than the social context, and that success is defined as having both careers and families."[33] The inability to change their outcome causes frustration and sadness, underlining their inherent inability to control their bodily selves.

Hurd Clarke and colleagues suggest that women tend to hold themselves responsible for their inability to conceive, that they have done something wrong that has caused what they interpret as failure. Women "are fearful that the control they exercised over their bodies in the past through the use of contraceptives may have led to their current inability to conceive and bear children." For those women who seek treatment for their infertility, the pathologization of this condition causes them to experience a sense of alienation from their bodies, where the women feel "hostages to their bodies, infertility and infertility treatment."[34] Women have "the perception of the embodied self as deviant, shameful and inadequate," and "the loss of control of the embodied self that they experience through infertility is often devastating and difficult to reconcile with their socialization and the dominant social constructions of femininity and womanhood."[35] Overall, the article suggests that women interpret their nonreproducing bodies as deviant, experience anger at their inability to control their bodies, find themselves alienated from their bodies through the medicalization of infertility, and strive to attain a pregnancy in order to fulfill their so-called maternal desires. This chapter shows how this theory of the discontinuity of the embodied self in infertility, when applied to Nanclares's novel, elucidates the process of the protagonist's experience of coming to terms with her own infertility and how the medical field treats her.

In addition to how women are treated in the area of assisted reproduction, for centuries the medical field has been controlled by men. During the Renaissance era in Europe, women healers and midwives were rebranded as witches and replaced by male physicians who still dominate the profession today, even in areas concerned with women's health, such as gynecology and obstetrics.[36] Gynecology is, says Nuria Varela, "una profesión en España copada por varones" [a profession in Spain headed by men].[37] As a result, "las mujeres seguimos pariendo en los hospitales para comodidad de los ginecólogos" [we women continue giving birth in hospitals for the comfort of our (male) gynecologists] and not the comfort of the women themselves.[38] Silvia Federici explains that once childbirth was removed from the oversight of women, women became enslaved to procreation, and "their wombs became public territory, controlled by men and the state, and procreation was directly placed at the service of capitalist accumulation."[39] These same controls exist today for women's infertile bodies, which are medicalized, pathologized, and treated as if sick, contributing to a sense of distance or disembodiment between the women themselves and the bodies that they gradually come to see as deviant.

Medicalization, defined as "the process by which scientific and medical expertise becomes valued over experiential knowledge and is used to categorize aspects of social life in terms of disease and abnormality," prioritizes scientific observations over lived experience and erases the person, leaving only the patient.[40] As Silvia Tubert says, the subject of fertility treatments "se borra y deja lugar al cuerpo anatómico, a un cuerpo sin referencias subjetivas, sexuales, que será abordado como ajeno a toda estructura, práctica o discurso que no sea el discurso médico o el discurso social de la maternidad" [is erased and leaves an anatomical body, a body without subjective or sexual references that will be approached as external to all structure, practice, or discourse that is not medical discourse or the social discourse of maternity].[41] Infertility has been deeply medicalized owing to advances in scientific understanding and a field dominated by people who lack the experiential knowledge of those they are treating. Jensen explains that "the medicalization process did not acquire significant traction [in fertility treatment and assisted reproduction] until the 1930s, when rhetoric circulating from and around the new field of reproductive endocrinology defined sterile bodies as chemically activated machines in need of technical intervention."[42] Bodies were mechanized and medicalized: women's bodies came to be perceived as machines whose sole desired output was pregnancy.

Jensen explains that by insisting on pregnancy as the ultimate outcome, "women who are deemed 'infertile' face nothing less than a technological mandate to alter their behavior—sometimes endlessly—to achieve pregnancy and parenthood."[43] Dysfunctional machines require technological fixes, and there is no shortage of products and behaviors being sold and promoted as solutions to the "dysfunction" that infertility has been turned into. Due to the wide variety of options available, "infertility clinics, products, and services have become a thriving international 'baby business' into which billions of dollars are devoted each year."[44] As women delve deeper into offered fertility products, they become more separated from their bodies, leading to a feeling of alienation. Contemporary medicinal practice allows for the medicalized machine-body to be deconstructed, understood, and controlled. Mechanization further separates the concepts of body and person by dehumanizing the body so that when pregnancy is medicalized, the woman becomes detached from her physical embodiment of fertility or infertility.[45]

The feminist discourse surrounding how women attain motherhood presents a difficult paradox: On one hand, reproductive technologies are seen as "merely another strategy for unnaturally coercing women into performing what are, under patriarchy, their natural roles," but on the other hand, feminism "celebrates those roles when they are performed without artificial intervention."[46] Helena Michie and Naomi Cahn present what they call the "patriarchal reproduction" perspective on fertility treatment, which emerges from matriarchal feminist theorists such as Gena Corea.[47] According to this viewpoint, women are compelled to participate in reproductive technologies due to cultural norms that depend on the binarism mother/woman because reproductive technologies "perpetuate and reinforce patriarchal powers over women." Matriarchal feminists believe that "reproductive technology interferes with the natural processes of pregnancy and childbirth, is symptomatic of the medicalization of the women's bodies, and reflects patriarchal society's emphasis on women as childbearers."[48] A natural mother, who becomes pregnant without technological aid, is viewed positively as a pillar of femininity, but those who seek medical intervention for the same goal are rejected as mechanized and controlled by patriarchal interests. Indeed, suggest Michie and Cahn, "infertile women are socialized into wanting biological children" and therefore do not "choose the new reproductive technologies so much as they are coerced to choose."[49] *Quién quiere ser madre* echoes this struggle as the protagonist, Silvia, processes her experience with the commercialization of motherhood.

The novel follows Silvia's "odisea" [odyssey] of trying to become a mother, closely following the author's own experience.[50] With multiple doctors, a variety of attempted assisted reproduction techniques, and even more treatments to try to make medical intervention more successful, Silvia repeatedly comes up against medicalized infertility. From the beginning, her medical professionals treat motherhood as simply another piece of medical history.[51] She creates a notebook to detail her experiences and quickly fills it with new medical terms: "Sangrado, ovulación, hormona, test, síntomas. Términos técnicos que abultan mi nuevo cuaderno vital de 'Quedarme embarazada'" [Bleeding, ovulation, hormone, test, symptoms. Technical terms that take up space in my vital new "Getting Pregnant" notebook].[52] All of these terms are, she is told in the early parts of her odyssey, critical to maximizing fertility and the chances of successful pregnancy. It does not take much for her to become tied to a medicalized conception of her own fertility and potential pregnancy despite previously distancing herself from a naturalist definition of her body and her experiences: "Yo, que negué la biología como condicionante supremo, me arrodillo ahora ante sus manuales y rebusco los indicios que hagan de mi cuerpo una máquina bien engrasada" [I, who had rejected biology as supreme determinant, now kneel before its manuals and look for the signs that make my body a well-greased machine].[53] She negatively references the machine imagery that is used to describe fertility treatments and assisted reproduction, which creates a dehumanized image of a body whose sole purpose is the attainment of motherhood and the production of children. As the protagonist continues to seek out solutions to her inability to become pregnant, she discovers that, as Hurd Clarke and colleagues explain, "infertility shatters previously held perceptions of the body and self as healthy, whole, and normal."[54] This shattering of perceptions increases a woman's sense of alienation from her own body, causing her to experience a feeling of distance between who she was previously, a feminine identity based on reproductive potential, and her new perspective of a broken body.

The depersonalization of the female body creates a sense of disconnection from the body, which is defined as other and separated from the woman herself as her body and her desire to become a mother are medicalized and defined in disembodied terms of cycles, hormones, and medical history. Silvia describes, "A pesar de que mi ciclo es previsible y puntual como un reloj de veintiocho días, su llegada me ha pillado casi siempre por sorpresa. Debe de ser otro indicio de la desconexión entre mi cuerpo y yo" [Even though my cycle is predictable and punctual like a twenty-eight-day clock, its arrival has almost always caught me by surprise. It has to be another indicator of the disconnection between my body and me].[55] In the middle of all the tracking, measuring, and planning, her body no longer feels like her own. This sense of alienation is typical when treating infertility, as patients "tend to see the body and the self as engaged in a dynamic tension in which the body exercises moral authority over the self."[56] The infertile body acts as a broken machine, separated from the embodied self that had previously been connected to it. This rupture of the body and the self challenges the woman's identity and self-definition.

Substituting lived experiences for their medical equivalents also contributes to medicalization. A doctor tells Silvia that she should avoid stress, because "el cortisol es malísimo para [el] proceso" [cortisol is very bad for (the) process] of maximizing fertility and becoming pregnant.[57] The experience of stress—emotional by definition—is reduced to its hormonal products, an obvious example of the medical essentialization of lived experience. It becomes clear that "el objetivo de la odisea [es] modificar el ciclo para poder manipularlo cual mecanismo de relojería" [the objective of the odyssey (is) to modify the cycle in order to be able to manipulate it like a piece of clockwork].[58] Medicalization and mechanization take control of all aspects of the lives of Silvia and Gabi, her partner, and everything they do becomes dedicated to the goal of pregnancy and the control of Silvia's body in order to create the best possible outcome. As all things not related to the medical science of those two organs are pushed aside, Silvia says, "Me resisto a convertirme solo en cerebro y útero" [I resist becoming only a brain and uterus].[59] When the female body is reduced to only a few of its parts, the person is no longer prioritized, which means that she becomes disconnected from her body. This is what causes the "partos [que] no tienen madre" [births without mothers] that take place when women become patients instead of people.[60] The same risk exists with medicalized fertility treatments that ignore the person behind the condition.

The pathologization of fertility treats it as an illness, a failure to produce and reproduce. Emily Martin discusses how the viewing of menstruation and menopause as failures contributes to the negative societal perspective of them, and the same idea of illness and failure applies to infertility.[61] Sandelowski makes a similar claim when she explains,

> The cultural mandate to procreate in marriage, the longstanding association of fertility with normal adulthood (particularly womanhood), and the prevalent view that reproduction is part of the natural design of the human species are among the factors that make infertility an undesirable condition, place it outside of the boundaries of health and normality (if not wholly inside the domain of disease).[62]

While not technically a disease, infertility becomes pathologized because fertility is the norm.[63] Indeed, popular culture has demonized women without children, especially stepmothers.[64] In the novel, Silvia challenges this dominant perspective as she resists the idea that the most important goal for a woman is to become a mother. She attends a group meeting for "Maminfértiles" [Infertile Mommies], but she finds that she doesn't fit in with the way they describe themselves and tell their stories.[65] She says she does not want to define herself "como una persona enferma o inútil" [as a sick or useless person].[66] She also refuses to blame herself. The book concludes with her realization, "Esta batalla no me representa. Puede que la maternidad no sea el proyecto más importante de mi vida" [This battle doesn't represent me. It could be that motherhood is not the most important project of my life]. Silvia realizes that to move forward, she must "reformular los sueños" [reformulate (her) dreams] and stop viewing her infertility as a failure.[67] She might not become a mother, she says, but she will be something else, whatever that ends up being.[68]

Albarrán Caselles describes Nanclares's body as she tries to become pregnant as a "máquina deseante y productora [que] no funciona con la precisión y prontitud que ella quiere, le lleva a profundizar en el tratamiento sociocultural que se da en la actualidad a la fertilidad" [desiring and productive machine that does not work with the precision and timing that she wants, which causes her to delve into the sociocultural treatment that is currently given to fertility].[69] For the protagonist, this means allowing maternity not to be the end-all for her as a woman. Even though she eventually decides not to continue her pregnancy quest, the external market continues to pressure her into making different fertility choices. The constant cycle of new products, hope, and disappointment follows her throughout her journey until she can finally tear herself away from the influence of the market.

The concept of the baby market—marketing products to people with infertility—appears throughout the book, suggesting that if women buy certain products, they will have the sought-after outcome of pregnancy. Purchasing these products will disguise the fact that these nonmothering women inhabit deviant bodies. In the novel, Nanclares mentions how women feel pressured to buy into the next step, from fertility apps and tests to more invasive procedures, such as in vitro fertilization (IVF) and egg donation. By marketing products to women to help them in the process of becoming pregnant, the fertility industry takes what was once a personal aspect of a woman's life and makes it marketable, consumable, and (seemingly) necessary. In her article "Race(ing) to the Baby Market: The Political Economy of Overcoming Infertility," K. Animashaun Ducre explains how the market capitalizes on maternal desire and "how aggressively those who are unable or unwilling to have a child by conventional means have been courted and wooed by those in the baby market."[70] By appealing to women's desire to become mothers, advertisers sell products that encourage natalist tendencies. Nanclares's characters discuss the many ways that they become consumers of the fertility industry. While talking to her coworkers, Silvia recalls a song from the 1990s, whose lyrics say, "El Predictor se pinta de rosaaa en tu cuarto de bañooo y te dice que vas a ser madre a finales de mayoooo" [The pregnancy test turns piiink in your bathrooooom and it tells you that you'll be a mother by the end of Maaaaay],[71] referring to the Predictor brand of pregnancy tests that allow women to determine if they are pregnant in the comfort of their own homes. The lyrics of this song demonstrate the ubiquity of the pressure not only to become a mother but also to purchase items that promote pregnancy and fertility. Along with pregnancy tests, Silvia's friends tell her about the ovulation tests that are available: "Adquiero mi test de ovulación digital, siguiendo obedientemente las instrucciones de mis amigas" [I get my digital ovulation test, obediently following my friends' instructions] from "la farmacéutica que nos vendió Clearblue, test digital de ovulación, cincuenta pavos" [the pharmacist who sold us Clearblue, the digital ovulation test, fifty bucks].[72] Not only does the protagonist feel pressured by her friends to follow their instructions on how to get pregnant, but she must also buy the right products, including the name-brand $50 ovulation kit that contains "tiras mágicas" [magic strips]. As Silvia says, "Todas las amigas que las usan se quedan" [All my friends who use them get pregnant].[73] She and her friends become part of the baby market mechanism, each one pushing the others to try something new and spend more money.

Along with these purchasable items to help with the process of becoming pregnant, technological applications also focus on women's desire to become mothers by marketing apps that collect freely given data. Silvia's friends discuss the utility of various fertility apps, such as "*fertility tracking* (monitorización de la fertilidad)," "Obtener bebé" [Get a Baby], "Alerta de periodo" [Period Alert], "Love Cicles," or "Woom," where you tell "tu *tablet* lo que no le contarías a tu mejor amiga" [your *tablet* what you wouldn't tell your best friend].[74] In addition to the conversation about which app works best, the women discuss what happens to the data they provide, the secrets they share with the app. "¿Qué mierdas harán luego con los datos?" [What the hell do you suppose they do with the data?] asks one friend, to whom another replies, "Seguro que hay unos emprendedores en Denver, Colorado, forrándose a nuestra costa" [I'm sure there are some entrepreneurs in Denver, Colorado, getting rich off of us].[75] Both the women's need to rely on technology to help them get pregnant as well as their awareness of the fact that they are taking part in a capitalistic system where others benefit economically from their maternal desires appear in this scene clearly. Their recommendation of different products to each other shows that even though they are aware of the market using them, they are still influenced by it. When they continue to encourage one another to take the next step in the commercialized path to motherhood, they hope that participating in these data-driven products will eventually give them the success they seek in order to become "normal," child-producing women.

Friends impact consumerist choices about overcoming infertility, but the medical system also reinforces the capitalist market of consumerism. As Charis M. Thompson explains in her chapter "Fertile Ground: Feminists Theorize Infertility," "The market for new reproductive technologies, atypical in medicine, was also crucial. Most patients were high-paying consumers not suffering from life-threatening conditions but pursuing life-defining goals," which meant that "the cutting edge of the field developed more like a consumer-oriented business than a state-sponsored social service."[76] Ducre comments about a similar idea when she says that "while the issue of money exchanges for children is a very uncomfortable topic for most, it is the basis for exchange for all ART services and private adoptions. Therefore, it is fair to conclude that the baby market—a multibillion-dollar global industry—is unregulated and largely commercial."[77] Spanish fertility clinics are recognized worldwide as among the most widely used and respected for fertility treatments and egg donation, with over 211 private clinics where anyone, even women over forty, the age cutoff for public health, can access reproductive aid.[78] For Silvia, since she is over forty, she must finance her own fertility journey, a concept that appears several times in the novel, such as when she mentions that she and her partner chose a low-cost franchise fertility clinic called Lilith because "simplemente es la que tiene precios más bajos" [simply it is the one that had the lowest prices].[79]

After their first visit to a private clinic, Silvia can only think of the cost of IVF: "Entre cinco y seis mil euros, ponedle siete mil, para redondear" [Between €5,000 and €6,000; let's say €7,000 to round off].[80] At each clinic she and her partner visit, the price of the intervention becomes a central part of what they learn. The Lilith Clinic has a deal for its patients: "Un plan de financiación muy asequible a quien lo subscriba antes de un mes" [A financing plan that's affordable for those who sign up within a month].[81] The plan includes affordable monthly payments, without interest, for up to a year—if they make a down payment of €2,500.[82] The price includes "primera consulta . . . , análisis de los dos con nuestro laboratorio de confianza, punción ovárica, ICSI, vitrificación de óvulos e implantación" [the first appointment . . . , analysis of the two people in our own lab, egg withdrawal, ICSI (intracytoplasmic sperm injection), vitrification of the eggs, and implantation], but it does not include the prescription medicine, which costs around €1,000 without insurance.[83] The marketing of the clinic, offering no-interest financing, affordable monthly plans, and colorful brochures and packets to take home, alludes to the consumerist aspect of fertility treatments. Silvia describes the private clinics as "un Harrods de la fertilidad: tenemos el producto adecuado para ti, da igual tu patología o tu condición" [a Harrods of fertility: we have the product that's right for you, whatever your pathology or condition].[84] By relating private clinics to Harrods, the world's leading luxury department store, Nanclares suggests not only that these clinics are selling products to fulfill dreams of normalcy but also that anything is accessible—if you have the economic level to pay for it. Women are not just asked to choose a method to try to become pregnant; they are given the chance to shop for one.[85] The awareness of the monetary cost of motherhood is made an integral (and accessible, with financing) part of a woman's experience, and in this way, the fertility industry preys on women's desires to become mothers at any price. As Noemí López

Trujillo exposes, however, this idea of being a mother at all costs causes debt and financial stress among many women with limited wealth.[86] The consumer market of fertility presents each new product as a stepping stone toward becoming pregnant, urging women to make that next purchase, and the next one, in order to be successful.

In her 2017 interview with *Pikara* magazine, Nanclares speaks to the commercialization of fertility treatments in Spain. The interviewer posits, "Cuando nos acercamos a la reproducción asistida, muchas tememos llegar a comprometer nuestra salud física, emocional y nuestros ahorros por intentar ser madres 'a toda costa.' Pero luego cuesta echar el freno" [When we approach assisted reproduction, many of us fear compromising our physical and emotional health, along with our savings to try to become mothers "at any cost." But then it's hard to put on the brakes].[87] Nanclares responds that she and her partner decided to only do one round of IVF, but she agrees that it's hard to stop:

> Igual me envicio y acabo endeudada y hormonada hasta las cejas. Es verdad que hay un componente adictivo. Conozco a gente que ha hecho hasta siete intentos. Me parece una locura pero no te digo que yo no vaya a llegar a eso. Creo que hay que reconocer ese peligro y romper un poco el "a toda costa."[88]
>
> [It could be that I get hooked and end up in debt and pumped full of hormones. It's true that there's an addictive component. I know people who have done up to seven tries. It seems crazy to me, but I can't tell you that I won't end up doing that too. I believe that we have to recognize the danger and break out of the idea of "at any cost."]

By providing a smorgasbord of fertility treatments from which to choose, women begin to experience purchase momentum: If they have already spent €4,000 on this, why not spend another €4,000 to try again? Even if these steps leave the customers in debt, the clinics provide easy financing and low payments, allowing customers to assume the debt as part of the experience of becoming pregnant. Any price becomes acceptable as long as the woman achieves this desired state of normalcy in pregnancy.

Nanclares's novel clearly shows how each step of the fertility process leads to the next: If she just tries the next thing, maybe she'll be successful. The protagonist writes a blog post about the levels of reproduction, which I have summarized as follows:

Level 1: Unprotected sex
Level 2: Monitoring your cycle
Level 3: Ovulation test
Level 4: Semen
Level 5: A little push (visit your gynecologist)

Level 6: Analysis
Level 7: Artificial insemination (AI)
Level 8: In vitro fertilization (IVF)
Level 9: Egg donation
Level 10: *Betaespera* [waiting for pregnancy test][89]

There is always the next level or trying again at certain levels. There are always experts waiting to give more options, such as dietary changes, acupuncture, meditation, and yoga.[90] The dietary expert Silvia visits tells her to wait for eight months for the diet to make a change to the toxicity of her body.[91] The medical "knowledge" along with the never-ending supply of advice and alternatives, from friends and experts alike, leads to a system that perpetually commercializes women's experiences of infertility and preys on women's desires to fit into the social construct of a mother-based womanhood.

Quién quiere ser madre illustrates the difficulties experienced by Silvia as she tries to become a mother. Through the theoretical lens of embodiment, we see how the experience of the medicalization of women's bodies affects Silvia and makes her question her connection to her body. She begins to see her body as a nonproductive machine while trying to reject being reduced to a uterus and hormones. Tubert reaffirms these feelings about fertility treatments, stating, "Aunque la procreación, en el ser humano, es indisociable del deseo inconsciente, de la sexualidad y del cuerpo, las técnicas proceden como si sólo fuera cuestión de órganos y gametos" [Even though procreation, in a human being, is inseparable from unconscious desire, sexuality, and the body, the techniques proceed as if it were only a matter of organs and gametes].[92] Silvia struggles with the concept of being sterile even while embracing the word. She worries about the postponement of pregnancy and questions why women must be defined by their choice to become mothers or not. Throughout all of the experiences narrated in the novel, the medicalization of the female body and the commercialization of fertility products stand out in stark contrast to the emotional and philosophical wonderings of the narrator. The mother-versus-nonmother binary construct continues to influence the protagonist and cause her great consternation, even as she seeks to reject this binarism. She questions her desire to become a mother, asking, "¿Por qué quiero ser madre? ¿Por qué ahora? ¿Será solo porque no me queda mucho tiempo?" [Why do I want to be a mother? Why now? Is it only because I don't have much time left?].[93] When connecting this current desire to become pregnant to her past experiences, she remembers her first menstrual cycle: "[A] los once años me convertí en mujer. O así me lo dijeron. Convertirme en mujer significaba poder tener hijos. De pronto, mi vida se relacionaba con el fenómeno de la fertilidad y la capacidad reproductiva. A los once años" [At eleven years old I became a woman. Or that's what they told me. Becoming a woman meant being able to have children. Suddenly, my life became related to the phenomenon of fertility and reproductive capacity. At eleven years old].[94] The connection between a woman and her reproductive ability comes early and makes a lasting (and monthly) impression.

Combined with the medicalization of the body and the marketing of products to extend fertility, women feel pressure at a societal level to procreate. However, the protagonist rejects these pressures and decides not to participate in the fertility race, explaining that she and her partner do not want to spend their "mejores años sufriendo una decepción tras otra cada mes, o endeudándonos en tratamientos" [best years suffering one disappointment after another each month, going into debt for treatments].[95] She rejects the quest for motherhood and challenges the idea that privileges mothering and instead focuses on living her life child-free. In her analysis of the text, Albarrán Caselles suggests,

> *Quién quiere ser madre* pone en evidencia que las explicaciones psicoanalíticas sobre el deseo de los hijos no dan cuenta de la compleja construcción social del mismo: querer ser madre no es únicamente un deseo íntimo, sino un conglomerado de causas donde lo personal juega un papel más, puesto que no hay que desestimar los condicionantes sociales, laborales, familiares, culturales y económicos al decidir ser madre y cuándo.[96]
>
> [*Quién quiere ser madre* reveals that the psychoanalytic explanations about the desire to have children do not account for the complex social construction of motherhood: Wanting to become a mother is not only a personal desire but rather an aggregate of causes where the personal aspect is just one of many, since we should not dismiss the social, labor, familial, cultural, and economic factors when it comes to deciding if and when to become a mother.]

The novel provides an important countercultural perspective to the patriarchal script that sees motherhood as the ultimate accomplishment for women, while also delving into why motherhood has become such a fraught concept.

More subtly, the tie between motherhood and womanhood that Nanclares remarks upon throughout her novel is woven into the medical system, marketing, and even the interactions between friends. One must be a mother to be a woman, says society, and moreover, technological resources exist to help. The structures surrounding assisted reproduction and IVF support this ideal, teaching women to pursue motherhood at any cost. Nanclares's narrator reflects on her experience and the price she was asked to pay for just the chance to give birth to a child—not only monetary but also personal and emotional. She describes the growing disconnect between her and her body and the personal discomfort that led her to reject the dominant narrative about infertility and motherhood. While the novel ends with Silvia and her partner accepting their infertile state, the novel also shows the constant pressure, both medical and commercial, to continue to try to achieve the (natural, desired) outcome of motherhood.

As an interesting postpublication note to this novel, Nanclares did become a mother through a donated egg. In a 2019 article in *El Diario*, Nanclares disclosed her worries about being "una mala feminista" [a bad feminist] for using a donor egg to become pregnant. She said that she feels that "estamos condenadas a cobijarnos bajo el manto del capitalismo, en este caso, reproductivo" [we are condemned to shelter under the blanket of, in this case, reproductive capitalism].[97] She questioned what it means to be a mother, biological or otherwise, and how this is affected by carrying another woman's egg. She also probed the ethical implications of egg donation. She called it a "traición" [betrayal] of her "esencia feminista" [feminist essence], simultaneously accepting and challenging the predominant feminist viewpoint that she cites.[98] She explains that "la densidad emocional de esta decisión [. . .] no resulta nunca tan fácil como en los presupuestos teóricos" [the emotional density of this decision (. . .) is never as easy as the theoretical assumptions].[99] *Quién quiere ser madre* ends with a positive vision of a woman who rejects the cultural mandate of motherhood and lives, seemingly, happily ever after with her partner and no children. The narrator comes to terms with her infertility and sets out to enjoy her life as is, breaking the consumption cycle of fertility treatments. To then learn that the author herself, who has shared her story with her readers, has compromised these ideals by succumbing to the use of egg donation to achieve a pregnancy only reinforces how much pressure is on women to have children. Nanclares admits that when she says,

> Supongo que mi decisión de seguir adelante tuvo que ver la espiral de intentos fallidos y nuevas opciones en la que te metes cuando pones un pie en la reproducción asistida y acabas haciendo de tus principios algo tan maleable como el slime de tus sobrinas. Escribo desde ahí, desde aquí, desde la traición consumada. Desde la contradicción.
>
> I suppose that my decision to carry on had to do with the spiral of failed attempts and new options that you get into when you dip your foot into assisted reproduction and you end up making your principles as malleable as your nieces' slime. I write from there, from here, from the consummated betrayal. From the contradiction.[100]

The selling and marketing of fertility treatments to women who cannot conceive naturally is a central aspect of Nanclares's novel. By examining the financial, emotional, and physical impact of assisted reproduction as portrayed in this book, the contradictions between feminist theoretical perspectives, the business of fertility treatments, and the motherhood mandate stand out. Within the text, Silvia decides to remove herself from the baby market and accept her position as a nonmother even while mourning the death of both her father and her dream to procreate. In reality, the pressure to have a child exerted itself on the author, who chose to continue her pursuit of a child through egg donation. The complexity of these contradictory actions is hard to describe or understand, as the previous quote from Nanclares tries to show. The desire to be a mother—and to be successful at assisted reproduction—can be overpowering. As much as women might deny the cultural mandate of motherhood, the pressure to reproduce is ingrained in us. With the added pressure of marketing and sales techniques to entice women to buy their successful pregnancies, no one should be surprised by the success of the baby industry.

As we have seen in this chapter, the focus is on the business aspects of infertility: how solutions to infertility are marketed and sold to women who would like to become mothers. This aspect of infertility appears in the following chapters as well, with questions of wealth inequality, access to paid systems of medicine, and privilege in general being a uniting thread among all of the works analyzed in this book. Nanclares's novel in particular focuses on this aspect of infertility, while the other books studied here mention the infertility industry more obliquely. The experience with and doubts about egg donation will be explored in chapter 3 through the analysis of the book written by Samanta Villar. Chapter 2 uses a wider lens, viewing infertility through the perspective of a doctor who works in a fertility clinic and how her patients perceive their infertility.

CHAPTER 2

Infertility as Stigma

TENGO LOS ÓVULOS CONTADOS BY RAQUEL SÁNCHEZ-SILVA

No one imagines they will be infertile. Indeed, many women spend years preventing pregnancies or fearing an unplanned pregnancy. When it comes time to start a family, we think that since our parents were able to attain a pregnancy, we should also be able to. In her novel *Tengo los óvulos contados*, Raquel Sánchez-Silva's main character, Miranda Ortega, complains that women "esperan, esperan a tenerlo claro, esperan a sentirse absolutamente seguras de su decisión, esperan a disfrutar todo lo que creen que perderán con la maternidad y esperan a tener la tranquilidad económica y estabilidad laboral. Esperan. Esperan. Esperan" [wait, they wait to have it clear, they wait to be absolutely sure about their decision, they wait to enjoy everything they think they will lose with motherhood, and they wait to have economic tranquility and work stability. They wait. They wait. They wait].[1] But by waiting, Miranda tells us, there is the danger of decreasing egg quality and quantity: "Todos nacemos con un número concreto de ovocitos, cuando tememos que nos aterroriza quedarnos embarazadas a una edad temprana y que querríamos multiplicar cuando los años de la decadencia de nuestra fertilidad se aproximan" [We are all born with a specific number of eggs, when we fear that we are terrified of getting pregnant at an early age and that we would multiply when the years of decline of our fertility approach].[2] When women postpone motherhood, for whatever reason, this postponement can lead to infertility. Women who discover they are infertile feel stigmatized because they cannot fulfill the biological mandate of motherhood. In this chapter, I explore the concept of stigma as related to infertility. In chapter 1, "Infertility as Business," we saw that medical intervention leads women to interpret their "broken" bodies as deviant. In chapter 3, "Infertility as Crisis," the involvement of a third party to achieve a pregnancy calls into question the concept of donation as a solution to infertility. This chapter, however, devotes itself to exploring the concept of stigma and its relationship to infertility. First, I explore the reasons that women in Spain postpone childbearing. Next, I provide some context about fertility treatments in Spain. I then delve into the concept of stigma and its connection to infertility as seen in *Tengo los óvulos contados*.

According to information from the *Informe España 2018*, the birth rate of Spanish women is falling while the age of mothers at the birth of their first child is rising. Spanish women also have one of the lowest birth rates in the world, at 1.2 children per woman.[3] Agustín Blanco, one of the collaborators on the *Informe España 2018*, offers that

> la muy baja fecundidad española [. . .] está ligada a la creciente precarización laboral de los jóvenes (y no tan jóvenes), el escaso apoyo público a las responsabilidades de crianza de los menores de tres años, las dificultades para conciliar vida laboral, personal y familiar a lo largo del curso de vida, y a la persistente desigualdad de género en el trabajo de cuidados.[4]
>
> [the very low Spanish fertility rate (. . .) is linked to the growing labor precarity of the young (and not so young), the lack of public support for the responsibilities of raising children under three years old, the difficulties of reconciling work, personal and family life throughout life, and the persistent gender inequality in care work.]

The labor precarity for young people in Spain, along with the other social and economic changes in the previous quote, have affected fertility rates in Spain. Women find that they have postponed childbearing until they are in a strong financial situation that includes stable housing, a stable job, and many times, a stable partner. But there are consequences to waiting.

By postponing childbearing, more and more people find themselves unable to become pregnant through intercourse and seek help through assisted reproduction technology (ART). The Sociedad Española de Fertilidad [Spanish Fertility Society] states that a twenty-five-year-old woman has a 25 percent chance of achieving a pregnancy, and the possibilities fall from there: at thirty, women have a 22 percent chance; at thirty-five, 12 percent; at forty, 5 percent; and at forty-five, it is 1 percent.[5] Isidoro Bruna, from the Sociedad Española de Fertilidad, cited in *El País*, explains that women

> asumen que si su aspecto físico es bueno, también lo será su fertilidad y creen que lo lograrán al igual que las famosas que tienen hijos pero no explican que son fruto de la ovodonación, que son un tercio de todas las fecundaciones que se realizan. Es una pena que durante sus chequeos rutinarios los ginecólogos rara vez les informen de la caída de su reserva ovárica.[6]
>
> [assume that if their physical appearance is good, then their fertility will also be so, and they believe they will achieve (pregnancy) like the famous women

> that have children but do not explain that they are from egg donations, which are a third of all of the fertilizations done. It is a shame that during their routine visits, gynecologists rarely inform them of the decline of their ovarian reserve.]

These messages that point to the decline in fertility conflict with the idea that women can achieve whatever they want whenever they want it. This is not true: Women's fertility is inextricably linked to age. Raquel Sánchez-Silva's 2017 novel, *Tengo los óvulos contados*, addresses the particular issue of women who postpone childbearing and find themselves in need of assisted reproductive technology (ART).

Raquel Sánchez-Silva, born in Plasencia, Cáceres (Spain), in 1973, is a journalist and author who has worked for Televisión Española, Canal+, and Digital+.[7] She has published several books, with her most recent, *Dosmundos: Cuentos de mellizos, gemelos y otros hermanos sin igual* (2021), being an illustrated children's book dedicated to her twins.[8] She wrote *Tengo los óvulos contados* while pregnant with her twins, as she writes in the introduction to her book: "Espero mellizos y he escrito esta historia experimentando la maternidad en mi cuerpo, en mi mente y también a través del teclado de un ordenador. Es un libro escrito desde el deseo de ser madre y desde la propia maternidad" [I am expecting twins, and I have written this story experiencing motherhood in my body, in my mind, and through the keyboard of a computer. It is a book written from the desire to be a mother and from my own motherhood].[9] The novel tells the story of Dr. Miranda Ortega, a gynecologist who specializes in assisted reproduction in Madrid, Spain. Through the stories of her patients, the doctor recounts her experiences treating infertility, expanding on the psychological, economic, and social impacts of the quest to become pregnant. The author states that she hopes that this novel sends "un mensaje claro que rompa el tabú social que rodea la reproducción asistida y, además, ayude a muchas mujeres y hombres a tomar decisiones basadas en una información rigurosa y no en los rumores" [a clear message that breaks the social taboo that surrounds assisted reproduction and also helps many women and men make decisions based on accurate information and not on rumors].[10] In an interview with LDcultura, Sánchez-Silva tells us that she wants society to overcome the stigma associated with assisted reproduction and to be able to speak openly about it without judgment, explicitly calling infertility a stigma. The novel presents stories of different women who visit the IVI Clinic in Madrid as they pursue pregnancy. Not only does infertility affect the psychological and physical parts of the body, but it also manifests as a lived stigma that creates a feeling of not being good enough.

As I mentioned, this chapter analyzes how Sánchez-Silva presents the situation of infertility through her fictional story about Dr. Miranda Ortega. First, it is helpful to have a brief overview of access to fertility treatments in Spain, especially as this access relates to age. Fertility treatments only partially address the problem of a growing infertile population. Spain's socialized medicine covers fertility treatments, as explained in the introduction, but only for women under forty. Those over forty years of age must access assisted reproduction through private, full-pay clinics. According to statistics in *El País*, around 3.2 percent of children born in Spain in 2013 were the result of fertility treatments, and in 2013, over twenty-seven thousand patients underwent in vitro fertilization (IVF; at a cost of around 4,000 euros each).[11] Economic precarity partially explains why women put off pregnancy in Spain, but there is a much larger societal issue at play. Esther Vivas, in her book *Mamá desobediente*, tries to explain why maternity is complicated for Spanish women: "La maternidad está bien vista y aceptada siempre y cuando se limite al ámbito del hogar y a lo individual [. . .] y no cuestione las dinámicas del trabajo productivo, el modelo socioeconómico ni el sistema patriarcal" [Motherhood is well regarded and accepted as long as it is limited to the domestic sphere and to the individual (. . .) and does not challenge the dynamics of productive work, the socioeconomic model, or the patriarchal system].[12] When women were at home taking care of children, not speaking out about the difficulties that come with balancing childcare, domestic labor, familial relationships, and so on, motherhood could be viewed as simple only because no one spoke about it.

Now that Spanish women have lived through an extraordinary time of social and economic change, motherhood and its decline have become a central issue of discussion. Vivas tells us that "la crisis de los sistemas de bienestar y la mercantilización generalizada de la vida, por un lado, y el cambio del papel de la mujer en la sociedad y en la estructura familiar, por otro, han revitalizado las discusiones acerca de lo que implica ser madre" [the crisis of the systems of well-being and the generalized commercialization of life, on one side, and the change in the role of women in society and in the family structure, on the other, have revitalized discussions about what it means to be a mother].[13] When motherhood is freely chosen, it can be emancipatory, suggests Vivas, but the choice is fraught because "la fertilidad femenina [. . .] no sabe de cambios socioculturales" [female fertility (. . .) does not know about sociocultural changes].[14] As women wait to have children, trying to find an economic, relationship, and housing situation that would support the choice, their age advances, making pregnancy without intervention harder to achieve. Once they come to realize that medical intervention is necessary, deciding to enter into the world of fertility treatments can be overwhelming, raising questions about "cómo gestionas el proceso, lo cuentas o no, de qué modo lo enfrentas" [how you handle the process, whether you tell others or not, how you face it].[15] Vivas points out the difficulty in deciding whether to not to tell others about the experience of infertility, and the decision to remain silent, while understandable, makes the topic challenging to discuss. Indeed, while large numbers of women and men seek help in order to have a child, public conversation about this topic is still quite scarce. As Bruna stated earlier, most people believe that they will not have issues with fertility despite what the statistics say. When they do seek the help of assisted reproduction, many refuse to admit it because they see their infertility as a personal failure. The taboo of talking about reproductive issues has a direct connection with the study of stigma theory, since the silence around infertility adds to the feeling of being stigmatized.

Infertility is viewed as a stigma, referring to the original sociological term used by Erving Goffman in 1963, who defines *stigma* as an "attribute that is deeply discrediting," reducing the person "from a whole and usual person to a tainted, discounted one."[16] Bruce Link and Jo Phelan add that "stigma exists when elements of labeling, stereotyping, separation, status loss, and discrimination occur together in a power situation that allows them."[17] In their article "Perceptions of Women with Infertility on Stigma and Disability," Elizabeth A. Sternke and Kathleen Abrahamson present four types of stigma: *felt*, *enacted*, *self*, and *public*.[18] I use these terms to illustrate the experience of stigma felt by those who undergo fertility treatments in *Tengo los óvulos contados*. The connection between stigma and infertility is clear: Some women feel that in order to be seen as fully a woman, they must be mothers. Men also equate the ability to produce children with their virility. If society continues to stigmatize women who are unable to attain a pregnancy while not addressing the underlying issues that make maternity a burden, the birth rate will continue to decline as a result of these misogynistic social norms.

Women and men who struggle with infertility can feel less-than or discounted. Charlene Miall, in her article on "The Stigma of Involuntary Childlessness," tells us that "the negative impact of involuntary childlessness is undoubtedly related to the pronatalistic views of marriage that pervade western society."[19] She goes on to explain that "the fertility norms of having and wanting children [transcend] sex, age, race, religion, ethnic, and social class divisions," which she suggests is connected to "the Judaeo-Christian tradition which sees children as blessings from heaven and barrenness as a curse or punishment."[20] The taboo, then, is reinforced from a personal perspective of feeling broken, the hesitancy in admitting that one is seeking help, and the perception that infertility could be a cosmic sign of some larger proportion.

In addition to the pronatalist perspective on fertility, Candida Moss and Joel S. Baden, in their book *Reconceiving Infertility: Biblical Perspectives on Procreation and Childlessness*, address how fertility is viewed in the Christian tradition, offering, "The Bible is read as an academic text, a work of literature, and a spiritual and theological handbook. When it comes to infertility, however, these disparate readings have coalesced around a single idea: that God instructed humanity to 'be fruitful and multiply.'"[21] When those raised in such a tradition find themselves unable to procreate, they perceive this lack as a "sign of divine judgment and moral failure," since in the Bible, "fertility is a sign of divine blessing."[22] Moss and Baden relate infertility to stigma, explaining that "all childless couples, including the infertile, are socially disabled by this stigmatization of childlessness as selfish."[23] When a woman admits that she is dealing with infertility or choosing not to have children, "she unwittingly reinforces a system that judged her as inadequate and potentially immoral."[24] These authors present infertility as a "subtle social stigma" that "extends the biological shortcomings and perceived character flaws of infertile couples into moral and political subversion."[25] According to this interpretation, those who suffer from infertility face a double stigma: the taboo of admitting their infertility, which could be read as a sign of moral failure or divine punishment, and the social stigma of not following natural law and procreating.

Along with being interpreted as a stigma, infertility is also seen as a disease and a disability. Disease generally refers to the opposite of health, with *health* defined as "a state of complete physical, mental and social well-being, not merely the absence of disease or infirmity."[26] Article 1 of the United Nations Convention on the Rights of Persons with Disabilities says that "persons with disabilities include those who have long-term physical, mental, intellectual, or sensory impairments which in interaction with various barriers may hinder their full and effective participation in society on an equal basis with others."[27] The World Health Organization (WHO) defines infertility as a "disease of the reproductive system" that results in disability, suggesting that people who struggle with infertility do not fully participate in society.[28] Miranda, in *Tengo los óvulos contados*, questions the definition of infertility as an illness, stating,

> Es una pregunta muy difícil de responder. La OMS cataloga la infertilidad como una enfermedad crónica no tanto por sus síntomas, sino por la pérdida de bienestar que supone. Pero de eso, seamos sinceros, no se muere nadie, no es un peligro para la supervivencia. Otra cosa es que la sociedad te haga sentir como un enfermo. A eso es mejor llamarlo «tabú social», mucho más acertado que enfermedad.[29]
>
> [It's a hard question to answer. The WHO catalogs infertility as a chronic illness not due to its symptoms but for the loss of well-being it brings. But let's be real, no one dies, it's not a danger to your survival. One thing is that society makes you feel like a sick person. That should be called a social taboo, which is much more accurate than disease.]

The definition of the term matters, because by equating infertility to disability, we see the connection between infertility and the "cultural ideas that we use to narrate and interpret physical, cognitive, and emotional differences."[30] The labeling of infertility as a disability, though, is a more complex question, since the feeling of stigma also accompanies the label of disability.

In an unexpected interpretation, those who suffer from infertility find that the term *disability* validates the struggles of being infertile. Sternke and Abrahamson explain that "individuals with a relatively invisible but stigmatizing condition (infertility) are requesting to be formally acknowledged by society as disabled."[31] This might seem counterintuitive, since "the main body of literature on disability indicates that stigma increases when one 'becomes' disabled."[32] However, the women interviewed in their study believe that "there was a perception that the label [of disability] would provide evidence of their pain and legitimize their condition, thus lessening the perception they were somehow less than whole women."[33] By recognizing their infertility as a disability instead of a stigma, women can remove the blame from themselves, distancing themselves from the idea of infertility as divine punishment or moral failure. In the United States, having infertility recognized as a disability could aid in access to insurance coverage for fertility treatments (something that has not proven to be the case, according to Sternke and Abrahamson). However, in Spain, the idea of infertility as a disability would have no effect on the ability to access socialized medicine. Spain's Ley General de derechos de las personas con discapacidad y de su inclusión social [General Law of Rights for People with Disability and Their Social Inclusion] recognizes infertility as a disability, saying, "Las personas con discapacidad tienen derecho a recibir protección de su salud" [People with disabilities have the right to receive protection for their health] and that "la salud mental, la salud sexual y la posibilidad de tener hijos tienen especial atención" [mental health, sexual health, and the possibility of having children have special attention].[34] The right to procreate sits among other reproductive rights, and "infertility as a description of childlessness embodies perfectly the modern definition of a disability."[35] Though disability can be interpreted differently through a cultural lens, the concept remains that "women felt that having the label of disabled would provide them with the necessary means to arm themselves to challenge both public and enacted stigma in order to better manage their own identities as women."[36] If infertility could be seen as a disability and not a choice or failure, women could divert the blame of childlessness from their own decisions (to postpone childbearing, for example) to a medical disability that makes them incapable of reproducing. Women could then subvert societal pressures to conform to motherhood by identifying an alternative culprit—the disability, not the woman. Blaming infertility, however, only underlines that "normal" women bear children and does not remove, only displaces, the social imperative to procreate.

Sternke and Abrahamson show that both men and women are equally susceptible to infertility, and both interpret their infertility as a failure. However, most fertility treatments affect women more, since men's contribution is solely linked to the quality of their sperm.[37] The authors explain that "not fulfilling motherhood expectations is often grounds for women with infertility to experience a deep sense of distress and incomplete womanhood."[38] Sternke and Abrahamson record that the women they interviewed for their study reported a "feeling of non-normalcy and discredited social status surrounding the childless state, and concerns regarding the disclosure of status that would arise from a public label."[39] The pressure on people to conform is great; the pressure on women to conform to motherhood can be enormous, and those who don't fit into the mold can suffer from feelings of lack or missed opportunity. The authors present four types of stigma found in their investigation: *felt*, *enacted*, *self*, and *public*. After defining each term, I illustrate how each of these stigmas appears in the novel, underlining the common experience of stigma felt by those who undergo fertility treatments. By analyzing how stigma is both experienced and presented in the novel, we will better understand the complicated process of fertility treatments and their effect on those who undergo them.

The first category of stigma, *felt* stigma, "involves perceptions of the stigmatized person that they are being labeled, stereotyped or isolated from/by others."[40] Sternke and Abrahamson emphasize that in felt stigma, "this person may self-stigmatize, incurring negative beliefs about themselves, loss of self-esteem and self-efficacy, and thus tend to isolate themselves from others, including their own in-group."[41] While *Tengo los óvulos contados* narrates many stories of women and couples, the theme of felt stigma appears most clearly when talking about men's sperm. In a conversation between Miranda, the doctor protagonist, and one of the other workers at the clinic, Miranda considers the absurd idea that men view their virility as linked to their sperm count, while she insists, "Nosotros no medimos virilidad, medimos normalidad" [We do not measure virility; we measure normalcy]. She continues to explain that "el universo del semen está muy mal, y eso que no tiene nada que ver con lo que le está pasado a él" [the universe of semen is really bad, and that has nothing to do with what is happening to him (the patient)].[42] However, the men in the novel interpret their lack of ability to engender a child as a stigma that makes them less of a man, much like women reported feeling less of a woman.

In a study about men's sperm, Randi Sylvest and coresearchers find that men "felt less masculine because they were unable to achieve two common expectations of men: they were unable to impregnate their partner and unable to become a father. These dual failures made them feel worthless as men and threatened their sense of masculinity."[43] Many men found the use of a sperm donor distasteful and would have a "difficult time reconciling that another man would be involved in the conception of their child."[44] Sylvest and colleagues suggest that this negative sense of self-worth "can be perceived as a threat to the masculine identity, closely related to stigmatization."[45] In one case in the novel, when called upon to produce his sperm sample to use for IVF, the man is unable to comply. Miranda imagines the man:

> Encerrado en ese cuarto con un lavabo, un inodoro, una silla y una pantalla situada en lo alto en la esquina. Nada más. Un espacio pequeño en el que ya no hay revistas pornográficas por razones higiénicas y se mantienen las películas pornográficas. Me imagino a mí misma intentando alcanzar un orgasmo en ese lugar y me parece del todo imposible.[46]
>
> [Shut in that room with a sink, a toilet, a chair, and a screen up high in the corner. Nothing else. A small space in which there are no longer pornographic magazines for hygienic reasons and there are pornographic movies. I imagine myself trying to reach an orgasm in that place, and it seems totally impossible to me.]

When his partner finds out that he is unable to produce his sperm sample for the fertilization, she increases the feeling of stigma by calling a friend to tell her that her husband "no vale, que no vale y ya está" [is worthless; he's worthless and that's it].[47] The performative aspect of producing a sperm sample with the pressure of eggs waiting to be fertilized, added to the stigma of needing to use outside help to impregnate one's wife, plus the final piece of the wife's belittlement of her husband, clearly illustrate the feelings of worthlessness that define felt stigma in infertility. Nevertheless, felt stigma is not the only stigma that occurs when investigating how infertility affects those who suffer from it.

The second definition of stigma within infertility studies used by Sternke and Abrahamson is *enacted* stigma, which "refers to actual status loss and specific acts of discrimination towards an individual."[48] While in many of the stories recounted in the book, felt and enacted stigma go hand in hand, such as in the previous example of a woman belittling her husband's ability to produce sperm, Miranda's perception of how mothers treat nonmothers exemplifies how this stigma is acted upon. She lists various comments that women make that are hurtful and callous, such as "Cuando seas madre, lo entenderás" [When you're a mother, you'll understand] or "Y vosotros, ¿para cuándo?" [And you all, when?] or "Por fin he cumplido el gran sueño de mi vida" [Finally I have achieved the great dream of my life].[49] Each cast-off statement painfully strikes women undergoing fertility treatments. Women who receive fertility treatments experience physical, emotional, and economic trauma, and when treatments fail, they must relive that failure each month during menstruation. Sternke and Abrahamson report that women in their study "noted that infertility is unique because sufferers must experience the failure of their treatment, the ensuing disappointment, on a monthly basis."[50] Along with the emotional drain associated with fertility treatments, women also struggle with gender norms. Miall explains that "when cultural norms and values encourage reproduction and celebrate parenthood, childlessness becomes a potentially stigmatizing status which can adversely affect the identities and interpersonal relationships of married persons."[51] While Sánchez-Silva's novel does not attempt to analyze the impact of these treatments on the relationships of heterosexual married couples, it does emphasize that many women come alone to the clinic, placing the onus on women to get pregnant, even though the male partners are half of that equation.

Miranda shows how the women who visit her clinic interpret enacted stigma. They share stories about other women who ask about their private business, with "palabras que hieren y destruyen, camufladas en un absurdo y obsceno interés social" [words that hurt and destroy, camouflaged as an absurd and obscene social interest].[52] The women who visit the clinic see themselves as "mujeres de segunda, todas esas No Diosas de la fertilidad" [second-class women, all of the Non-Fertility Goddesses].[53] The particular story of one client, Clara, shows how hurtful other women can be when enacting stigma. She talks about the process of fertility treatments, saying that while going through the treatments, it seems like everyone around her is pregnant, that "las embarazadas serán como una plaga de zombis que no puedes dejar atrás; ellas serán entonces el recuerdo de lo que deseas y no logras, y su presencia será dolorosa" [pregnant women will be like a plague of zombies that you cannot leave behind; they will be the reminder of what you desire but can't attain, and their presence is painful].[54] When friends call to tell Clara that they are pregnant, she says, "No podrás alegrarte, ni podrás compartir su ilusión, y eso te dolerá" [You will not be able to be happy, you cannot share their excitement, and that will hurt you].[55] She continues, "Te sientes . . . menos. En ese momento te gustaría poder decirle: 'Mira, me parece completamente innecesario que me des los detalles de tu concepción. Me está doliendo lo que cuentas. ¿Qué tal si me ahorras las puntualizaciones y me dejas disimular cierta alegría por ti?'" [You feel . . . less. In that moment, you'd like to be able to tell her, "Look, it seems completely unnecessary that you give me all of the details of your conception. What you're telling me is hurting me. How about if you save the explanation and let me fake some happiness for you?"].[56] While the other women might not mean to enact stigma or make the infertile women feel less-than, their comments still cause pain and create a situation where the infertile women feel the stigma of being unable to conceive naturally. Linda Whiteford and Lois Gonzalez describe how "infertile women come to see themselves as the 'other,' and that stigmatizes them for failing to fulfill the cultural norm."[57] When people question those who do not (or cannot) procreate, they create an environment of enacted stigma, where women not only feel judged by others for not being able to have children but also judge themselves for failing to conceive.

Motherhood is the cultural norm for women, and any woman who cannot or decides not to have children falls outside of that norm and finds herself stigmatized and, many times, judged by those around her, as the examples above illustrate. However, this judgment does not exist only externally. Many women judge themselves harshly for their inability to procreate. In addition to the two previous types of stigma, self-stigma in infertility is related to how an individual with infertility interprets her own situation. In the case of the study done by Sternke and Abrahamson, "infertility has also been described as a 'secret stigma,' one that causes individual women to feel distress, a loss of self-esteem and self-efficacy," which are tendencies of self-stigma.[58] Miranda talks with disgust about blogs where women write about their struggles attaining a pregnancy, as those forums reproduce inaccurate information. She states that every once in a while, she explores Google to see what people are saying. She explains that if you search for "infertilidad" [infertility], you can find mostly useful information, but if you search "No me quedo embarazada, ¿qué puedo hacer?, irás directamente a los blogs en donde los casos particulares te contaminarán. Las mujeres escriben su frustración y su inseguridad. Su ansia por encontrar algo que cada día que pasa ven un poco más lejano" ["I can't get pregnant, what can I do?" you will go directly to the blogs where personal cases will contaminate you. Women write their frustrations and insecurities. Their longing to find something that each day that passes seems more unlikely].[59] Miranda sees a recurring theme of self-stigma in comments like "Cuestionaba a DIOS, que he hecho mal? porqué [*sic*] a mí?" [I asked GOD, "What have I done wrong? Why me?"] or "Creo q la del problema soy yo [. . .], y la verdad es q me tiene muy mal . . . cuando me indispongo me cambia la cara, me pongo de miy [*sic*] mal humor, me enojo conmigo misma" [I think I'm the one with the problem (. . .), and the truth is that it's really bad . . . when I get sick my face changes, and I get in a really bad mood, I get angry with myself].[60] While women suffer from the societal pressure to conform to pronatalist norms, they also encounter self-inflicted suffering that lowers their self-esteem. For some women, the use of blogs to share their situation and find support, while still maintaining their anonymity, allows some release but also reinforces unhealthy ideas, such as medicinal self-treatment, and false myths, like the idea that eating sushi can help women get pregnant.[61] Better to seek professional help to understand the process of assisted reproduction, claims the novel, than to refer to "contaminated" information on the web.

Along with finding (at times misleading) information about infertility online, women discover self-stigma in their past actions and choices. The self-blame encounters many avenues, with women asking, What if?

> ¿Si no hubiera tenido tanto miedo? [What if I hadn't been afraid?]
> ¿Si no me hubiera tomado la píldora del día después? [What if I hadn't taken the morning-after pill?]
> ¿Si hubiera sido mamá en aquel momento? [What if I had become a mother back then?][62]

All of these self-recriminations do nothing to assuage the anguish women feel: "Cuando el tiempo pasa y el deseo de ser madre no se atenúa, sino que crece, aparece la angustia, las preguntas y los reproches no se irán" [When time passes and the desire to be a mother doesn't go away but grows, anguish appears, and the questions and reproaches will not go away].[63] Whiteford and Gonzalez explain that "the frequent lack of a clear etiology for infertility denies women a recognized illness category to blame for their stigmatization. This denial is especially significant in a society where the validation of social identity is formed by the cultural construction of gender roles linked to reproduction," which leads to women not having a specific problem they can blame for their infertility.[64] Even when they are diagnosed with the disease of infertility, there is rarely an explanation for what has caused it. That, in turn, leads them to blame only themselves, a characteristic of self-stigma.

The final type of stigma exemplified in *Tengo los óvulos contados* is *public* stigma, defined as when the loss of social status associated with being childless is used in a discriminatory way toward the stigmatized group.[65] The authors of "Stigma: Advances in Theory and Research" define public stigma as "people's social and psychological reactions to someone they perceive to have a stigmatized condition," which, in this case, is being infertile.[66] When thinking about infertility as a public stigma, the examples of unwitting comments, such as the previously mentioned "Y vosotros, ¿para cuándo?" [And you all, when?], illustrate how fertility is the underlying norm by which all heterosexual couples are judged.[67] People who have sex and get pregnant do not understand the very personal sense of failure that accompanies an inability to become pregnant or impregnate. Therefore, while pronatalist comments might not purportedly be mean-spirited, they are hurtful to those experiencing difficulty attaining a pregnancy.

One example of these discriminatory practices in the novel occurs when a woman, who is thirty-four years old and has been married for three years, visits the clinic with her mother. The mother, who had six children, does not understand why her daughter cannot get pregnant. She wonders, "¿Puede ser que no sepan cómo hacerlo bien?" [Could it be that they don't know how to do it right?], a ludicrous notion that belittles both her daughter and the group of women labeled infertile.[68] The doctor discovers that the woman does not want to become pregnant—is actively preventing pregnancy—but cannot tell her mother due to the stigma of wanting to remain childless. Speaking of her mother and sisters, the patient explains, "Creen que debo tener hijos ya y les da igual si lo deseo o no. Yo no me imagino embarazada, pero eso es impensable para mis hermanas y mucho más para mi madre" [(They) believe that I should have children already, and it doesn't matter to them if I want them or not. I do not imagine myself pregnant, but that is unthinkable for my sisters and even more so for my mother].[69] While the question here may not relate directly to infertility, it does connect directly to stigma.[70] Miall "argues that the childless by choice are more likely to be stigmatized than the infertile," and she quotes another researcher who states that "the subfecund may be considered unfortunate and hence deserving of sympathy, but the voluntarily childless are considered immoral and hence deserving of censure."[71] The public stigma exemplified here relates to the concept that women who do not have children, either voluntarily or involuntarily, experience discrimination as a group. One way to combat this stigma is to reimagine how families are formed and what parenting means.

Patients seeking treatment often make the choice to use gamete donation. How Miranda's patients receive the idea of gamete donation is another example in the novel of how public stigma affects those seeking fertility treatments. Miranda gives the background about Spain's anonymous system of donation, both of eggs and sperm. She tells one client, "Nuestro sistema de donaciones es uno de los más importantes de Europa precisamente por el anonimato. Si el anonimato no fuera garantizado, el número de donantes caería de forma estrepitosa" [Our system of donations is one of the most important in Europe precisely because it is anonymous. If anonymity were not guaranteed, the number of donors would drop precipitously].[72] However, using the genetic material of an unknown donor causes stress for many of the patients. They question how others might perceive them (i.e., as failures for being unable to become pregnant without intervention), how they might perceive the child born to them through donation, and how the child might perceive them as nonparents due to his or her status as coming from donated genetic material.

One of the patients, a woman named Yaiza, talks about her hesitancy in receiving a donated egg. She states, "Pienso sobre todo en si seré capaz de querer a mi hijo o si mi hijo o hija me querrá a mí teniendo en cuenta que no será . . . [. . .] del todo . . . mío" [I think the most about whether I will be capable of loving my child or if my child will love me, keeping in mind that she will not be . . . (. . .) totally . . . mine].[73] Yaiza, then, bases her concept of motherhood on the traditional idea of a genetic relationship being the main connection between mother and child. While Miranda recognizes that the decision is difficult, for the doctor, the outcome outweighs the complication: "Las tasas de embarazos de embriones procedentes de óvulos donados son más altas, incluso, que las de fecundaciones in vitro con microinyección espermática [. . .]. Los resultados médicos son fabulosos, aunque no [se puede] obviar que es una decisión difícil de tomar" [The rates of pregnancies from embryos coming from donated eggs are higher, even, than in vitro fertilization using sperm injection (. . .). The medical results are fabulous, even though you can't overlook that it is a difficult decision to make].[74] Miranda confronts the worry that many have by explaining that while we might imagine the donor as "una persona desaprensiva que, únicamente por dinero y procedente de un ambiente marginal, decide depositar sus gametos en manos de otros. Una vez más, la realidad es otra" [an unscrupulous person who, only for money and coming from a marginalized position, decides to deposit their gametes in others' hands. Once again, the reality is different].[75] Each person who chooses to donate undergoes extensive physical and psychological testing in order to assure the clinic that she or he is appropriate.[76] While these tests are meant to be reassuring, those who accept the donated genetic material still feel the stigma of not being able to achieve pregnancy without intervention.

Accepting gamete donation is another example of public stigma, since the lack of a genetic relationship can lead to questions about the child's parentage. The concept of creating a child with the involvement of a third person can be complicated, as we will see in chapter 3. On the one hand, no one needs to know how the pregnancy was achieved. As Hudson and colleagues show in their study about the public perception of donation, "a couple would not reveal the use of third party genetic material outside of the couple" for "fear of the stigma that it would attract."[77] On the other hand, openly addressing the need to access fertility treatments such as donation allows space to start a conversation about a taboo subject. Both men and women confront public stigma when it comes to gamete donation, and for both parties, the use of a third person can be hidden from those outside of the relationship. Men's experience with pregnancy, however, lacks the lived and embodied experience that women enjoy, since they do not participate in the gestation of a child. One of Miranda's colleagues sees this as a problem for men: While women who receive donated eggs experience pregnancy even if the child is not genetically related to them, men have neither the genetic relatedness nor the embodied experience. He states,

> Al menos, vosotras engendráis en una donación de óvulos, pero ellos tienen que crear el vínculo emocional desde la nada. No he puesto mi semen, no voy a engendrarlo. [. . .] Eso me parece más difícil de construir y lo logran. Crean una proximidad afectiva de la nada porque hasta que el niño llega son puro acompañamiento.[78]
>
> [At least you (women) procreate in egg donation, but they (men) have to create an emotional attachment from nothing. I didn't give my sperm, I'm not going to gestate it. . . . This seems to me more difficult to build, and they do it. They create emotional proximity from nothing because until the child arrives, they are purely accompaniment.]

While men who have low-quality sperm experience self-stigma, they also could interpret their stigma as public, as their self-interpretation of less-than or less masculine could also be seen on a societal level, where men could be judged as broken when unable to engender a child. According to Shanna Swan and Stacey Colino in *Count Down*, sperm count decline "in Western countries is unabating" and shows "no signs of tapering off," having dropped by 50 percent over the last four decades.[79] While men might identify their underperforming sperm as a stigma, it is also a fact that "a high proportion of infertility issues can more clearly be placed at men's feet."[80] It is therefore understandable that infertile people choose to keep their silence in order to avoid feeling stigmatized for their inability to reproduce.

Many women and men choose not to disclose how they approach their infertility. They fear a "discredited social status surrounding the childless state, and concerns regarding the disclosure of status that would arise from a public label."[81] While many access ART to overcome childlessness, there are still taboos around the treatment, especially as related to the use of donated gametes. One couple worries about telling their child about his or her origins, saying, "Creo que nosotros no tendríamos ningún problema en contárselo a nuestro hijo en un futuro, pero pensamos que la donación de gametos sigue siendo un tabú social" [We believe that we wouldn't have any problem telling our child in the future, but we think that gamete donation is still a social taboo].[82] While the doctor insists that the child born to them will be in all realms theirs—grown in the mother's womb and raised, loved, and educated by them—the couple doubts that they can make the decision to give up the genetic relationship to their child (although the child will be genetically related to the father). A combination of two types of stigma occurs in this example: the self-stigma of the woman who cannot produce a viable egg and the public stigma that surrounds the taboo of using donated sperm or eggs to attain a pregnancy.

Feminist perspectives on the use of fertility treatments are complicated and have a clear relationship to stigma. In her article "Fertile Ground: Feminists Theorize Infertility," Charis M. Thompson explains that for feminists, discussions about fertility are twofold. On the one hand, "involuntary childlessness is recognized as one of the greatest forms of unhappiness and loss an adult woman might endure," while on the other hand, feminists are interested in "disrupting the gendered role expectations and the essentialist connection between motherhood and women's identity that greatly intensify infertile women's suffering."[83] Both of these perspectives connote stigma: first, self-stigma, and second, public stigma. Women who cannot have children but who would like to find that they feel less-than, and women who choose not to have children feel judged for their choice. *Tengo los óvulos contados*, told from the perspective of Miranda, a woman who both already has a child and ends the novel unexpectedly pregnant and who also embodies the industry of getting women pregnant for a hefty fee, detracts from the feminist argument aspect of the narrative. However, the novel's wealth of information researched by Sánchez-Silva at the IVI Clinic in Madrid while she herself underwent fertility treatments expands what is currently a small field of literary texts that delve into the cultural and social effects of the increasingly large number of women who want to talk and learn about the subject of infertility and involuntary childlessness.

By analyzing the ways in which we can interpret the varied forms of stigma as related to infertility and childlessness, we see that, for each example, the people seeking assisted reproduction struggled with accepting their infertility and their status as childless. They approached assisted reproduction from a place of lack, seeing the need to overcome "the physical constraints of the body through access to and use of assisted reproductive technologies vital to overcoming the stigma of failed motherhood."[84] For each of the stigmas analyzed here, the novel's examples reinforce how the stigmas are lived by people accessing fertility treatments. As an example of *felt* stigma, men who had sperm deficiencies felt that they were stereotyped as nonmasculine, nonvirile men. At times, even the women they were involved with interpreted their low-quality semen as making them worthless. *Enacted* stigma, how people discriminate against infertile people, was illustrated by how deeply ingrained cultural norms of motherhood are and how women who have children discriminate, sometimes unwittingly, against those who are childless through their hurtful comments. *Self*-stigma is best seen in how women talk about themselves when experiencing difficulties achieving a pregnancy. From blaming God to feeling guilty about previous choices, women embody self-stigma, which leads to a lack of self-esteem. The final stigma analyzed here, *public* stigma, shows how others discriminate against those who are childless. The examples in the novel vary from a mother wondering if her adult child is having sex correctly to couples deciding not to use gamete donation in order not to be judged by those around them. All of these types of stigma illustrate the complications that accompany infertility and its treatments.

Both women and men struggle with what it means for them, psychologically and socially, to be infertile—men doubting their virility and women questioning what it means to be a woman and not a mother. Meanwhile, societal and commercial pressures encourage them to continue on an ever more invasive and expensive path to fertility. Miranda touches on her concern about the medicalization of fertility treatments when she offers,

> Trabajo en una clínica en la que cada vez es más difícil poder mirar a una pareja y decirle: el "no" también existe; no debo ni puedo prometer un bebé; no quiero pero debo decirle a una mujer de 40 que ya es una madre añosa y que de "debería haber venido antes"; tengo que explicar que el azar juega una parte fundamental en una ciencia que no es exacta y, todo eso, tengo que hacerlo sin vapulear la ilusión de los que vienen hasta mí como si fuera el oráculo de la fertilidad y tuviera en mis manos el poder de la creación.[85]

> [I work in a clinic where every day, it is more difficult to look at a couple and tell them that "no" also exists; I shouldn't and can't promise them a baby; I don't want to, but I should tell a woman who is forty years old that she's already a geriatric mother and that she should have come earlier; I have to explain that fate plays a fundamental part in a science that is not exact; and all of that I have to do without killing the dream of those who come to me as if I were the oracle of fertility and had in my hands the power of creation.]

Our belief in science erroneously allows us to think that all diseases are treatable, and our capitalistic beliefs teach us that any problem can be overcome with economic resources. While scientific advances in fertility treatment have indeed allowed many women to experience pregnancy who would not have been able to without intervention, there are still limits to science and to best practices when it comes to these interventions. But once again, age-based infertility is only a symptom of a larger societal problem.

When women put off childbearing and need medical intervention to attain a pregnancy and when the medical system steps up to help these women possibly achieve said pregnancy but all of these topics are not freely spoken about—people do not want to share their perceived failures—this causes the root problem to remain unresolved. Age and fertility in women are linked; that is a fact. If society cannot change its pronatalist, mother-norming position, and if women see motherhood as a burden or a choice to be delayed as long as possible, the outcomes (low birth rates) will not change.

Chapter 1, "Infertility as Business," examined how infertile women feel less-than for not being able to procreate. *Quién quiere ser madre* illustrated how the fertility industry preys upon women's desires to be mothers and demonstrated how the industry uses marketing concepts to entice women to continue to submit to fertility treatments. This chapter focuses on the concept of stigma when related to how women (and men) feel when confronting their infertility and how that stigma manifests in various areas of life. Chapter 3, "Infertility as Crisis," delves into research about the specific area of egg donation in Spain as a way of overcoming infertility. Changing perspectives from fictional writing to nonfiction, Samanta Villar's *Madre hay más que una* narrates Villar's personal experience with infertility in Spain.

CHAPTER 3

Infertility as Crisis

MADRE HAY MÁS QUE UNA BY SAMANTA VILLAR

Samanta Villar is a Spanish journalist and author of *Madre hay más que una* [There is more than one mother], published in 2018. Villar's journalistic career has allowed her to investigate many aspects of Spain and Spanish culture. During her tenure recording *21 días* [21 Days], Villar spent twenty-one days embedded in each area of her investigation, such as "21 días en la industria del porno" [21 Days in the Porn Industry] or "21 días fumando porros" [21 Days Smoking Joints].[1] Most recently, however, Villar is known for her journalism and books published about motherhood in Spain. In *Madre hay más que una*, Villar narrates her experience with assisted reproduction technology (ART) and relates how she became pregnant with twins through egg donation. The book, along with narrating her personal experience, is also a form of investigative journalism about fertility in Europe. As well as writing the book, she also decided to film her pregnancy and birth in the television program *9 meses con Samanta* [9 Months with Samanta].[2] Using a third party to achieve pregnancy (through the use of either an egg, sperm, or a surrogate) depends on the generosity of an altruistic donor. However, altruism, when related to body parts, is complicated and, in the case of egg donation, calls into question the concept of motherhood. Villar's book illustrates the example of a woman who accepts egg donation to achieve pregnancy and the emotional consequences of participation in what is really the purchase and sale of eggs.

This chapter uses the case presented in the book *Madre hay más que una* to show how the concept of altruistic donation impacts the assisted reproduction market in Spain. The chapter also presents the challenges Villar faces as a recipient of donated eggs. I start by situating the question of egg donation within the European Union in general and within Spain in particular. Next, I explore the concept of altruistic donation in the Iberian Peninsula. Thus, by analyzing the situation of egg donation in Spain, I show a system in crisis that is based on the economic precarity of young Spanish women. I suggest that the concept of motherhood, according to Villar's experience, has to change in order to include more than one woman.

The title of the book, *Madre hay más que una*, presents the context: Villar's pregnancy through the use of a third person via egg donation. At the beginning of the book, Villar explains that she and her husband have spent four years "buscando el bebé y sin ayuda de la ciencia tendría[n] unas posibilidades en torno al 5 por ciento de lograrlo" [trying for a baby and without the help of science would have a 5 percent chance of getting one].[3] She begins to question what it means to be a mother in a system that depends on the commercialization of the bodies of other women. Villar recognizes this fact when she reports that "solo un 15 por ciento de las mujeres que tienen una baja reserva ovárica e intentan una fecundación *in vitro* a partir de los treinta y ocho años" [only 15 percent of women that have a low ovarian reserve and try in vitro fertilization (IVF) after thirty-eight years of age] achieve pregnancy, which is what brings her to seek an egg donation.[4] Villar's book discusses the state of fertility in Spain specifically and Europe in general, and it is as much investigative journalism as it is a diary recounting her experience becoming pregnant and giving birth to her twins. Neither Villar's book nor the television show speaks from the perspective of the donor; rather, they speak from the recipient of the eggs, Villar herself. It is important to note that the voice of the woman who donates, absent in this case, would be necessary in order to be able to deeply analyze the failures and accomplishments of the donation system. It is not surprising that a wealthy, famous woman could write about her experiences as a recipient of donated eggs, while the silence of the donor woman exemplifies the inherent inequality in a capitalist system based in social neoliberalism.[5] Unlike organ donation, egg donation calls into question these systems whereby those with purchasing power can become pregnant and those without economic resources donate.

The concept of the donation of human body parts (like kidneys, livers, or plasma) has long been socially accepted. In fact, Spain has the highest rate of organ donation in the world, according to the statistics listed in the *Actividad de donación y trasplante España 2019* [Activity of Donation and Transplant Spain 2019]. In contrast, the donation of gametes, eggs or sperm, is comparatively new and has different rules and interpretations throughout the countries of the European Union. The European Union's Charter of Fundamental Rights, article 3, clearly states, "Everyone has the right to respect for his or her physical and mental integrity," which includes "the prohibition on making the human body and its parts as such a source of financial gain."[6] Spanish law regarding human ART (Law 14/2006) is also clear, indicating that "la donación nunca tendrá un carácter lucrativo o comercial" [donation shall never have a profitable or commercial character] and adding, "La compensación económica resarcitoria que se pueda fijar solo podrá compensar estrictamente las molestias físicas y los gastos de desplazamiento y laborales que se puedan derivar de la donación y no podrá suponer incentivo económico para esta" [Any economic compensation that might be established will solely compensate for physical discomfort and costs related to displacement and work that might be caused by donation and will not assume economic incentive for donation].[7] There is no doubt about this law's interpretation: In Spain, donation can only be done for altruistic motives, not economic reasons. However, in various European countries like Germany, Norway, and Switzerland, egg donation is prohibited, while in others, like Denmark and Sweden, while the practice is permitted, it is considered a health risk for donors due to possible complications, such as hyperstimulation of the ovaries.[8] In contrast, sperm donation is legal (and compensated) throughout the European Union, illustrating the gendered nature of so-called donation.

Due to differing interpretations of the legality of egg donation in Europe, markets for eggs do exist in countries where donation is possible. As previously cited, Spanish egg donors receive compensation only for "physical discomfort and costs related to displacement and work," and this amount ranges from €700 to €1,000, which makes it difficult to interpret donation as fully altruistic.[9] Regardless, as a result of the described differences among European countries, Spain has seen a fertility tourism boom, in which "el 62,2% de la atención reproductiva transfronteriza corresponde a tratamientos con donación de ovocitos" [62.2 percent of cross-border reproductive attention corresponds with egg donation treatments].[10] In her article about Danish travel to Spain for egg donation, Charlotte Kroløkke explains that Danish women go to Spain because Spanish clinics "are among the most widely used and the most respected foreign clinics with which private Danish fertility clinics collaborate and to which Danish women travel for egg donation."[11] She situates this fertility tourism in a larger European framework, offering that "Italians, Swedes, and Norwegians travel to Denmark for anonymous sperm donation, while Danes, Norwegians, and Germans travel to Spain, Greece, the Ukraine, or the Czech Republic for anonymous egg donation."[12] This imbalance among countries calls into question the concept of altruistic donation.

Egg donation is a problem with multiple facets, like the identification of the woman-mother binary, the complexity implied by the sale of a part of the body, and the inequality in reproductive labor. According to Guido Pennings, the emphasis must be placed on altruistic motives for donation in order to avoid the commodification of the human body, and we as humans must insist on the fact that donation to help others is a moral act.[13] His reasoning is echoed by other voices, such as those of Michelle Leve and Laura Mamo. In her article "Reproductive Bodies and Bits: Exploring Dilemmas of Egg Donation Under Neoliberalism," Leve asks if "the technology of egg 'donation' is oppressive or libratory, perpetuates 'motherhood mandates' or subverts biogenetic notions of motherhood, and whether it commodifies women's bodies or offers women new ways to join the labor market using their reproductive body parts."[14] Leve's questioning of the concept of egg donation illustrates how complicated the situation is. Egg donation allows women to become pregnant who likely could not otherwise, but they only can carry that pregnancy based on the paid labor of the young women who sell/donate their eggs. Leve affirms that, within the neoliberal global economy, the reproductive female body is fragmented and commodified, which involves the exploitation of the female body as a "mother machine," a term borrowed from Gina Corea.[15] In so naming the female body, Corea associates women's bodies with the biological mandate that women feel to become mothers, at any cost. This pressure to become a mother leads them to explore alternative ways of attaining a pregnancy, including the willingness to pay another woman to provide an egg.

In agreement with Leve's position, Laura Mamo explains that fertility biomedicine constitutes a neoliberal ethos because it is "another do-it-yourself project enabling us to transform ourselves, identities, and social lives through consumption."[16] While the biological mandate to reproduce puts pressure on heterosexual and same-sex couples, few people can afford to pay to attain a pregnancy outside intercourse with a male counterpart. Women who are unable to become pregnant due to the low quality of their own eggs or who have partners with low-quality sperm and who can afford to pay a donor to provide the missing gamete may be able to become mothers. In agreement with Mamo's position, Ana María Rivas, Fernando Lores, and María Isabel Jociles indicate that "resulta difícil interpretar la producción de ovocitos como 'donación,' más bien podríamos argumentar que el discurso de la 'donación' es una estrategia para legitimar un acto que comprende una relación salarial encubierta, un trabajo productivo no reconocido y la mercantilización completa de la vida humana" [it becomes difficult to interpret the production of eggs as 'donation'; rather, we could argue that the discourse of 'donation' is a strategy to legitimize an act that comprises a covert wage relation, an unrecognized productive job, and the complete commodification of human life].[17] The word *donation*, then, hides the economic problems that create a broken system of motherhood: Older women whose eggs no longer have the quality needed to produce a pregnancy look to younger women to sell their eggs to overcome their financial instability.[18] Leve also interprets the situation of the so-called donation in neoliberal code and adds the following: "Yet herein lies a paradox of egg selling: egg providers attempt to improve their economic status and gain a sense of dignity within global capitalism by selling their eggs, yet these desires are indicative of contexts that promote agency through participation in markets, whether as buyers or sellers."[19] The paradox of donation as remunerated work and personal choice implies a change in the concept of motherhood, because egg donors participate in reproductive work along with the women who gestate.

If one woman provides the genetic material necessary to create an embryo while a second woman provides the womb to grow the fetus, both women can be considered mothers. Indeed, the question of gender arises when considering the concept of motherhood through egg donation, since both the donor and recipient of the donated eggs are women. Effectively, donation is considered a gift from one person to another, but egg donation is an offering that can only be given from one woman to another. It is intimately tied to the female gender. Susana Silva and Helena Machado, in their article about egg donation in Portugal, point out the difference between the genders in relation to donation, expressing the following: "There is an underlying gender ideology to this distinction, which promotes egg donation as a duty, as opposed to the donation of semen, seen as a benefit for which there should be symbolic gratitude for the inconvenience caused for men."[20] By understanding egg donation as a duty for women and sperm donation as a benefit for men, we discover a gendered difference between what the act of donation entails for men and women. Even though both provide essential cells for the creation of an embryo, the situation for the woman (which involves a more invasive, medicalized, and costly donation) is different, not only because of the complex process required to donate an egg, but rather due to the interpretation of the donation in terms of a deeply medicalized and expensive gift.

For the women who donate, the concept of gifting an egg to another woman who wants to become a mother is essential. According to Rene Almeling in her book *Sex Cells*, "The gift rhetoric in egg agencies serves to highlight the importance of what the egg donor is doing for the recipient, making it possible for her to have a child and become a mother."[21] Almeling explains that women create a distinction between biological maternity and social maternity, while the agencies that recruit women donors stress this separation, "de-emphasizing the importance of the egg in favor of highlighting the gestational or caregiving components and pointing to the recipient as the 'real' mother, the one who nurtures."[22] These distinctions between motherhood as labor (care work) and motherhood as corporeal (gestation, egg extraction, conception, etc.) signal that motherhood, with its various functions, could include more than one mother and more than two people.[23] In this way, egg donation can be interpreted as reproductive work.

Women in Spain donate more eggs than women in any other European country. One fertility website suggests that Spain is "the undisputed leader in Europe for egg donation, with around 50% of all European donation activity being performed there and Spain is recognised as a key global destination for infertility treatment."[24] According to Lima, Plaza, and Vega, in Spain,

> La donación de óvulos representa el 35% de los tratamientos realizados y aproximadamente el 40% de la facturación de los centros de reproducción. Constituye más de la mitad de los tratamientos con ovodonación efectuados en Europa y ocupa el primer lugar del ranking de países europeos.[25]

[Egg donation represents 35 percent of treatments carried out and approximately 40 percent of reproduction centers' billing. It constitutes more than half of treatments with egg donation carried out in Europe and occupies the first place in the ranking of European countries.]

According to Sara Lafuente Funes, 40 percent of babies born in Spain in 2017 thanks to IVF were the result of donated eggs, making up 3.5 percent of total births that year.[26] Lafuente Funes affirms that we cannot know why so many young Spanish women decide to donate, "pero está claro que la mezcla de precariedad y mandatos de género allana el camino a que una forma tan profundamente feminizada de obtener ingresos haya logrado expandirse tanto" [but it is clear that the combination of precarity and gender norms paves the way for such a feminized way of earning money to grow so much].[27] These numbers mark not necessarily generosity on the part of Spanish women but rather their precarious financial situation.

Research on the factors that motivate egg donors continues to be poorly represented. Nevertheless, recent studies give some ideas as to why Spanish women choose to donate eggs. In a survey of donor women that included the question "¿Por qué se decidió a ser donante de óvulos?" [Why did you decide to be an egg donor?], one study found that "para el 41% de las mujeres la motivación era económica en primer lugar junto con la idea de ayuda, y un 10% alegó que la motivación principal era la compensación económica" [for 41 percent of women, the primary motivation was tied between economic motivation and the idea of helping, and 10 percent alleged that their primary motivation was economic compensation].[28] It is impossible to see these statistics and interpret that Spanish women only donate for altruistic reasons.

Not only do economic precarity and the lack of job stability help explain the high number of Spanish egg donors, but the concept of the social value of helping another woman be a mother serves as an impetus for donation.[29] Rivas, Lores, and Jociles explain it in this way:

Se construye un imaginario en el que la donación aparece como un acto solidario entre mujeres, homogeneizadas por su "condición natural" derivada del mandato biológico de la maternidad, independientemente de las circunstancias económicas, políticas, sociales, culturales de cada una de ellas. De este modo se oculta la estratificación social dentro del colectivo de mujeres, la desigualdad entre las productoras y las receptoras de ovocitos.[30]

[An imaginary is constructed in which donation appears as an act of solidarity between women, homogenized by their "natural condition" derived from the biological mandate of motherhood (and) independent of economic, political, social, or cultural circumstances of each of them. In this way, social stratification within the collective of women and the inequality between producers and receptors of eggs is hidden.]

This hidden inequality between donors and recipients affects not only the women of Spain but also those of many other countries. Since Spain is a destination for reproductive tourism, these young Spanish women provide genetic material to produce the children of women in various parts of Europe and the world. Wealthy older women who come from northern European countries where egg donation is prohibited travel to Spain to buy eggs donated by Spanish women.[31] The reproductive tourism between the north and south of Europe reveals that "el trabajo biomédico, clínico y reproductivo actual es inseparable de cuestiones de raza, imperialismo e intercambio desigual, incluidas las relaciones de poder que existen entre las mujeres" [current biomedical, clinical, and reproductive work is inseparable from questions of race, imperialism, and unequal exchange, including the power relations that exist between women].[32] Unpaid reproductive work makes up "un entramado de relaciones desigualitarias de clase [que] se articula en las dinámicas de la bioeconomía reproductiva para que jóvenes mujeres de bajos ingresos constituyan el ejército de reserva reproductivo de las parejas o mujeres infértiles acomodadas, de mediana edad" [a network of unequal class relationships that are articulated in the dynamics of the reproductive bioeconomy such that young, low-income women make up the reproductive reserve army for well-off, middle-aged infertile couples or women].[33] These descriptors match the situation of Samanta Villar, a woman in her late thirties who recounts her experience with egg donation in her book *Madre hay más que una*.

Thanks to the story told by Villar, we can at least access one side of the egg donation experience, that of the egg recipient, from a woman who declares herself not to be "lo bastante valiente para tomar la determinación de no tener hijos" [brave enough to have the determination not to have children] but does not long to be a mother.[34] Her words echo what the previous authors analyzed in this book also grapple with: the societal pressure to become mothers. Here, Villar's lack of bravery to go against societal norms and not be a mother, added to the unknown but substantial amount of money spent to be a normal (mother) woman, creates a paradox: If Villar does not necessarily want children, why go to such lengths to become pregnant? Once her mind is made up, however, she begins her journey through multiple assisted reproduction interventions. From her perspective as a recipient, there are three difficulties related to accepting the donation: genetic grief, worries for the future of the child, and remorse. Although Villar understands her privileged position of being able to pay another woman to donate her eggs, Villar's work delves not into the why of the donation but, instead, into the situation of being a recipient and its consequences. Therefore, by using her book as a case study, we can see the complex process of accepting a supposedly altruistic gift, with the moral, ethical, and emotional consequences it involves. While traditionally, motherhood has been interpreted as monolithic, meaning that there is only one way to interpret who is the mother of a child, the use of another woman's eggs leads Villar to question this concept.

The notion of genetic grief permeates the narration of Villar. Upon accepting that she would have a greater chance of being pregnant with donated eggs, the author mentions that she passed through a stage of "duelo genético" [genetic grief], which she describes as the moment "cuando [las mujeres] son conscientes de que sus hijos no contendrán su misma carga genética, [y] pasan por una etapa de dolor, de sensación de pérdida irreparable e incluso depresión" [when (women) are conscious of the fact that their children will not possess their (the women's) own genetic material, (and) they pass through a stage of pain, the sense of irreparable loss and even depression].[35] She admits that it was difficult for her to accept that "[sus] hijos no serán hijos [suyos]" [her children will not be her children].[36] She tells the story of her grandmother and her fascinating life as a woman in the postwar period, and it saddens her to think that the "cadena de ADN" [DNA chain] that unites her and her grandmother "a pesar de la muerte se pierda definitivamente" [despite death would be definitively lost].[37] She understands that what she carries in her DNA is not what will be carried by her children, something that, for her, represents a sad moment within her experience with donation. When she looks for more information about genetic grief and finds almost nothing, she is surprised and asks, "¿Que la Wiki no diga nada del duelo genético es una prueba de que el tabú de la infertilidad está más extendido de lo que creo?" [Is the fact that Wikipedia doesn't say anything about genetic grief proof that the taboo of infertility is more extensive than I think?].[38] From the perspective of the receiving woman, one consequence of donation is that she experiences grief for the loss of who her son or daughter might have been with her genetic makeup.

For Villar, this genetic grief follows her throughout the book. For example, when Villar thinks about the moment of giving birth, she fears that when the twins are born, she will only see "la viva imagen de esa desconocida" [the spitting image of that unknown woman].[39] For the woman who becomes pregnant via egg donation, Kroløkke says that "motherhood is restored through efforts put into achieving pregnancy, as well as shared blood and space."[40] Comparing the idea of the mother as the woman who gestates with the earlier idea that the mother is the woman who provides the DNA, Kroløkke underlines that the donor "is explicitly framed as a gift giver and not a mother."[41] The rupture between these two faces of motherhood is reflected here: If the woman who donates is not the mother, and the woman who gives birth also does not feel like the mother, how can we define the concept of motherhood? According to Spanish law, the woman who gives birth is the mother.[42] Villar, when she asks herself who the mother or father is or what defines the role of mother or father, responds that, from her point of view, "lo único que lo define es la voluntad de serlo y la ejecución de esa voluntad" [the only thing that defines it is the desire to be it and the execution of this desire].[43] Villar struggles to coexist with the uncertainty caused by her pregnancy through donation. She believes that the desire to be a parent is enough while she mourns the fact that she is not genetically related to her children. Her genetic grief causes her to accept the concept of "voluntad" [free will], a notion that fits into a neoliberal system: With the right conditions, anything can be bought or sold, including an ovum. Structural inequalities that allow some women to "donate" eggs while others "buy" them are not questioned, which allows the system to perpetuate these inequalities. Nevertheless, Villar works to come to terms with her purchased pregnancy.

To mitigate the sense of doubt about selling an egg, the marketing in the clinics in Spain focuses on donation as an altruistic act. Examples of marketing material to this effect include "Tu ayuda es un regalo para la vida" [Your help is a gift for life] and "Dona ilusión, dona vida" [Donate hope, donate life].[44] In an interview, Carlos Simón, director of the IVI Clinic in Valencia, explains that the idea of egg donation is based on "giving of 'excess' tissue or tissue drawn from a 'natural reserve' of eggs that otherwise would have gone to waste."[45] By promoting donation as a natural concept of unneeded or wasted material, the clinics separate the idea of motherhood from the work of supplying the egg, wherein the egg has nothing to do with being a mother, and by promoting selflessness, where the donor helps another woman achieve her dreams of becoming a mother.[46] However, from Villar's perspective of a woman who has become pregnant with a donated egg, the concept continues to be nebulous because, as Villar exemplifies, the gestating woman knows that the children from the donated eggs are not genetically hers. By framing donation as a giving away of excess, unneeded materials and interpreting egg reception as a period of mourning for the woman who gives up her genetic connection to her child, women who participate in the system of donation open the interpretation of motherhood to include more than one woman, even if only one of these women is recognized as the mother.

The other sides of this conversation do not appear in this book: How does the egg donor feel about her genes in someone else's children? How does the child produced by a donated egg feel about the way he or she was conceived? In order to separate the genetic relationship between the donated egg and the child produced by that egg, egg donation is marketed as a gift. Egg donation is not recognized as remunerated work or as paid labor, even though Spain's dire financial situation encourages young women to donate in order to receive limited compensation. In this sense, Kroløkke, in her chapter "The Golden Egg: The Business of Making Mothers Through Egg Donation," discusses the concept of donation as a gift, saying, "Women donating eggs will be perceived as altruistic helpers who want nothing more than for recipients to have families."[47] Villar also alludes to the eggs as a gift, explaining that she fantasized "con un modelo de familia en el que los que aportamos nuestra biología, los que [la] ayudan con su material genético y los que participemos en la crianza de [sus] hijos podamos sentarnos a la mesa de vez en cuando y compartir una amistad" [about a model of family in which those who provide our biology, those who help her with their genetic material, and those who participate in the raising of her children can all sit at the table from time to time and share a friendship].[48] Later she says that she, not the woman who "cedió sus óvulos" [surrendered her eggs] to her, is a mother "a todos los efectos" [for all purposes].[49] This comment opens the question of how to define a mother: Is she the person whose genetics are passed down? The woman who gestates and gives birth? The woman who takes care of and raises the children? The title of the book, then, introduces this concept of varying categories of maternity. Yet this multiplicity of maternal definitions becomes further complicated when viewed through the lens of neoliberal economics. A fundamental conflict exists in the concept of motherhood with donated eggs: The ovum marketed as an altruistic gift is, more truthfully, an egg sold as one mode of participation within the reproductive labor market, especially in Spain, where the unemployment rate is very high for young women.[50]

The fact that the donation is anonymous and that the information about the donating woman is scarce creates a situation that causes the receiving woman to worry about the genetics of the donor woman.[51] Villar admits that "[l]e habría encantado ver una foto de la donante de los óvulos que han servido para engendrar a [sus] hijos y conocer algo más de ella que los pocos rasgos físicos y alguno médico de los que la ley [le] permite disponer" [she would have loved to see a photo of the donor of the eggs that have served to beget (her) children and to know more about her than just the few physical and medical traits that the law permits (her) to have].[52] While knowing the donor is impossible due to obligatory anonymity in Spain, Villar verifies that other women also suffer from the same worries that she does. In an online forum, a woman says, "Me siento como si le fuera a robar ovocitos a la donante" [I feel as if I stole eggs from the donor].[53] The author shares her worry about the long-term results of the donation when she says, "Empecé a pensar que mi manera de plantearme las consecuencias de la ovodonación podría acabar generando un fantasma que contaminase mi vínculo con mis hijos" [I began to think that my way of considering the consequences of egg donation could end up creating a ghost that would contaminate my connection to my children].[54] She comments that while she grappled with the consequences of donation, other people around her "creían que le daba una importancia excesiva al tema [. . . porque l]a mayoría de la gente considera que la donación de óvulos es algo minúsculo en comparación con la gestación y la crianza" [believed that she was giving too much importance to the subject (. . . because) the majority of people consider egg donation to be minuscule in comparison with gestation and parenting].[55] As seen earlier in Kroløkke's study, the definition of mother includes parenting and gestation, but it becomes complicated with the introduction of donation.

Thus, one of Villar's worries, connected to genetic grief, is physical dissimilarity with her sons or daughters, since in Spain, women cannot choose a donor, unlike in other countries like the Czech Republic and the United States. Rivas, Lores, and Jociles explain that "la ley de 2006 prohíbe la selección de las donantes por parte de los receptores, asignando a los equipos biomédicos esta tarea" [the 2006 law prohibits the selection of donors on the part of the recipients, assigning this task to biomedical teams], concluding the following: "En todo caso, el equipo médico correspondiente deberá procurar garantizar la mayor similitud fenotípica e inmunológica posible de las muestras disponibles con la mujer receptora" [In any case, the corresponding medical team should seek to guarantee the most phenotypic and immunological similarity possible of the available samples with the recipient woman].[56] For Villar, who has light eyes and is rather tall, it is more difficult to find a donor with those characteristics.[57] Phenotypic matching allows parents to hide the fact that they used donated materials to have a child, and it also obscures the lack of a genetic relationship between parents and children by trying to match physical characteristics.

Even though Villar says that phenotypic similarity isn't important for her, the clinic must match her appearance. The Spanish law requires it in order to "renaturalizar la relación entre los padres y los hijos, dado que la presunción cultural derivada del sistema del parentesco occidental es que los hijos son continuidad biogenética de los padres, que supone la continuidad de los rasgos fenotípicos" [renaturalize the relationship between parents and children, given that the cultural presumption derived from the Western kinship system is that children are the biogenetic continuity of their parents, which means the continuity of phenotypic traits].[58] The idea of phenotypic resemblance is promoted in order to hide the third-party intervention in the pregnancy in case the family of the child born does not want comments about whether the child resembles the parents.[59] In this way, from the perspective of the donor, problems arise because a young woman who has certain physical traits that are more socially valued, like being tall, blonde, and light-eyed, might be hard to find. According to Priscila Rivera in her study about women who donate eggs in Barcelona, the majority of donors are between eighteen and twenty-one years old; 84 percent were born in Spain, with 5 percent of the donors from Romania followed by lower numbers from other countries; and 17 percent are university students.[60] Not only do these statistics speak to the precarity of the women involved in donation; they also show how different genetic traits are preferred.[61]

Another complication for women using egg donors arises from the difficulty of matching physical characteristics as well as chromosomal viability. For many women, including Villar, this means several attempts with eggs from several egg donors. The cost per cycle for using an egg donor allows only the wealthy to persist. When the clinic calls Villar to tell her they have a possible donor, they say that "ha sido una casualidad" [it had been a coincidence] that they had found a donor with similar physical characteristics to hers, to which she responds, "Viva la suerte. Viva la donante" [Long live luck. Long live the donor].[62] In the end, that donor is ruled out for some reason, but they find another, and although the author manages to get pregnant, she loses the pregnancy after nine weeks.[63] Upon arriving at the clinic to have an ultrasound, her doctor asks her, "El embarazo no va bien, ¿eh?" [The pregnancy isn't going well, huh?] to let her know that the pregnancy isn't viable.[64] Consequently, they perform a curettage to analyze the gestational sac, and they discover that there was a chromosomal anomaly.[65] Finally, they find a third donor, and through that donation, Villar gets pregnant with what will be her twin children. After two failed attempts at IVF and three attempts with donated eggs from three different donors, she achieves her goal. From the perspective of Villar, who is in a comfortable economic situation and has a partner who supports her, the pregnancy is a success. In contrast, if we analyze it from another perspective—for example, considering the donors and their situations or the inequality that exists between women belonging to wealthy classes and those who donate—the system is a failure.[66]

The reproductive market is built on a system of inequality, as only those with financial resources can access the most reliable techniques, such as egg donation. As Lafuente Funes indicates, the reproductive market not only affects the infertile women or the young women who donate their eggs; rather, "está en juego la normalización de nuevas formas de comprender el cuerpo, el trabajo, el género y la reproducción tanto familiar como social" [the normalization, both familial and social, of new ways to understand the body, work, gender, and reproduction is at stake].[67] We do not want a reproductive market that is intertwined "con los procesos de estratificación reproductiva" [with processes of reproductive stratification] or for infertility to become resolved "de forma privatizada, tecnológica y mercantilizada" [in a privatized, technological, and commodified way] and externalized.[68] Villar's story exemplifies the inequality of access to ART, where a woman can resort to a private health system thanks to her privileged economic situation. However, the story does not end with the attainment of the pregnancy.

Once she becomes pregnant, Villar begins to worry about the future. During her pregnancy, she suffers from nausea and other problems characteristic of a complicated pregnancy. Her experiences lead her to question motherhood as essential for women, eventually regretting her condition. According to Orna Donath in her book *Regretting Motherhood*, "We need to rethink the axiom that motherhood is necessarily experienced as worthwhile by all mothers everywhere."[69] Villar demonstrates this feeling when she admits, "El embarazo no siempre es esa experiencia maravillosa y casi mística que te cambia la vida" [Pregnancy is not always that wonderful, almost mystical experience that changes your life].[70]

But in addition to questioning the value of a motherhood that she struggled to obtain, the author feels deceived, confessing, "Me he tragado la historia de que la maternidad es maravillosa y ahora estoy condenada de por vida" [I've bought into the story that motherhood is wonderful, and now I'm condemned for life].[71] Villar is not the first woman to express such opinions, and those opinions are not only for mothers who use ART. In her book about motherhood, Isabel García-Zarza also admits to believing that she was a "bicho raro" [strange bug], stating, "No me sentía en absoluto identificada con la imagen que me vendían de la maternidad, ese mundo almibarado de felicidad permanente. Primero me sentí un monstruo, pero luego fui descubriendo que no era yo la única" [I didn't identify at all with the image they sold me of motherhood, that sweet world of permanent happiness. At first I felt like a monster, but then I discovered that I wasn't the only one].[72] Donath understands women's regrets when it comes to motherhood and explains that the issue is not whether motherhood is worth it; rather, "regret is an alarm bell that not only should alert societies that we need to make it easier for mothers to be mothers, but that invites us to rethink the politics of reproduction and the very obligation to become mothers at all."[73] By questioning the value of motherhood, Villar points to the crisis that mothers face: The lack of societal support for women as mothers encourages women to either not become mothers or postpone motherhood until traditional pregnancies are not viable.

Furthermore, Villar also mentions the social difficulties of having children and the lack of recognition of the work needed to care for them. She explains, "Ahora entiendo las reivindicaciones feministas de valorar económicamente los cuidados, exigir su incorporación al producto interior bruto, reclamar una compensación económica y digna. Siento haber despreciado ese papel durante tanto tiempo y me da vergüenza ser consciente de su importancia solo ahora que me lo vivo en carne propia" [Now I understand the feminist demands to economically value caregiving, to require its incorporation into the gross domestic product, to demand worthy economic compensation. I feel sorry for having scorned this role for so long, and I'm ashamed to be conscious of its importance only now that I'm living it in my own flesh].[74] Before becoming a mother, when she was investigating issues for her previous television programs, she admits that she never worried about work-life balance. Now that she has experienced it in "en carne propia" [in the flesh], she understands that the situation is unsustainable and that the work of caring for children is part of being a mother and should be recognized at a societal level. This declaration echoes other feminist critiques that demand social changes in Spain, such as that of Inés Campillo and Sandra Ezquerra, who say,

> Tras décadas de hegemonía de las políticas neoliberales, las cuales contribuyen a la mercantilización del cuidado y agravan su invisibilización, y después de una gestión austeritaria de la crisis económica que ha impuesto recortes y

> retrocesos particularmente en el ámbito de la reproducción social, el feminismo reivindica la importancia del cuidado con una insistencia y una vitalidad renovada.[75]
>
> [After decades of hegemony of neoliberal politics, which contribute to the commodification of care and exacerbate its invisibility, and after austerity-based management of the economic crisis that has imposed cuts and rollbacks, particularly in the sphere of social reproduction, feminism demands the importance of care with renewed insistence and vitality.]

When motherhood is difficult or impossible to attain, the social system does not support families, and caregiving is made invisible, the reproductive system enters into crisis.

The term *crisis*, then, comes into play in multiple areas of concern: The lack of support systems, lack of economic stability, and lack of fertility are just a few. Lafuente Funes uses the term *crisis* "no como sinónimo de la caída de la natalidad, sino como forma de señalar que la reproducción de la vida, al igual a su sostenibilidad, se ha dejado en los márgenes de lo que se prioriza socioeconómicamente" [not as a synonym for the declining birth rate but as a way to signal that the reproduction of life, just like its sustainability, has been left in the margins of what is socioeconomically prioritized].[76] This crisis affects not only biological reproduction but also social reproduction, which creates precarity by externalizing reproduction and caregiving.[77] Villar's crisis stems from her own experience in accessing medical interventions to become pregnant, her use of other women for their eggs, and subsequently, her comprehension of the state of motherhood and its lack of support at a societal level. Add to this her internal crisis of genetic grief and concerns about her future as a mother of twins from donated eggs, and the term *crisis* expands to encompass the entire concept of motherhood.

Motherhood as a crisis exists when only one woman serves as mother. Examining this situation from the perspective of Villar, money can resolve many of the problems mentioned above, such as "buying" eggs and buying the domestic help of another woman to help meet the demands of motherhood. For Villar, her experience improves when she finds a nanny who helps her with her twins. By outsourcing the care work that falls to most mothers, Villar becomes more comfortable with her own motherhood. She admits that her life began to go back to normal when she employed a woman who collaborated "con el trabajo doméstico y los bebés" [on domestic work and the babies].[78] Villar's privilege is obvious, as she has at-home help while she continues working and recovering from the birth. But here we observe the inequality in motherhood: While some women have the financial capability to purchase whatever they need to make their maternity work (eggs, nannies, etc.), others supply the goods needed (the eggs and domestic help). The system always fails for women with few resources. Women who do not have secure careers, supportive partners, and access to financial resources face a separate type of crisis than Villar, whose crisis stems more from her recognition of motherhood as work.

Villar's perspective on the work of motherhood causes her to question if children are worth the cost to her career and lifestyle. For Villar, who works as a journalist, her job is secure, but her work schedule must change. She expresses that her "trabajo viajando quince días al mes es incompatible con criar a dos hijos" [work traveling fifteen days a month is incompatible with raising two kids], but she wants "hacerlo todo, como tantas mujeres" [to do it all, like so many women].[79] Nevertheless, although she logically understands that she cannot keep working as she had done before, emotionally, she does not want to give it up: "Así que me quiero—escribo *me quiero* y no sé si la expresión más honesta es *me debo*—dedicar a ellos" [Although I want to—I write *I want to*, and I don't know if a more honest description would be *I should*—focus on them].[80] She understands that social pressure obligates her to dedicate herself to her children, and because of this, she says, "Me he metido en la cárcel yo sola. He cometido el error de mi vida y no hay marcha atrás" [I alone put myself in this prison. I've made the biggest mistake of my life and there's no going back].[81] In this way, with that negative reflection on her own motherhood, Villar presents us with a conflicting version of her experience as a mother. Regardless, she cannot end the book without changing her mind because, as Donath explains, it is difficult for a woman to admit she regrets being a mother.[82] At the end, Villar says, "Nunca más he vuelto a pensar que me he equivocado escogiendo la maternidad" [I have never again returned to thinking that I was wrong to choose motherhood]. This is meant to reassure the reader that having children really is worth it, even with the changes that accompany motherhood.[83]

In 2019, Villar published her third nonfiction book, *La carga mental femenina* [*The Female Mental Burden*], "un conjunto de historias cotidianas protagonizadas por madres, con el que se pretende dar visibilidad al problema que tienen las mujeres tras la maternidad, que viven con el doble peso su vida laboral y familiar" [a collection of everyday stories featuring mothers, which attempts to give visibility to the problem women have regarding motherhood, who live with the double weight of their work and family lives].[84] After several interviews about her book, the headlines shouted that Villar said, "La maternidad es un horror" [Motherhood is a horror] and "Mi vida es peor desde que tengo hijos" [My life is worse since I had children].[85] In an interview in *La Vanguardia*, Villar speaks "sin tapujos" [no holds barred] about the difficulties of being a mom and states that mothers are "encantada[s] porque quiere[n] a [s]us hijos y porque [les] gusta cuidarlos" [happy because they love their children and like taking care of them]. She continues, "¡Como yo! ¡Pero claro que mi vida es peor! En términos de calidad de vida, de descanso, de libertad, de ausencia de conflictos" [Like me! But of course my life is worse! In terms of quality of life, of sleep, of freedom, of absence of conflicts].[86] Like the quote from *Madre hay más que una*, Villar's headlines show how complicated a lived maternity can be. While her voice truly represents the situation of mothers in Spain (and elsewhere), Villar speaks from a position of privilege, and it is impossible to ignore that aspect.

By being the recipient of eggs from three different donors, by regretting her motherhood because of its effect on her professional and social life, and by questioning the concept of motherhood when the mother is not the carrier of the same genetic material as her children, Villar presents an unusual perspective on motherhood. Villar's motherhood is based on an unequal system of access: She has access to ART, the eggs of a young woman who chose to donate, and a nanny to whom she subcontracts domestic tasks. By contrast, her motherhood embodies the problems of inequality of women living in Spain. Regardless, her positionality does not detract from her motherhood. She continues suffering from "una perpetuación tanto de la centralidad de la economía considerada productiva como de la marginación e invisibilización de la reproductiva" [the perpetuation of both the economic centrality of work considered productive and the marginalization and invisibility of reproductive work] because that is the situation for each woman who is a mother.[87]

Villar's writing highlights that the economic context of Spain presents a problem regarding reproductive work. With such a high unemployment rate for young people and the rising age of first-time mothers,[88] Spain is a country with an unsustainable population decline. If women delay motherhood and later cannot have children by traditional means, then cannot access the public health system because of wait times between eighteen and twenty-four months for an appointment, the situation is critical.[89] Young women who do not have many alternatives, "impulsadas por la necesidad económica, acceden a someterse a tratamientos hormonales y punciones ováricas. De no encontrarse estas mujeres en estado de vulnerabilidad social, tal vez no accederían a participar" [motivated by economic necessity, allow themselves to be subjected to hormonal treatments and egg retrievals. Were these women not in this state of social vulnerability, perhaps they would not agree to participate].[90] The female burden, then, is a double-edged sword. The woman who enjoys a more comfortable position, like Villar, must use her own financial resources to achieve pregnancy, but in order to do so, she has to use other women who live in precarious situations to achieve and sustain motherhood. That is to say, she has to use the donor woman and the woman who cares for her children. Young women who cannot (or choose not to) have children because of their economic situations enter into the system of commodification of the body by selling (donating) their eggs to women who can subsidize the donation.[91]

For this reason, motherhood is in crisis. Motherhood is "menospreciad[a] en una sociedad capitalista, mercantilizada e individualista como la actual. Visibilizar y dar centralidad a la maternidad, la crianza y los cuidados es lo que tanto molesta. No es el hecho de ser madre en sí, sino una determinada manera de entender cómo serlo" [disparaged in a capitalist, commodified, and individualist society like ours today. Making motherhood, parenting, and caregiving visible and central is what is so bothersome. It is not the fact of being a mother in itself, but rather a certain way to understand how to be one].[92] If society does not support women having children through access to dependable income and housing, assisted reproduction, and care work, we will continue to see fewer children born because the societal context does not permit it. Lafuentes Funes declares, "Es evidente que un sistema que no prioriza la sostenibilidad de la vida, sino la acumulación de capital y el crecimiento económico, no es un sistema que facilite la reproducción de la vida" [It is evident that a system that does not prioritize the sustainability of life, but instead the accumulation of capital and economic growth, is not a system that facilitates the reproduction of life].[93] Thus, Spain is in a reproductive crisis "porque existe una desigualdad profunda en el acceso a las condiciones básicas de las que reproducimos" [because there exists a profound inequality in access to the basic conditions for we who reproduce].[94] Women's unequal access to jobs, housing, income, medical care, and societal support all contribute to the current situation in Spain that allows some women to pay to become mothers while others sell their eggs to make ends meet. In order to change this situation of inequality, Sandra Ezquerra explains that a starting point would be to recognize care work as a central part of socioeconomic life and to promote the co-responsibility of all involved in care work, for, as we see in Villar's narrative, it takes a village to care for (and have) a child.[95]

Villar's situation illustrates the complications of infertility and the difficulties that accompany pregnancy through assisted reproduction. Although she leaves us with a positive perspective "de puro amor" [of pure love] that she feels toward her children, she also shares that her reconciliation with motherhood has not been simple.[96] As Marina Bettaglio explains, books written about motherhood always express "discontent and bewilderment but also a sense of inadequacy and guilt, since regardless of what women as mothers decide to do, whether they go back to work or retreat to the domestic role, they are doomed to self-recrimination."[97] Villar never offers a completely sugarcoated version of motherhood, but she does make us reflect on the reproductive crisis in Spain and the consequences that egg donation has on both the donor and the recipient. This new model of motherhood takes advantage of the precarious situation of other women to provide, at first, genetic material to achieve a pregnancy, and then, once the baby has been born, care for the children as domestic help. This situation is also based on a broken system of unequal access, where some women pay to procreate while others are paid for their eggs. Those who provide the genetic material try to better their lives by working within a system that devalues their contribution to capitalist society.

While the previous chapters explored assisted reproduction through a fictional (although autobiographical) lens, Villar's book narrates her own experience and includes statistics and stories about many other people who need outside help—such as lesbian mothers and mothers who lose a pregnancy or a child—as well as interviews with employees and donors at a mail-order Danish sperm bank. Her investigative journalism adds much to our understanding of fertility issues in Europe and Spain. The first three chapters of this book have in common in-depth descriptions of the process of accessing fertility treatments in Spain, with varying outcomes. They also all speak to the financial aspect of these treatments and their accessibility. The following chapter explores the concept of adoption as an alternative to ART.

CHAPTER 4

Infertility as Classist

A MÍ NO ME IBA A PASAR BY LAURA FREIXAS

In 2005, Angelina Jolie adopted her daughter Zahara from Ethiopia.[1] In 2006, Madonna adopted her son David from Malawi. Each of these women subsequently adopted other children internationally. In Spain in 1999, the famous singer and actress Rocío Jurado, at the age of fifty-five, adopted two children from Colombia.[2] In 1996, the Spanish singer Isabel Pantofla adopted a daughter from Peru.[3] These high-profile international adoptions created new conversations about adoption in general and international adoption in particular. Indeed, Benyam Mezmur's article reminds us that Zahara, who was said to be an orphan, actually had a living mother who had not consented to her daughter's adoption.[4] Mezmur also tells us that Madonna was said to have donated £1.7 million to the orphanage in Malawi to bypass the adoption regulations of that country.[5] These examples show the complexities of international adoption: the heartwarming stories of families finding the child of their heart versus the idea of stealing children from their countries of origin.[6]

This chapter examines adoption as an alternative to fertility treatments. Whereas in previous chapters, I have examined how women who are diagnosed as infertile utilize assisted reproduction technology (ART), here I show how, in this case, after trying several rounds of fertility treatments, the author chooses to expand her family through international adoption. The 2019 autobiography *A mí no me iba a pasar* [It Wouldn't Happen to Me] by Laura Freixas tells her personal story of her life with her French husband, Étienne, from the beginning of their relationship to its end, including the process of building their family. After some medical intervention, they are able to have one child, a girl, but they encounter problems becoming pregnant a second time. At first they resort to fertility treatments to attain their second pregnancy, but after years of attempts, they choose to adopt a boy internationally from Russia. This chapter analyzes the narration of the author's struggle with infertility and the process of adoption.

Using Karen Dubinsky's tropes of adoption as rescue versus adoption as kidnapping, the analysis shows how Freixas recognizes her position of privilege yet still embraces the discourse of maternal savior. While initially questioning the value of motherhood due to the inequalities faced by women who are mothers, Freixas concludes that motherhood can be a rewarding experience and that rescuing a child from an alcoholic biological mother has increased her maternal desire for her son.

Laura Freixas, born in Barcelona in 1958, along with being a writer, is also a literary critic, a translator, and an editor.[7] Her first novel, *Último domingo en Londres* [Last Sunday in London], was published in 1997. She is perhaps best known for her work supporting women authors in Spain, with anthologies such as *Madres e hijas* [Mothers and Daughters] (1996) and *Cuentos de amigas* [Stories of Friends] (2009). The oldest author included in *Narrating Infertility in Spain*, Freixas also stands out as the most established writer of the women included here as well as the most influential in opening the publishing industry for women like Diana López Varela and Silvia Nanclares, who, like her, also work as journalists. In her 2015 book *El silencio de las madres y otras reflexiones sobre las mujeres en la cultura*, Freixas calls out the need for more women to write about their experiences with motherhood, saying, "Es una cultura en la que falta una voz: la de las madres pensantes" [It is a culture in which there is a voice lacking: that of thinking mothers].[8] In this book of essays, she not only encourages women authors to write about motherhood but also narrates about her own experience to add her voice to the growing number of works in Spanish about this topic. In an interview about *El silencio de las madres*, Freixas explains that motherhood is rarely represented in great literature or other intellectual writings. When maternity is mentioned, it is presented "como algo maravilloso e ideal y a las mujeres como felices de sacrificarse por sus hijos. Se perpetúa el mensaje de la maternidad como algo impersonal, como si las madres no fuéramos seres humanos con nuestras dudas, nuestras incertidumbres y nuestras reflexiones" [as something marvelous and ideal and women as happy to sacrifice themselves for their children. The message of motherhood as something impersonal is perpetuated, as if we mothers were not human beings with our own doubts, our uncertainties, and our reflections].[9] Having thought and written about motherhood extensively, and belonging to a different generation of women than those in the previous chapters, Freixas's perspective on motherhood is unique in that her choice to become a mother came before the Great Recession and before anyone spoke openly about ART. However, the publication date of the text, as well as its storyline, fit well into the scope of this book. When asked why she waited until 2019 to publish this autobiography, Freixas answered,

> Porque es una etapa cerrada en mi vida, desde que conozco al que iba a ser mi marido hasta que nos separamos (1985–2003), que ha quedado atrás y que me

permite hablar de esa Laura como si no fuera yo. Necesitaba escribirla. Y no lo veo tanto como un proceso de desnudez personal sino como de interrogación colectiva.[10]

[Because it is a closed chapter of my life, from when I met the one who would be my husband until we separated (1985–2003), that has stayed behind and that allows me to talk about that Laura as if it weren't me. I needed to write it. And I don't see it so much as a process of personal nakedness but as a process of collective interrogation.]

While the main storyline of her autobiography recounts the years from 1985 to 2003, including her marriage and how it ended, Freixas also narrates not only her difficulty in attaining her first pregnancy but also her decision to adopt internationally after discovering her secondary infertility. By positioning international adoption as a viable option to become a mother, Freixas both questions the system of international adoption and benefits from it, underlining the unequal impact on those who adopt and those who give up their children for adoption.

Freixas's story illustrates the difficulty one encounters at many stages of adoption. She goes between seeing her son's adoption as a rescue from the poverty and disgrace that awaited him as an orphan in Russia and as a kidnapping. While both positions are presented in her autobiography, she accepts her adopted child as hers and minimizes the backstory that accompanies him. The analysis of an autobiographical text proves fruitful when examining Freixas's recollection of her adoption of her son. According to Genevieve Lloyd, "Autobiography purports to present the truth of a self as grasped by itself."[11] Lloyd notes that not only does the concept of truthful retelling define an autobiography but the concept of time does too:

Much of the perplexity of the relations between self as subject and as object, spring from the self's peculiar relations to time. An autobiography is as much the expression of a present self as it is the representation of a past one. The narrator is the creator of the protagonist, although it is also true that the protagonist is the model to which that creation is supposed to conform. Autobiography can illuminate questions about the relations between truth, time, and selfhood.[12]

Autobiography, then, contains both aspects of truth: as remembered by the writer herself and as a representation of the past (or fiction) as the writer reexamines the experience as she writes about it. Since "the distinction between fiction and autobiography is not an either/or polarity," I analyze Freixas's work recognizing that it is autobiography but interpreting it as fiction.[13] Laura Freixas is both the author and the protagonist of her autobiography. As Paul De Man explains,

"The name on the title page is not the proper name of a subject capable of self-knowledge and understanding, but the signature that gives the contract legal, though by no means epistemological, authority."[14] In this analysis of Freixas's work, I at times interchangeably refer to both the author and the character of the book as the same person, which they both are and are not.

In Spain, adoption happens frequently. In fact, one out of every ten adopted children worldwide comes to Spain.[15] In 2005, Spain held first place for the number of adoptions per capita.[16] According to Peter Selman, Spain ranked second in the world in receiving children through international adoption in the early 2000s, after the United States, with that number falling precipitously after the 2008 Great Recession.[17]

Between 2008 and 2017, Spain's birth rate went from 1.46 to 1.31 children per woman, positioning Spain as one of the lowest birth rates in the world.[18] According to the article "El desafío de la baja fecundidad en España" [The Challenge of Low Fertility in Spain], one explanation for this drop is the economic crisis that began in 2008 and caused labor precarity throughout Spain. The authors suggest that the effects of the crisis will leave "una huella más duradera en la fecundidad" [a long-lasting impression on fertility] that is much more serious than a "mero aplazamiento de los nacimientos" [a mere delay in births].[19] They also signal other factors, such as "el aumento del desempleo y de la precariedad laboral" [the rise in unemployment and in labor precarity] and "la reducción del gasto público impuesta por las políticas económicas de austeridad" [the reduction of public spending due to economic policies of austerity] that affect the willingness of women to have children.[20] In their article "Homework and Transnational Adoption Screening in Spain: The Coproduction of Home and Family," Jessaca Leinaweaver, Diana Marre, and Susan Frekko study adoption in Spain and explain that for many young people, the difficulty in becoming economically independent and establishing their own homes delays adulthood, which then affects the age of primiparity.[21] These factors help explain why Spain has one of the lowest birth rates, but economic factors are only one part of a much larger equation.

Along with the economic aspect, the delay of primiparity also affects the birth rate in Spain. The change in age of the mother at the birth of the first child has gone from 25 in 1980 to 31 in 2016.[22] While this is the average age, more than 30 percent of women were 35 years or older at the birth of their first child in 2016, and 7 percent were 40 years or older.[23] The number of women in their fertile years, defined as women aged 15 to 49, is also lower, which results in a tendency toward low numbers of births.[24] Another change in cultural norms is the average age of marriage for Spanish women, which is 36.6, several years past the prime age to attain a pregnancy. While 2022 registered more births by unmarried women than by married women in Spain, demographers still cite the age of marriage as part of the study of population numbers, as seen in the 2022 publication by the Instituto Nacional de Estadística (INE).[25] These numbers point out that women are less likely to have multiple births, since the later age of primiparity can also cause secondary infertility. The American Society for Reproductive Medicine defines secondary infertility as infertility in a woman who has had one or more pregnancies.[26] Secondary infertility rates have been estimated globally to affect 10 to 35 percent of women.[27]

Even though the economic and cultural factors have an obvious correlation to the low Spanish fertility rate, social factors also affect it. A higher level of education, access to multiple methods of birth control, and a change in social norms influence fertility as well.[28] The age of a mother with university studies at the birth of her first child was 33.8 in 2016.[29] By delaying the age of maternity, the likelihood of involuntary infertility rises, which carries with it a need for "un incremento de la necesidad de recurrir a técnicas de reproducción asistida" [an increase in the need to use assisted reproduction techniques].[30] When faced with the inability to attain a pregnancy, women turn to alternative methods such as ART and adoption in order to become mothers.

Spain's low birth rate, the high average age for Spanish women at the birth of their first child, and the country's economic situation that does not promote a sustainable work-life balance are some of the reasons for Spain's interest in adoption. However, the precarious state of the economy begs the question of the financial impact of adoption. A guide for parents, *Adopción internacional en la Comunidad de Madrid*, mentions that there is not a fixed price for adopting a child, as it depends on the country the child comes from, the number of trips to and from the child's birth country that the prospective adoptive parents must take, the translation of documents, and a long list of other minor expenses.[31] An article in *La voz de Galicia* says that the price of adopting a child from Russia averages around €30,000.[32] This large quantity of money is inaccessible to most Spaniards, where the average yearly income is €23,000.[33] In a society with high unemployment numbers for young workers (in 2021, the rate of unemployment was 30.29 for workers under the age of twenty-five), the decision to have children is unlikely, but the decision to adopt is economically impossible.[34] However, Beatriz San Román and Karen Rotabi explain that "international adoption emerged as a reproductive strategy" that was more affordable since it had higher success rates than assisted reproduction.[35]

For those who are financially able to adopt, like Laura Freixas, many choose to do so internationally. In her article "Intercountry Adoption: A Global Problem or a Global Solution?," Judith Masson gives the background on international adoption, explaining that in "receiving countries, the decline in fertility associated with postponing marriage, the limited success and high cost of infertility treatment and a lack of domestic adoption opportunities have made intercountry adoption an alternative to childlessness."[36] Masson continues, "In states of origin (sending countries), extreme poverty, lack of contraception and attitudes to birth outside of marriage are three major factors leading to the abandonment of children to institutions."[37] In 1993, the Hague Convention on the Protection of Children and Co-operation in Respect of Intercountry Adoption was created to outline a framework for international adoption.[38] Masson explains that in the Hague Convention, which was ratified by ninety-nine countries in 2019, "states of origin take responsibility for ensuring that children are 'adoptable,' (i.e. that all the legal requirements have been met) and receiving states take responsibility for the suitability of the applicants."[39] Jessaca Leinaweaver calls the late 1990s "a period full of promise and excitement," naming the decade as that of "Spain's international adoption boom."[40] As a receiving country, Spain works through the different autonomous regions to ready parents for international adoption.

For those Spaniards who choose to pursue international adoption, Russia is a popular location. Between 2003 and 2010, 47,864 children were adopted from Russia worldwide.[41] During these years, Spain adopted over 20,000 children in total from sending countries.[42] Leinaweaver shares that in 2003, the annual number of children adopted in Spain from Russia topped 1,000.[43] Lilia Khabibullina states that "Russian children adopted abroad go to the United States (26 percent), Spain (17 percent), and Italy (8 percent)."[44] Peter Selman suggests that Russia cannot afford to send its children abroad, nor can it afford to keep them in institutions, as many children in orphanages are victims of fetal alcohol syndrome and have been abandoned by their mothers.[45] While Russian children are popular because their foreignness is not obvious to Western European parents, Russian adoptions have a reputation for offering children with serious special needs, and the country has a "notorious history of adoption fraud in which bribery is a known expectation of moving the paperwork along for a child's departure."[46] While Russian adoption has its own specific concerns and benefits, adoption theorists clarify that all international adoptions present areas of concern.

These expectations of unwell children and institutionalized bribery in Russia bring to the forefront the two contrary theoretical perspectives on international adoption. Many adoption theorists view international adoption in one of two ways: humanitarian rescue or imperialist kidnapping.[47] Two prominent theorists, Karen Dubinsky and Patricia Sawin, agree that international adoption is a complicated premise that can provide an alternative way to form a family. Dubinsky, in *Babies Without Borders: Adoption and the Symbolic Child in a Globalizing World*, explains that adoption is normally viewed in polar ways and writes her book to "move our understandings of interracial and international adoption beyond the false dichotomy of imperialist kidnap or humanitarian rescue."[48] She offers that "international adoption [is] the most privileged form of immigration in the world today" and that our "enthusiastic embrace of adopted children stands in stark, and perverse, contrast to the immigration policies aimed at others from their countries."[49] While Dubinsky examines adoption from a more global perspective, Sawin, herself the mother of a child adopted from Guatemala, offers a more personal one:

> In depicting a process that can be bewildering, exhausting, and enraging, adoptive parents position themselves as those with morality on their side and with rights to children born in another country to other parents, while often situating the legal systems intended to safeguard children's and birthparents' human rights and civil liberties as the enemy.[50]

Sawin admits that adoptive parents can add to the interpretation of international adoption as a flawed system, and she offers her article as a way to make "ethical sense" of international adoption by "using stories to negotiate reciprocal responsibilities" between those who adopt and those who give up their child.[51] Sawin explains that those who support adoption emphasize the needs of the children, while those who criticize it focus on the system of privilege and wealth that allows some people to adopt while others reproduce.[52] She goes on to explain that she sees adoptive parents not as "self-sacrificing saviors" but just as simple parents, and she argues against the "assumption that international adoption is inevitably exploitative and corrupt."[53] Both Sawin and Dubinsky recognize the complications that occur when parents from wealthy countries adopt children from poor nations. Freixas's book mirrors some of the positive aspects of international adoption that both Sawin and Dubinsky express while also acknowledging the more negative aspects.

On the other side of the argument, those who see international adoption as imperialist kidnapping argue that it can never be acceptable due to the imbalance of power between receiving nations and sending nations. Sung Hee Yook and Hosu Kim, in their article "Decolonizing Adoption Narratives for Transnational Reproductive Justice," assert,

> We thus contend that transnational adoption discourse achieves its humanitarian facade through a narrative in which birth mothers are only legible as victim-mothers, perpetuating a colonial narrative in which they are backwards, unliberated, unenlightened, and economically dependent, and thus ineligible to perform motherhood. This victimology justifies a transnational adoption practice in which one person's reproductive access and privileges are inevitably intertwined with another's reproductive dispossession.[54]

While this quote echoes Sawin's comment about the dichotomy between those who reproduce and those who adopt, not only do those who adopt do so for the benefit of the child, but they also tend to silence the voices of those who gave birth. As is the case with Freixas's autobiography, the voice of the birth mother is absent, with only blame and recriminations about her appearing in the recounting of the adoption.

Like Yook and Kim, Kristen Cheney and Stephen Ucembe emphasize the lack of the voice of the birth mother and of any account of the child's life before being adopted. They explain that "biblical commands and nationalist fervor" justify rescuing poor orphans from squalor while also causing the "pathologization of poverty, the vilification of birth mothers, and the erasure of orphans' life histories before adoption."[55] This system causes "a clear and uneven pattern [. . .] of privileged people in developed countries targeting children in developing countries whom they perceive as in need of rescue."[56] Cheney and Ucembe call this "The Orphan Industrial Complex," a system that requires the production of orphans who are available for adoption for those in the global north, which then causes a network of criminals who want to take advantage of these do-gooders who want to help these poor orphans.[57] Likewise, Kathryn Van Doore, in her article "Paper Orphans: Exploring Child Trafficking for the Purpose of Orphanages," explains that

> orphanhood becomes the commodity, and the creation of the orphan through fraudulent documentation of legal guardianship is akin to legal ownership. The trafficking of the child is critical in this instance, as the payment for the child initiates a process of commodification. The paper orphan becomes a tradeable commodity bought and sold by orphanages as product to utilise to garner funding.[58]

This leads to what basically becomes the purchase of children, if adoption is interpreted as imperialism. The exchange of money, a complication seen also in the concept of egg donation, creates a feeling of commerce in what could or should be a question of family formation.

The financial aspect of adoption, which, as stated earlier, is around €30,000 in Spain, begs the question of how to distinguish between adopting a child and purchasing a child: Where does the money go? Diana Marre explains that women who bear the children receive no benefit from adoption; instead, "los beneficios son para una larga cadena de profesionales, técnicos, intermediarios, administraciones y gobiernos" [the benefits are for a long chain of professionals, technicians, intermediaries, administrations, and governments].[59] According to her field research, Marre finds that the women who put their children up for adoption generally do so due to

> falta de recursos económicos, familiares o personales con que criar un hijo o hija, porque no pueden acceder a la contracepción, porque su pareja masculina ha tenido que emigrar interna o internacionalmente o porque una relación

> temporal con la que sobrevivir económicamente o estar acompañada la ha dejado con un hijo o hija que no puede mantener a su lado.[60]

> [lack of economic, familial, or personal resources with which to raise a child; because of lack of access to contraception; because their male partner has had to emigrate internally or internationally; or because a temporary relationship has left them with a child that they cannot maintain.]

These findings, then, refute the idea that orphans are created for a waiting market of buyers; instead, they are created by a sexist and patriarchal hierarchy that leaves women with few choices when they become (unexpectedly) pregnant. Even so, within this system of unequal access, the adoptive parents can be viewed as "kidnappers" who support an illicit baby market. When analyzing Freixas's autobiographical perspective on adoption, the complications surrounding international adoption become clear: Freixas herself wavers between love for her adopted child, worries about his genetic background, and a sense of superiority about both Spain (versus Russia) and her parenting skills (versus those of the birth mother).

In *A mí no me iba a pasar*, the adoption story begins when Laura discovers that she is unable to attain a second pregnancy several years after the birth of her daughter. Although her first pregnancy was achieved after a surgery for her endometriosis, Laura questions whether she can participate again in the process of assisted reproduction. Through her questioning of the occupation of motherhood and her recognition of her position of privilege, the narrator recounts her story of adoption using both the savior and the kidnapper tropes to deconstruct the story of adoption. Before deciding to adopt, Laura again needs to explore the role of motherhood and its impact on her life.

Laura's first encounter with motherhood is the decision to try to have children. While she is not necessarily against having a child, she recognizes that motherhood is an expectation more than a choice. She states, "Querer tener hijos es la obviedad, es la evidencia, ¿quién lo ha dicho?, todo el mundo, es la naturaleza, si no lo entiendes no te lo puedo explicar" [Wanting children is the obvious choice, it is the evidence, who has said this? The whole world; it is nature, if you don't understand I can't explain it to you].[61] The assumption that women become mothers is ingrained in society and considered the natural state for women. Such is the pressure to conform that the narrator explains why she decides to have children: "Porque no necesitaba razones para el sí (nadie me las pedía), pero habría necesitado razones para el no, y no estaba segura de tenerlas" [Because I didn't need reasons for yes (no one asked me for them), but I would need reasons for no, and I wasn't sure I had any].[62] She feels like everyone around her exerts pressure on her to conform and that everyone else is starting their families:

"Explícita o silenciosa, aquella voz que venía de tantos canales a la vez, envolvente como unos altavoces estéreo *surround* a todo volumen, me estaba volviendo loca" [Explicit or silent, that voice that came from so many channels at the same time, enveloping like one of those surround sound speakers at high volume, was driving me crazy].[63] When she begins to question her hesitance to become pregnant, she discovers that giving birth does not constitute the major drawback of motherhood; the chores and responsibilities that accompany it cause her reluctance.

Freixas calls out the difference between men and women in childcare, explicitly stating that she does not want to be a mother; she would rather be a father. From her perspective, a father's interaction with children is minimal:

> Quería tener hijos sin que eso me impidiera pasarme los días fuera de casa trabajando. Quería tener hijos y verlos a llegar, cinco minutos, cenados y bañados y oliendo a colonia o, mejor aún, ya en la cama, darles las buenas noches y un besito y ya, a cenar, a hablar entre adultos.[64]
>
> [I wanted to have children without it impeding me from spending the days out of the house at work. I wanted to have children and see them when I arrive, five minutes, having eaten dinner and bathed and smelling fresh or, even better, already in bed, tell them good night with a kiss, and then eat dinner and have adult talk.]

She comes to the following conclusion: "No es que yo no quisiera tener hijos. Sí quería tener hijos, lo que no sabía si quería era ser madre. Prefería ser padre" [It's not that I didn't want to have children. Yes, I did want to have children; what I didn't know was whether I wanted to be a mother. I preferred to be a father].[65] Her struggle between wanting to have children and not wanting to be a mother illustrates the inequality Spanish women experience in care work with their male partners.

Her perceptions of care work are supported by statistics. Sandra Ezquerra cites a study by Institut d'Estadística de Catalunya [Institute of Statistics of Catalonia] (IDESCAT) from 2011 that shows "la duración media diaria que las mujeres en Catalunya dedican al hogar y a la familia es de 4 horas y 14 minutos, mientras que la de los hombres es de 2 horas y 35 minutos" [the average daily time that women in Catalonia spend on household chores and the family is four hours and fourteen minutes, while that of men is two hours and thirty-five minutes], confirming that "las mujeres continuamos en la actualidad teniendo un papel preponderante en la provisión del cuidado familiar en diferentes momentos del ciclo vital" [we women today continue to have the principle role in the provision of family care in different moments of the life cycle].[66] Ezquerra points out that the feminization of care work is a major part of the economic distinction between men and women, insisting that "la identificación social del cuidado como algo inherentemente femenino, así como su invisibilización, refuerzan la discriminación laboral de las mujeres y su situación de desventaja en relación con los hombres" [the social identification of care work as something inherently feminine, along with its invisibilization, reinforce labor discrimination of women and their disadvantageous situation in relation to men].[67] She goes on to explain the cycle that reinforces these gender differences:

> Si la construcción social del cuidado como algo femenino promueve la desigualdad de género en el mercado laboral, la situación de inferioridad de las mujeres en el mercado laboral favorece en muchos casos, a su vez, que en situaciones de necesidad de cuidado familiar seamos nosotras las que reduzcamos nuestra jornada laboral o abandonemos nuestra trayectoria profesional para dar respuesta.[68]
>
> [If the social construction of care work as feminine promotes gender inequality in the labor market, the situation of inferiority of women in the labor market favors in many cases, at the same time, that in times of need for family care work, we women are the ones who have to reduce our work day and abandon our professional trajectory to meet that need.]

The circularity of the inequity between men and women in caring for children affects both men and women in the labor market, as women generally sacrifice their careers to do care work, while men spend more hours at work to make up for women's unpaid labor.[69] The couple experiences this, as Laura gives up her publishing job for her husband's more lucrative job in finance in order to care for their daughter. When talking about their division of labor, she explains that her husband, Étienne, is in charge of "lo que se piensa, se negocia, se discute" [what is thought, negotiated, discussed], while she takes care of "lo que se toca, se abraza, se saborea" [what is touched, hugged, savored], a traditional division of work that she both embraces and despises even though it makes caring for her daughter easier.[70]

When she and Étienne decide to have another child, their interaction with secondary infertility is different. Étienne approaches having a second child with a business plan:

> Posibilidad 1: se produce un embarazo natural. Posibilidad 2: a falta de embarazo natural, se acude a consulta ginecológica y se efectúa tratamiento según indicación facultativa, lo que a su vez abre varias posibilidades: 2.1: embarazo; 2.2: gestación subrogada; 2.3: adoptar; 2.4: cualquier otra cosa, lo que fuese, ¡todo antes que darse por vencidos![71]
>
> [Possibility 1: a natural pregnancy is achieved. Possibility 2: in the absence of natural pregnancy, a gynecologist is consulted and treatment is carried out according to indication, which in turn opens up several possibilities: 2.1: pregnancy;

> 2.2: gestational surrogacy; 2.3: adoption; 2.4: any other thing, whatever it may be, anything before giving up!]

After four years of not impeding pregnancy, they decide to try in vitro fertilization (IVF), with "inyecciones, ecografías [. . .], análisis de sangre, anestesias generales para extraer óvulos, fecundación en laboratorio, implantación de los óvulos fecundados en el útero" [injections, sonograms (. . .), blood analysis, general anesthesia to extract the eggs, fertilization in the lab, implantation of the fertilized eggs in the uterus].[72] After the second failed attempt, Laura decides that she does not want to be pregnant again, and she complains, "Estoy harta de que me trataran como si fuese un trozo de madera colocado encima de una camilla. Como una probeta esterilizada. Como un jarrón chino roto, que los mejores especialistas tratan de reparar" [I'm tired of being treated as if I were a piece of wood placed on top of a stretcher. Like a sterilized test tube. Like a broken Chinese vase that the best specialists try to repair].[73] As seen in previous chapters, women's bodies, when medicalized, are treated as separate from their person, as broken pieces needing repair. Silvia Tubert affirms that this process of medical intervention leads to a loss of self:

> Se pueden programar los nacimientos, controlar los cuerpos y su funcionamiento a favor de una mayor eficacia, pero todo esto conduce necesariamente a la pérdida de la posición de sujeto, a la alienación, a la ilusión de satisfacer los deseos a escala industrial, a la abolición de la palabra, del símbolo, de la temporalidad, es decir, de todo aquello que nos define como especie.[74]
>
> [Births can be programmed, bodies and their functioning controlled in favor of greater efficiency, but all this necessarily leads to the loss of the position of the subject, to alienation, to the illusion of satisfying desires on an industrial scale, to the abolition of the word, of the symbol, of temporality—that is, of everything that defines us as a species.]

Instead of continuing on their pursuit of a second child through ART and being made to feel like a nonperson, when the second attempt at IVF fails, they decide to adopt.

The decision to adopt comes with many additional choices and concerns. According to *Adopción internacional en la Comunidad de Madrid*, the first thing adoptive parents must do is say goodbye: "Adiós al hijo que siempre imaginé que tendría, adiós al embarazo, adiós al parto, adiós a ser lo primero que verá mi bebé, adiós a reconocer en el recién nacido lo mejor de mí mismo, de mi pareja o de mi familia" [Goodbye to the child that I imagined I would have, goodbye to pregnancy, goodbye to giving birth, goodbye to being the first that my baby will see, goodbye to recognizing in the newborn the best of me, my partner, or my family].[75] The guide also warns that adopted children always carry a *mochila* [backpack]—"ese trocito de vida que el niño trae consigo y del que nosotros no hemos formado parte" [that little piece of life that the child brings with them and that we have not formed part of].[76] The guide explains that the work of adoptive parents is to "sacar de [la mochila] todo lo positivo y aligerar el peso de lo que haya de doloroso y de negativo" [take (from the backpack) all of the positive and lighten the load of what has been painful or negative], as many times, the adopted children have lived through some form of neglect or lack.[77] The guide also signals that adoptive parents should not forget the child's past because "el recuerdo, la reconstrucción o la imagen de 'otros padres' formará parte de la vida de [su] hijo" [the memory, the reconstruction, or the image of "other parents" will form part of the life of their child].[78] Laura and her husband in *A mí no me iba a pasar* experience these aspects of international adoption on their journey to find their second child.

Others' rejection of their idea to adopt confronts the narrator and her husband. When she shares their plan with her parents, they react negatively, since the new child will not be genetically related to them. The narrator states,

> Ese intruso que yo estaba planeando meter en casa, a saber de quién era hijo: desde luego, no de los Freixas, ni tampoco de «los» esto, «los» aquello, «los» de más allá, familias de confianza, de los nuestros, burguesía catalana con denominación de origen; ese desconocido, que yo iba a sacar de un orfanato (¡de un orfanato!), sería hijo de unos pobretones, o algo peor.[79]
>
> [This intruder who I was planning to bring home, who knows whose child it is? Definitely not a Freixas, or one of ours, those, or those over there—Catalan bourgeoisie with an appellation of origin. This unknown person, who I was going to get from an orphanage (an orphanage!), would be a child of poor people or something worse.]

The ironic tone of this passage, with its nod to class implications and the shame of poverty, also allows Freixas to portray her parents' concern about international adoption. Their perceived superiority and the fear of an adopted child carrying an illustrious Catalan surname do not negate how difficult it is to say goodbye to the genetic relationship with an adopted child, much like Samanta Villar's concept of genetic grief. The idea that the child does not belong creates a layer of difficulty, especially when the extended family does not support the idea of adoption.

The parents also experience ups and downs as part of their adoption story. They see both perspectives of adoption, rescue and abduction, as they choose their child from the orphanage. The first emotional response, that of excitement in connecting with their new son, quickly diffuses after they experience the orphanage in Russia. Laura says they started their journey believing "que la adopción era una historia de amor. Que empezaría con un flechazo, como en las películas:

un amor fulminante, inmediato, total, por ambas partes" [that adoption was a love story. That it would start with a love at first sight, like in the movies: an overwhelming, immediate, total love on both sides].[80] She sees herself and her husband as knights coming to the rescue of a poor child: "Con nuestro poder, nuestro dinero, el halo dorado de nuestra condición de occidentales, veníamos a rescatar a un niño, subirlo a un avión, llevarle a una vida mil veces mejor que la que le esperaba" [With our power, our money, the golden halo of our condition of Westerners, we were coming to rescue a child, take him on a plane, and bring him to a life that was a thousand times better than the one that was waiting for him].[81] As Freixas comments on these past feelings of expectation and joy, the irony of her tone stands out, contrasting the high expectations she had with the sad reality of the Russian orphanage where she and her husband would rescue a poor child and make his life better. Her tone continues as she describes them as being "extraordinariamente generosos" [extraordinarily generous] and protagonists in a story where they, "ante un niño mendigo boquiabierto, iba[n] a hacerle la limosna de un futuro radiante" [before an open-mouthed beggar child, were going to give him the charity of a brilliant future].[82] However, the reality they experienced differed greatly. What the Madrid adoption guide describes as the fantasy of adoption, where the child's life begins with being adopted, is not and should never be the case.[83] Each child has a lived experience before being adopted, which leads to difficulties with the processes of adoption and adaptation.

Laura and her husband travel to Russia to find their child, and their experience illustrates how far from the fantasy the reality is. Laura describes the orphanage as a market, saying, "¿Nos están ofreciendo niños como si fueran alfombras en un mercado persa?" [They are offering us children as if they were rugs at a Persian market?] when the director of the orphanage asks if they want a boy or a girl.[84] While the international laws of adoption guarantee a child in good health under three years old, the director of the orphanage offers child after child with health or other problems.[85] The emotional and physical states of the children available cause her to question their decision to adopt, understanding that she is not capable of taking care of "un niño con problemas graves de salud" [a child with major health problems].[86] This barrage of difficulties continues until she says that "no podía más, quería volver a casa, tiraba la toalla, pero imposible, había[n] llegado demasiado lejos" [she couldn't take any more, she wanted to go home, she was throwing in the towel, but it was impossible, they had come too far].[87] Their imagined joy at finding the one child who sparked love in them seems to be impossible to attain. Their hope to rescue a child and provide him with a home seems unlikely. However, as with any story, there must be conflict to find resolution.

Just when the couple has had enough, they meet their child, Sasha, and their expectations of rescue return. When the orphanage brings Sasha to them, Laura goes to him and holds him, describing him as "muy pequeñito, flaco, amarillento, demacrado" [very small, skinny, yellowish, emaciated].[88] She instantly connects with the child and wonders, "¿Cómo no íbamos a aceptar al niño?, al que yo había abrazado casi llorando, que nos necesitaba tanto" [How would we not accept the child? The one who I had hugged almost crying, who needs us so much].[89] Finding the child was an emotionally draining process, and then the actual process of adopting him internationally begins. They must leave Sasha in Russia while the paperwork is processed and then return to get him. When they return to Russia, they sign paperwork that affirms this transaction is permanent and that they cannot return the child for any reason, including underlying health issues.[90] Freixas narrates the experience of signing the forms and receiving the baby at the consulate as panic-inducing: "Fui a firmar que ese bebé flaco, apático, amarillo (pero, ¿cómo?, ¿los bebés no eran todos rojizos, suaves, sonrientes?, entonces, ¿mentían los anuncios de potitos?) era mi hijo (no se admiten devoluciones BAJO NINGÚN CONCEPTO)" [I went to sign that this skinny, apathetic, yellow (But how? Aren't all babies reddish, soft, and smiley? Then are the ads for creams lying?) was my child (returns are not accepted UNDER ANY CONDITION)].[91] Even with her concerns about the state of the child, his yellowish skin and slight weight, she accepts the baby as her own. With the baby in her arms, she begins to feel righteous again, returning to the savior trope of adoption stories.

The concept of adoption as saving a needy child causes conflict for families who adopt. Sawin explains,

> We squirm at the praise that casts us as self-sacrificing saviors, rather than simply parents, of that "lucky baby." Yet we are stung by unbidden criticism of our family composition based on, depending on the politics of those we encounter, scarcely veiled racism [. . .] or an assumption that international adoption is inevitably exploitative and corrupt.[92]

While Sawin admits that the process of adopting a child internationally is narrowed to one of two options, either parents as saviors or parents as kidnappers, she points out that really, parents of adopted children are just that: parents. Laura takes some time to come to that realization, first recollecting her experience of adoption ironically, as if she and her husband were gods, "milagrosamente llegados desde el olímpico Occidente a resolverlo todo con salud, dinero y amor a manos llenas" [miraculously arrived from the Olympic West to solve everything with hands full of health, money, and love].[93] She recalls with irony how she and her husband feel righteous due to their choice to adopt: "Qué gusto daba mirarnos en ese espejo: todopoderosos, resplandecientes, llegados para rescatar al pobre niño perdido en el bosque. De la madre borracha, del padre ausente" [How good it felt to look at ourselves in this mirror: all powerful, shining, arrived to rescue the poor child lost in the woods. From the drunk mother, from the absent father].[94] She understands that the concept of childhood differs from country to country, and she assumes that her adopted child will benefit from living in Spain, "donde a los bebés se les trata como a jarrones chinos, frágiles y valiosísimos, como a diosecillos caprichosos en sus cunas-altares" [where babies are treated like Chinese vases, fragile and valuable, like capricious little gods on their cradle-altars].[95] The comparison between the yellowish, emaciated child she adopts and the small, godlike, soft babies of Europe creates a feeling of superiority between "us" (the adoptive parents) and "them" (the poor, alcoholic biological parents).

This perspective of self-righteousness quickly changes when Laura is faced with the reality of parenting a child who lacked care as an infant. Due to Sasha's time in the orphanage and his recovery from being born to an alcoholic mother, he does not respond like her first child. She talks about trying to play trains with him: "Cuando lo hacía con mi hija ella se reía a carcajadas [. . .]. Pero este niño no" [When I did this with my daughter, she laughed out loud (. . .). But this child, no].[96] She begins to question why she decided to adopt:

> ¡Ay, Sasha! ¡Qué he hecho! ¿Para qué estoy haciendo toda esta comedia? ¿Para quién? Todos esos, yo qué sé: la gente, las revistas, la agencia, todos los que me animaban a ser madre, adoptando o como fuera, con una sonrisa y una lagrimita, que me decían que era maravilloso, ¿dónde se han ido? Déjame llorar ahora que no nos ve nadie . . . Qué hago yo sola en Moscú con un niño extraño, arisco, que no sonríe, que no me mira, que se tira por el suelo y se da cabezazos contra los muebles.[97]
>
> [Oh, Sasha! What have I done? Why am I doing all of this comedy? For whom? All of them, how should I know: people, magazines, the agency, all of those who cheered me on to be a mother, adopting or however, with a smile and a tear, who told me that it was marvelous, where are they now? Let me cry now that no one can see us . . . What am I doing alone in Moscow with a foreign, unsociable child who doesn't smile, who doesn't look at me, who throws himself on the ground and hits his head on the furniture.]

The pressure she experienced not only to become a mother the first time but also to continue to try for a second pregnancy causes her to break down and recognize that everyone, from friends to magazines to her husband, made her feel incomplete without trying the step of adoption. When faced with his inability to respond to stimuli, she wonders, "¡Ay, Sasha, qué va a ser de nosotros! ¿Por qué me he metido en esto, dios mío? Yo era feliz . . . lo he estropeado todo . . . ¿Qué va a ser de mí?, Sasha, Sasha . . ." [Oh, Sasha, what will become of us! Why did I put myself in this, my God? I was happy . . . I've destroyed everything . . . What will become of me? Sasha, Sasha . . .].[98] While the child has no agency in the choice to be adopted, the adoptive mother blames herself for not rising to meet his needs.

Her initial ambivalence about being a mother, combined with the difficulties of adopting a child, changes when viewed in retrospect and causes a sense of longing for the past, which, viewed from a distance, seems easier. She can now look back at her life with one child and interpret that she was happy even though she did not experience that happiness at the time, since she was unable to conceive a second time due to her secondary infertility.

As with all things, as time passes, Laura begins to forget her concerns about adoption and returns to the concept of having saved a child. The child psychologist she visits explains that Sasha hits his head on furniture to "saberse vivo, de sentir su cuerpo" [to feel alive, to feel his body], which he stops doing once he becomes incorporated into the family.[99] She begins to see other changes in him, such as gaining weight, growing, and beginning to smile.[100] In her article about international adoption in Spain, Marta Bertran affirms that the adopted children "had often lived in conditions which visibly affected their health, often caused by basic needs that went unmet."[101] When talking about the experiences of parents with adopted children, Bertran says that the parents she interviewed questioned the concept of "the affective bonds created between parents and children (culturally unquestionable parent-child love)."[102] At first, Laura does not feel this innate, intimate attachment to her adopted child. But as he begins to recuperate from his time in the orphanage, those feelings change. She and her family begin to accept Sasha as part of their family. She even comes to the realization that she has bought into the cultural norm of motherhood, saying, "En una revista femenina, hojeada en alguna sala de espera, leí la frase de una mujer que decía: 'Lo más importante que tengo en manos es mi familia.' Yo también, pensé. Pero me fastidiaba estar de acuerdo con una revista femenina" [In a woman's magazine, flipping through in a waiting room, I read a phrase where a woman said: "The most important thing I have is my family." Me too, I thought. But I was irritated that I agreed with a woman's magazine].[103] After the pressure exerted on her by her parents, her husband, her doctors, and society at large, Laura accepts the cultural norm of motherhood as essential.

While the narrator generally conforms to the norms of adoption "as rescue from a life of squalor," she does occasionally refer to the opposite side of the adoption argument, adoption as stealing a child.[104] As Sawin notes, adoptive parents expect "to help our children mourn their lost birth family, struggle over identity formation because they are perceived as racially or ethnically different from their adoptive family, and possibly deal with aftereffects of early malnutrition, lack of medical care, or orphanage life."[105] She also offers that "the experience of international adoption clearly requires adoptive parents and adopted children to reimagine their identities."[106] Laura begins to experience life with her adopted child, and she also recognizes that his identity is fraught due to his position as adopted. She worries, "A él le estábamos robando. Le robábamos su apellido, su historia, su lengua" [We were stealing him. We stole from him his last name, his history, his language].[107] This one nod to her understanding of adoption as theft is then incorporated into the concept of rescue when she notes, "Con la promesa de una vida limpia y noble, culta, rica, libre, despierta y feliz, le estábamos robando su patria. Pobre, sucia, triste, desgraciada, pero suya" [With the promise of a clean and noble, educated, rich, free, bright and happy life, we were stealing his country from him. Poor, dirty, sad, disgraced, but his].[108] The comparison between Western countries like Spain, filled with light, joy, and freedom, and Russia, filled with dirt and poverty, illustrates Laura's inability to interpret Sasha's adoption as anything but positive for him.

The process of negotiating between taking a child from his original home and bringing him into a new country and new environment appears in many narratives of families who adopt. Sawin explains that "stories that assist in identifying a child and getting her or him home are arguably the only accounts that the adoptive parents' own internal family-building story of disappointment, frustration, search, and hoped-for success can reasonably accommodate."[109] In order to begin to build a family, the adoptive parents must learn to accept the stories that existed before they appeared. They must not focus on their adoption story as a perfect fantasy, and they must resist

> the inclination to exaggerate [their] expertise or let [their] accounts of the search for a child eclipse imperfectly known stories of birth families and emerging stories of adopted children. Likewise, [they] must refuse to let a sense of psychic connection with birth families, however sincerely felt, obscure actual power relationships.[110]

The privilege that accompanies the ability to adopt or seek out ART allows families to focus only on their side of the story and forget that the child they have adopted was relinquished by his birth family.

Freixas's recounting of her early married life and childbearing and child-rearing years is written years past the actual events even though the story is based on journals she wrote at the time. The distance between what she remembers and narrates and the time she lives in now allows her to create perspective and tell her truth as she sees it in retrospect. In a time of Instagram stories and TikTok videos where people constantly keep track of what everyone else is doing, a published autobiography allows the author to curate her thoughts based on diaries she wrote at the time and weave a story from those memories. On 13 June 2022, Freixas posted this about her son on Instagram:

> Cuando recuerdo a aquel bebé raquítico, angustiado y amarillo, y veo el mocetón de metro noventa, sano, deportista, políglota, trabajador, y sobre todo (es lo que más me gusta de él) buena persona y cariñoso, en el que se ha convertido, pienso que algo habré hecho bien en la vida.[111]

> [When I remember that rickety, anguished, yellow baby, and I see the young man of 6′2″, healthy, sporty, multilingual, hardworking, and above all (and what I like best about him), a good, caring person that he has become, I think that I must have done something well in my life.]

Her use of some of the same descriptors found in her book reinforces the idea that she did the right thing in adopting him, but in this post, the focus is on her mothering as something she has done well.

This chapter examines motherhood through adoption as described by Laura Freixas in her autobiography. From her lack of interest in becoming her mother, to her difficulties attaining her first pregnancy, to her decision to adopt a second child, Freixas struggles with the inequality of care work between women and men. In her experience, women shoulder the burden of childcare, and motherhood comes accompanied by sacrifice in the workplace. When delving into her portrayal of the adoption of her son Sasha from Russia, Laura struggles with the tropes of rescue and kidnap that surround stories of adoption, only to come to the conclusion that she loves her adopted child as much as her biological child. However, the book ends with the author questioning her life, "esa vida de maruja de lujo" [that luxurious life of a housewife]: "Odiaba el chalé adosado, odiaba las vacaciones en Australia, [. . .] odiaba estar casada con una cuenta corriente" [I hated the semidetached house, I hate the vacations in Australia, (. . .) I hated being married to a checking account]. These feelings lead to her eventual divorce.[112] In *A mí no me iba a pasar*, Laura's adoption story begins with questioning the occupation of motherhood and her recognition of her position of privilege as a rich, white Westerner and ends with her accepting that her story of adoption is both about being a savior and a thief, adding to the complicated issues that underlie any international adoption. The distance between her experience of adoption and the publishing of her memoir allows for a kinder, more accepting perspective of both herself as a mother and her children. Her recollections utilize irony to create space between her written self and her writer self, who reworks her diary entries to be published for a wider audience.

While adoption has a much higher success rate (also known as the take-home baby rate) than all other ARTs, adoption does not allow the adopting woman to experience pregnancy, nor is there a genetic relationship between the adopting mother and her adopted child. In Samanta Villar's narrative, she called this concept "el duelo genético" [genetic mourning] and thought about what was lost by not carrying on her genetic line. Silvia Nanclares's story talked about the mourning that accompanied both the loss of her father and her decision not to continue seeking a pregnancy in the fertility clinic, even as that meant the end of her genetic line. Even Raquel Sánchez-Silva's novel addresses the fear that accompanies raising a child that is not genetically related, through gamete donation.[113] Positing consanguinity as the most reliable source of bonding detracts from the concept of chosen family formation that has gained popularity as movie stars and other famous people, such as Villar, form families through alternative routes.

The next chapter diverges somewhat from the previous chapters, as it explores structural infertility and not the inability to conceive but the choice not to carry a pregnancy. Entering into the world of nonmothers, Diana López Varela illustrates the struggle of deciding when and if to become a mother due to financial instability in Spain post-2008. López Varela's narrative, also a work of nonfiction, encourages us to deconstruct the mother-equals-woman construct and to question the concept of freely made reproductive choices.

CHAPTER 5

Infertility as Choice

MATERNOFOBIA BY DIANA LÓPEZ VARELA

Books analyzed in the previous chapters focus on different ways women diagnosed with infertility in Spain can have children, including adoption and assisted reproduction technology (ART), but this chapter widens the definition of infertility to include the concept of structural infertility. Bruna Álvarez and Diana Marre define structural infertility as "low fertility for social, political, and economic (rather than biological) reasons."[1] In other words, structural infertility explains that even if a woman might physically be able to become pregnant, her social or economic position makes it impossible, or ill-advised, for her to do so. Defining infertility beyond biological functions becomes especially important in a world of reproductive technology where terms like *donor* and *mother* also need to be questioned and analyzed, as seen in previous chapters. By expanding my study on infertility to include structural, not only biological, infertility, I illustrate both the pressure on women to have children as well as the lack of support that women face when postponing or forgoing motherhood. For many women in Spain, it is difficult to obtain the level of stability necessary for motherhood for several reasons: job inequalities, the lack of affordable housing, the lack of public family support policies, and unequal participation in household work and family care, among others.[2] This groundbreaking idea explains that fertility is complicated and cultural and must be investigated and understood as more than a biological condition. Diana López Varela, in her 2019 book *Maternofobia: Retrato de una generación enfrentada a la maternidad* [Maternophobia: Portrait of a Generation Faced with Motherhood], discusses how the issues that comprise structural infertility led her to choose not to have a child. López Varela becomes pregnant and therefore is not biologically infertile, but her lack of dependable income, the newness of her relationship, and profound doubts about her desire to become a mother all worked to make pregnancy at this juncture impossible for her. This chapter, then, extends the definition of *infertility* in Spain to encompass not only women who cannot become pregnant but also those who, due to structural infertility, feel like there is no way they can successfully navigate motherhood at this time in their lives. The concept of choice, or feeling like there is no choice, however, becomes complicated, since women's reproductive decisions live within a patriarchal, neoliberal structure that makes choice a fraught concept. I suggest that women who choose not to have children due to structural infertility belong in the study of infertility, since they too receive societal backlash for their choices, especially because their choices are dictated by societal structures and deficits.

Within a neoliberal structure, individual choice is posited as the ultimate freedom. Neoliberal rhetoric, according to David Harvey, places "foundational emphasis upon individual freedoms" and "require[s] both politically and economically the construction of a neoliberal market-based populist culture of differentiated consumerism and individual libertarianism."[3] Indeed, choice becomes the "definition of a free modern individual in the neoliberal context, a figure who stands in contrast to people of the past who supposedly had no choices."[4] In relating choice to politics, Ana de Miguel offers that "los argumentos individualistas han calado fuerte en una sociedad que defiende el relativismo y el deseo personal como criterio último, tanto en moda como en política" [individualist arguments have had a strong impact in a society that defends relativism and personal desire as the ultimate criterion, both in fashion and politics].[5] De Miguel assures us that "los fines del feminismo son incompatibles con el neoliberalismo" [the goals of feminism are incompatible with neoliberalism], since feminist theory "es una teoría crítica del poder y no una teoría neoliberal de la preferencia individual" [is a critical theory of power and not a neoliberal theory of individual preference].[6] To connect the concept of neoliberal systems to procreation, Tejaswini Ganti observes that within neoliberalism, "freedom of choice also extend[s] to individuals who should have the right to plan their own lives."[7] Added to that, "the rhetoric of choice, responsibility, and self-regulation has become the means through which a neo-liberal state can disclaim responsibility for social welfare, while at the same time ensure that individuals, and in this case individual women, adhere to notions of proper behavior."[8] Proper behavior means that women might believe they have options, but they actually face "choiceless choices," such as "a pregnant person who wants to have a child but who lacks adequate housing and a secure job."[9] However, as de Miguel assures us, most reproductive decisions are based not on free choice but on systems of power that do not allow women to choose freely.[10] Instead of choice, the neoliberal system "holds individuals solely accountable for their reproductive health instead of reconsidering the role that governments and public institutions might play in informing, educating, and ensuring the well-being of the population."[11] López Varela conveys these same concerns in her narrative about her choice not to become a mother.

The term *reproductive choice* falsely suggests that women make decisions about their fertility without societal pressures suggesting (or forcing) certain choices on them. In their book *Confinements: Fertility and Infertility in Contemporary Culture*, Helena Michie and Naomi Cahn point out that "the paradox of choice reappears in the image of women who choose to have careers and defer childbearing, in the midst of a culture that fostered this choice but then, later, blamed the women for having made this choice."[12] Their perspective speaks to the issue of structural infertility, as women who wait to establish themselves are sometimes unable to conceive. Society then marks them as selfish for not putting family first, offering that waiting is a choice, not a consequence of a structure in place that prohibits actual choice. Expanding on the concepts of motherhood, blame, and infertility, Michie and Cahn certify that

> because individual women are perceived, and may indeed perceive themselves, as creating their own infertility, this masks the cultural production of the metanarrative of infertility and provides, yet again, an example of the policing of women's bodies into appropriate roles. Society assumes that only when women make inappropriate choices do they become infertile, and this definition of appropriate choices disciplines women's fertility. The discourse of autonomy, under which women are free to choose their own reproductive destiny, is ultimately paradoxical, because women are still judged and blamed for whatever choices they make.[13]

Álvarez echoes this concern, offering that there is no true reproductive choice; "instead, it appears that there is an accepted choice (having children) and a deviant one (not having them)."[14] De Miguel, in a longer argument about prostitution and women "choosing" to be prostitutes, explains that "se apela a la libre elección como si esta fuera el fundamento del feminismo, y se resta valor al análisis de una estructura social generizada y patriarcal que actúa determinando de forma coactiva las elecciones de las personas" [free choice is appealed to as if this were the foundation of feminism, and value is detracted from the analysis of a gendered and patriarchal social structure that coercively determines people's choices], which leads to a distortion of the feminist message that power structures limit choices.[15] Yet again, women face difficulties with the concept of choice because "choice comes with or can act as a cover for blaming women for the things over which they actually have no control and for deflecting that blame from social conditions."[16] This chapter analyzes the concept of choice within structural infertility in *Maternofobia*, looking at both structural impediments that limit fertility and the rejection of motherhood as necessary for women.

Diana López Varela was born in 1986 in Pontevedra, Galicia, Spain. In 2016, López Varela published her first book, *No es país para coños* [Not a Country for

Pussies], a feminist manifesto that presents a humoristic view about growing up in Spain and the need for a feminist society. A columnist, playwright, and writer, López Varela is also known for her blog *Suspenso en religión* [Failed in Religion], where she published "Mi coño" [My Pussy], an article about women's rights that quickly went viral.[17] Her first theatrical work, *No es país para coños*, premiered in 2015, and her short film *Feminazis* premiered in 2018 (and is available on YouTube).[18] Along with her work writing books and scripts, she also works as a journalist.[19] *Maternofobia* depicts how structural infertility affects women in Spain. López Varela narrates the difficulties of choosing a motherhood bounded by patriarchal structures that reduce women's ability to make choices about whether or not to have children. Through her narrative, she explores the choice not to become a mother along with the choice to end a pregnancy. From her position as a nonmother and someone who thinks deeply about the decision not to become a mother, López Varela's book illuminates the social and economic situation in Spain for young women as they decide whether or not to become mothers within a system of structural infertility.

Maternofobia is a collection of essays and ideas that the author ties together by narrating her decision not to have a child. She interviews both men and women who do not want to have children, and she shares stories about women who have had abortions, which in Spain are called an "interrupción voluntaria del embarazo" [voluntary interruption of pregnancy] (IVE). While focusing on the right of a woman to freely choose motherhood, the book also examines other feminist issues, such as salary inequality, work-life balance, and education. López Varela's takeaway, however, is that the choice to become a mother, or the decision not to become a mother, is limited by unequal political and economic structures that curtail choice. She explains, "La maternidad es la columna vertebral del sistema patriarcal. En torno a ella se ha construido la desigualdad de derechos entre hombres y mujeres, su relato, su justificación, su fe" [Motherhood is the backbone of the patriarchal system. The inequality of rights between men and women has been built around it, its story, its justification, its faith].[20] She would like us instead to see women without the lens of motherhood as central to a woman's life:

> Hablo de identidad femenina al margen de la función reproductiva. Hablo de desafiar las estructuras de poder que durante siglos nos han tenido invisibilizadas, mudas y ocupadas de lo doméstico mientras los hombres reinaban en lo público. Nos ha costado tantas generaciones definirnos al margen de los otros que tiemblo si me imagino siendo exclusivamente la mujer de . . . la madre de . . .[21]
>
> [I speak of feminine identity away from the reproductive function. I speak of challenging the power structures that for centuries have kept us invisible,

> mute, and busy with domestic work while men reigned in public. It has taken us so many generations to define ourselves apart from others that I tremble if I imagine being exclusively the wife of . . . the mother of . . .]

López Varela enters into an ongoing feminist discussion about the place of motherhood in a woman's life. While she determines that society has changed significantly in the past generations, she still recognizes that power structures exist that keep women from freely exploring alternative identities.

Her book points out the social pressure to have children, the ubiquitous marketing surrounding reproductive technology, and the deeply embedded essentialist belief that women are only complete when they become mothers. López Varela also reveals her decision to end a pregnancy and the effects this decision has had on her. In an interview in *La Vanguardia*, when asked about her abortion, López Varela answers, "Ninguna mujer quiere acabar pasando por un aborto, por eso es un derecho tan necesario. Un aborto es la decisión más meditada que toma en su vida una mujer. Y juzgarla no ayuda a evitar abortos" [No woman wants to have an abortion, and that's why it is a necessary right. An abortion is the most meditated decision a woman makes in her life. And judging her does not help avoid abortions].[22] As López Varela explains, "Las mujeres no necesitamos saber su opinión sobre lo que deberíamos hacer con nuestros órganos reproductores. Que sus comentarios son impertinentes, dañinos e innecesarios. Que no todas las mujeres quieren tener hijos" [We women don't need to know your opinion about what we should do with our reproductive organs. Your comments are impertinent, hurtful, and unnecessary. Not all women want to have children].[23] She works to deconstruct the idea that "mujer igual a madre" [woman equals mother] and to find new ways of defining what it means to be a woman.[24] In order to understand López Varela's perspective on ending her pregnancy, I situate the question of abortion within Spain in the legal arena.

Spain's position on abortion reflects the changes in society in post-Franco Spain. In 1985, the Ley Orgánica [Organic Law] 9/1985 became the first law outlining women's reproductive rights and decriminalizing abortion in cases of rape, problems with the fetus, or danger to the mother.[25] Then, several years later, the Ley Orgánica 2/2010 legalized abortion until the fourteenth week of pregnancy for any reason.[26] According to the Ministerio de Sanidad [Ministry of Health] of Spain, in 2017, the majority of abortions in Spain were performed on women between the ages of twenty and twenty-nine.[27] Granda Berridi and García Álvarez explain that the main conflict around abortion is the question of rights: the right of a woman to decide about her body versus the right of the fetus to survive.[28] For this reason, they suggest, the Spanish law allows for the right of women to decide until there is the possibility of a viable fetus.[29] In this way, the Ley Orgánica 2/2010 does not conflict with section IA, article 15 of the Spanish constitution, which states, "Todos tienen derecho a la vida y a la integridad física y moral, sin que, en ningún caso, puedan ser sometidos a tortura ni a penas o tratos inhumanos o degradantes" [Everyone has the right to life and to physical and moral integrity without, in any case, being subjected to torture or inhuman or degrading punishment or treatment].[30] Therefore, abortion before fourteen weeks of pregnancy is covered by the Spanish national health system, much like fertility treatments for women under forty. And like the situation for fertility treatments, many women, like López Varela, opt to use private clinics and pay out of pocket for access to quicker medical interventions. López Varela explores the difficulties that surround obtaining an abortion as well as the socioeconomic and cultural factors that affect that decision. Her narrative allows for an in-depth analysis of the ways that motherhood complicates women's position in society.

López Varela suggests that motherhood continues to reinforce inequality, with women seen as less-than due to the burden of childcare falling on mothers. In Spain, women comprise "el 91% de las excedencias que se concedieron en España para cuidar a un hijo o a otro familiar" [91 percent of the leaves of absence that were given in Spain to take care of a child or another family member], "el 80% del trabajo no remunerado en España está en manos de las mujeres" [80 percent of the unremunerated work in Spain is done by women], and a "brecha salarial del 24%" [24 percent salary gap] exists between women and men, and this gap grows to 37 percent when women become mothers.[31] These are the systemic problems in Spain that illustrate that "la desigualdad ya no se produce por la coacción explícita de leyes, ni por la aceptación de ideas sobre la 'inferioridad de la mujer,' sino a través de 'la libre elección de aquello a lo que nos han encaminado'" [the inequality is produced not by the explicit coercion of the law, or by the acceptance of ideas about the "inferiority of women," but rather through "the free choice that we have been directed to"].[32] These issues lead women to postpone childbearing until their prime fertility era has passed. According to "La reproducción asistida en España: Criterios para su priorización" [Assisted Reproduction in Spain: Criteria for Its Prioritization] from 2002,

> El factor de riesgo de infertilidad más importante en las sociedades occidentales es el retraso de la maternidad. Por tanto, se precisa abordaje amplio en el que se incluyan medidas no sólo asistenciales, sino de tipo social, económico y laboral que, tal como se ha demostrado en otros países del entorno, son realmente efectivas.[33]
>
> [The most important risk factor of infertility in Western society is the age of maternity. Therefore, a broad approach is needed that includes not only welfare measures but also social, economic, and labor measures that, as has been demonstrated in other surrounding countries, are truly effective.]

Indeed, López Varela points to many of these same issues, such as job instability and partner insecurity, when making her decision to terminate her pregnancy.

These complications urge her to postpone (or forgo) motherhood and face the judgment of a society that believes women should necessarily become mothers. While López Varela focuses on how the economic situation in Spain impacts women's decisions to delay becoming mothers, the societal pressure to be a "normal" woman who has children continues to influence this choice as well.

The connection between accepted female behavior (motherhood) and nontraditional behavior (nonmotherhood) continues to be debated, but the idea of motherhood as the ideal for women still predominates. Silvia Tubert offers that "la mujer que no es madre perturba, en cierto modo, el orden establecido, pone en cuestión aquello que regula las relaciones entre hombres y mujeres y atenta contra el sistema de exclusiones que rige el orden jerárquico establecido entre ellos" [the woman who is not a mother disrupts, in a way, the established order; calls into question that which regulates relations between men and women; and threatens the system of exclusions that governs the hierarchical order established between them].[34] Donna Haraway, in "A Cyborg Manifesto," posits a similar idea, saying, "Female embodiment seemed to be given, organic, necessary; and female embodiment seemed to mean skill in mothering and its metaphoric extensions," while Rosi Braidotti focuses on the fact that "we are all of women born."[35] These ties between womanhood, pregnancy, and birth reinforce López Varela's suggestion that women are not free to choose: Their choices have been limited by a society that sees the female body as a site for the creation of the next generation. Women's bodies are controlled by larger power structures.

In addition to the concept of behavior control, women's bodies are surveilled as part of reproductive control. Alys Einion and Jen Rinaldi offer that "mothering bodies are subject to significant oversight, judgment, criticism, political- and health-oriented control systems, and culturally constructed expectations. In and through these discursive frames and practices, corporeal boundaries are produced, contained and displaced."[36] Part of López Varela's experience obtaining an abortion involved a conversation with a doctor who asks her why she wants to terminate her pregnancy, since she is at a good age to have a baby. López Varela replies, "No lo sé, no sé qué quiero hacer con mi vida. No sé nada. No estoy preparada" [I don't know; I don't know what I want to do with my life. I don't know anything. I'm not prepared].[37] The doctor then responds, "Mi obligación es intentar que entres en razón. No sé qué os pasa a las mujeres de ahora, pero solo tienen hijos las chinas" [My obligation is to try to make you see reason. I don't know what is happening to women today, but only Chinese women have children].[38] Between her shock at the racist comment from the doctor and her own questions about ending her pregnancy, López Varela feels both judged by the doctor and enraged that she must submit to this meddling to control her reproductive decision-making. She explains, "Adivino en su mirada todo lo que piensa de mí. Mujer de treinta años abortando por no tomar anticonceptivos. Me siento avergonzada. Soy la homicida sentada ante ese tribunal popular" [I can guess in her eyes everything she thinks about me. Thirty-year-old woman having an abortion for not taking contraceptives. I feel embarrassed. I am the murderer sitting before that popular court].[39] By calling herself a murderer, the boundary between mother and fetus becomes more confusing. Is the fetus a person who deserves protection, or is the woman in charge of her own body? If women could freely decide to become mothers, it would be easier to answer these questions.

When motherhood is posited as a choice, notwithstanding earlier arguments that there is only one "right" choice, women should feel empowered instead of disenfranchised. By framing both motherhood and nonmotherhood as a choice, "the rhetoric of choice diverts attention from the constraints within which an individual choice occurs onto the act of the choice itself."[40] Choice does not recognize social, economic, or political demands on women. López Varela explains the cultural pressure that women, from childhood, feel to become mothers. She says, "Nadie me explicó que la maternidad era una opción, que había mujeres que no eran madres y que yo podría elegir cuando llegase el momento. No, definitivamente eso no nos ocurría a las niñas españolas en las décadas de los ochenta y los noventa del siglo pasado" [No one explained to me that motherhood was a choice, that there were women who were not mothers and I could choose when the moment arrived. No, definitely this did not occur to us Spanish girls in the decades of the eighties and nineties of the last century].[41] The previous quote focuses on a cultural aspect of young girls living in early post-Franco Spain in the 1980s and 1990s, when the author and her generation were growing up and when women were "empujadas a su destino materno" [pushed into their maternal destiny].[42] The author reinforces the idea of choice when she states that "el primer requisito indispensable e insustituible para gestar, parir, adoptar y criar tiene que ser el deseo personal y genuino de la mujer que decide ser madre. Ser madre es una decisión que sólo concierne a las mujeres, no una prueba de amor, ni un regalo o una obligación" [the first indispensable and unsubstitutable requirement for gestating, birthing, adopting, and raising has to be the personal and genuine desire of the woman who decides to become a mother. Being a mother is a decision that only concerns women, not a test of love or a gift or obligation].[43] López Varela stresses that women must be able to freely choose to become mothers. Women must not be defined by their childbearing capacity or by their decision not to become mothers.

However, the structural inequalities between men and women create obstacles that cause women not to be able to freely make the choice to become mothers. López Varela tells us,

> En un contexto de desigualdad patriarcal y neoliberal, el "sexo consentido" al igual que "la renuncia consentida" son realidades tramposas. La libre elección de las mujeres no deja de ser una entelequia cuando las oportunidades y posibilidades que tenemos están absolutamente cercenadas por razón a nuestro

> sexo. A veces, no es el amor de madre lo que nos permite cuidar a tiempo completo, es la imposible conciliación.[44]
>
> [In a patriarchal and neoliberal context of inequality, "consensual sex" as well as "consented resignation" are tricky realities. Women's free choice is still an entelechy when the opportunities and possibilities we have are absolutely curtailed due to our sex. Sometimes, it is not a mother's love that allows us to care full-time; it is the impossible conciliation.]

The concept of "realidad tramposa" [deceptive/tricky reality] speaks volumes about women's access to choice. While equality between the sexes receives lip service, the reality is that inequality still exists, and motherhood is a factor in this inequality. López Varela explains it like this: "Tener un hijo es la decisión más importante a la que se puede enfrentar una mujer en toda su vida, la que más pone en jaque nuestra independencia y más nos penaliza a nivel laboral y económico" [Having a child is the most important decision that a woman can face in her life, that which puts in check our independence and most penalizes us at work and economically].[45] If no equality exists in the labor market and to support children, then the choice to become a mother is fraught with decisions balancing one's career, economic sustainability, and motherhood.

If choice is, through societal pressures, not viable, then women must face the consequences of their decisions. The decision not to become a mother, especially once one is pregnant, causes a rift between being a woman and being a mother. The woman must submit herself to a medical intervention, which creates a distance between herself and the embryo she has conceived. This separation between one's personhood and the body's ability to gestate a new life advances a new way of interpreting a woman's body outside of motherhood. Haraway offers that "a woman is not simply alienated from her product but in a deep sense does not exist as a subject, or even a potential subject, since she owes her existence as a woman to sexual appropriation."[46] By constantly tying femininity to motherhood, society transforms women into baby-making machines that serve the purpose of reproducing future generations, not humans capable of making choices. Haraway muses over many of the same issues as López Varela, such as work, access, and choice, when she says, "Home, work-place, market, public arena, the body itself—all can be dispersed and interfaced in nearly infinite, polymorphous ways, with large consequences for women."[47] Once again, the connection between women and their reproductive capabilities has consequences for all other aspects of society, and the lack of choice for women, or a freely made choice, relates to how society interprets nonmotherhood.

Women's bodies are often seen as nurturing and therefore naturally prone to motherhood. In Susan Bordo's *Unbearable Weight*, the chapter titled "Are Mothers Persons?" investigates how the female body is interpreted when a woman seeks an abortion. Bordo tells us that "the essence of the pregnant woman [. . .] is her biological, purely mechanical role in preserving the life of another" and that in abortion cases, judges make decisions based on the "supreme role of the pregnant woman" being "incubator to her fetus."[48] Bordo's argument connects to López Varela's earlier statement about women's lack of free will when it comes to choice, especially the choice to terminate a pregnancy. Indeed, women must be kept from making their own choices for the (greater) good of societal procreation.

As a counterargument to the mother-as-incubator concept, Julia Hanigsberg, in her article "Homologizing Pregnancy and Motherhood: A Consideration of Abortion," posits abortion as what she terms a "mothering decision": "Abortion, and indeed all procreative decisionmaking, is about mothering in its broadest terms [. . .]. Even when a woman decides to have an abortion, she is still making a mothering decision."[49] Every decision a woman makes about her body when pregnant can be interpreted as a mothering decision, even the decision to end a pregnancy. By connecting abortion to motherhood, Hanigsberg recognizes the central point about women's choice: Women must be able to freely choose how, when, and if to become mothers. López Varela states the same when she says,

> Traer a una persona al mundo sin desearlo y sin estar completamente segura de que va a poder gozar de la estabilidad emocional y del amor de su padre es un acto egoísta e insensato. No quiero pasar por un embarazo no deseado, no quiero pensar que lo hice porque tocaba aun sin tocar.[50]
>
> [Bringing a person into the world without wanting it and without being completely sure about being able to enjoy emotional stability and the love of the father is a selfish and foolish choice. I don't want to have an unwanted pregnancy; I don't want to think that I did it because I was supposed to even though I wasn't.]

The decision to have a child has lifelong consequences, both for the mother as well as for the child. Deciding to have a child—or not to have one—is a mothering decision. Hanigsberg offers a novel interpretation of abortion by positing it as a choice women make about mothering, much like deciding how many children to have. From this perspective, ending a pregnancy is just one option among many that women could exercise.

López Varela focuses on the ability to make a choice, a maternal decision, about the well-being of the child (and herself) in the future. When society blames women for choosing not to have a baby, women "sufren las consecuencias de un sistema que demoniza a las mujeres por ser capaces de llevarle la contraria a su destino biológico. Nuestro silencio les permite vulnerar nuestros derechos" [suffer the consequences of a system that demonizes women for being able to go against their biological destiny. Our silence allows them to infringe on our rights].[51] However, as López Varela discusses, this choice is never free from doubt. By framing abortion as a choice that women suffer from making and inserting the concept of going against one's biological destiny, the decision not to mother is never easy, especially when economic and social barriers cause disparity between men and women.

Women's bodies are seen as either prosperous (creating babies) or failures (infertile or noncreators). Even worse than failures, women who terminate pregnancies are equated with murderers. López Varela explains, "Las [mujeres] que interrumpen un embarazo no deseado pasan al lado oscuro, el de las que reniegan la mística de la maternidad, a medio camino entre el asesinato y el homicidio imprudente [. . .]. A nosotras, nadie nos justifica. Nadie nos perdona" [Women who terminate an unwanted pregnancy go to the dark side, that of those who renounce the mystique of motherhood, halfway between a murder and a reckless homicide. No one justifies us. No one forgives us].[52] By going against the "natural" desire of women to have children, women who have abortions are never forgiven by society for rejecting their role as possible mothers, even in a country where early abortion access has been legally recognized for decades. López Varela conveys how society categorizes women who seek abortions:

> Las irresponsables, las putas, las asesinas, las no arrepentidas. Las arrepentidas y avergonzadas. Las que no han vuelto a pensar en ello y las que piensan en ello cada día de sus vidas. Las que nunca quisieron ser madres y las que querían serlo, pero no así. No entonces. No con él.[53]
>
> [The irresponsible ones, the whores, the murderers, the ones who are not sorry. The ones who are sorry and embarrassed. Those who have not thought about it again and those who think about it every day of their lives. Those who never wanted to be mothers and those who did, but not this way. Not then. Not with him.]

Each of these categories shows women from a negative, selfish perspective. If women are destined to be mothers, then interrupting a pregnancy can only be seen as deviant. However, this creation of deviant womanhood can be deconstructed by questioning the categories of womanhood and breaking the taboo of silence surrounding abortion.

Sharing stories about abortions is a way that López Varela suggests for women to conceptualize their experiences without the negative connotations associated with it. She states that, within the categories of women who have had abortions, there are also "las que querían contarlo para decirnos a todas que ninguna mujer está sola cuando hay otra capaz de entender su dolor" [those who wanted to tell it (her story of abortion) to tell all of us that no woman is alone when there is another capable of understanding her pain].[54] López Varela's second chapter, "¡Asesinas! Mujeres contra el mandato biológico" [Murderers! Women Against the Biological Mandate], discusses protesters outside of abortion clinics, the lack of information online, and the silence surrounding abortion. According to the statistics she shares, between 2010 and 2014 in Spain, an average of 11.6 women per 1,000 had an abortion, with an average age of 29.1 years old.[55] In 2015, 88 percent of abortions were performed in private clinics, even though the constitution guarantees access to free reproductive care.[56] The rest of the chapter includes personal testimonials from women who have received abortions. A consistent theme of these testimonials is the feeling of guilt and disbelief each woman experienced when contacting a doctor. According to López Varela, the guilt factor weighs heavily. Even during her own visit to the doctor's office, she felt judged by the female obstetrician.[57] The fact that the doctor in the clinic makes her feel uncomfortable reinforces the idea that a woman should want to have children; fighting against that mandate is unnatural. A fertile body should produce offspring or else it is a failure. Throughout her experience, these feelings of guilt remain, and López Varela suggests that "muchas veces el sentimiento de culpabilidad, tan arraigado desde la religión, las familias, la sociedad y la propia comunidad médica, retrasa la curación emocional de las mujeres" [many times the feeling of guilt, so ingrained from religion, families, society, and even the medical community, delays the emotional healing of women].[58] If women were able to speak more openly about their experiences, she says, then the sense of guilt would be less.

López Varela presents her decision to terminate her pregnancy as a choice based on structural infertility, albeit a choice no one wants to make. She sees her book as a way of processing what happened to her, a woman who did not want or felt like she could not afford to have a child, a feminist woman who had also judged other women who had received abortions. She realizes within the context of her writing that some choices, even those purportedly supported by the constitution, are imbued with societal pressure, judgment, and disdain. She analyzes some aspects of the psychological effects of her abortion, focusing on the feeling of loss that accompanies her as she writes her book. After her abortion, she realizes, "Mi antigua yo murió un poco en aquella clínica de cortinas verdes y aspecto de centro veterinario. No era trauma lo que arrastraba, tampoco vergüenza [. . .]. No todos los abismos que se abren con un embarazo no deseado se cierran con un aborto voluntario" [My old self died a little in that clinic with green curtains that looked like a veterinary clinic. It was not trauma that weighed, and neither was it embarrassment (. . .). Not all abysms that open with an unwanted pregnancy close with a voluntary abortion].[59] While the author accepts the feelings of loss that accompany her abortion, she also understands that, given her situation of structural barriers to her fertility, the decision was right for her. That doesn't negate the fact that the decision was hard. She shares,

> En mi caso, fue la decisión más difícil que tomé en mi vida. No sé si fue la correcta, y nunca podré comprobarlo. A veces me arrepiento y me culpo, o lo culpo a él, a todo el personal médico sin sensibilidad alguna que se cruzó en mi camino, a los astros, y a otras muchas, la mayoría, tengo un poco más de autocompasión y me repito que hice lo único que necesitaba hacer en aquel momento.[60]
>
> [In my case, it was the most difficult decision I've made in my life. I don't know if it was the right one, and I will never know. Sometimes I regret it and I blame myself, or I blame him, or all of the medical staff without any sensitivity that crossed my path, or the stars, and many others, the majority, I have a little more self-compassion, and I repeat to myself that I did the only thing I needed to in that moment.]

The author clearly identifies the reasons for her discomfort and sadness; she was made to feel guilty by those who surrounded her but, also, by her own feelings. She admits that she doesn't know if she made the right choice; the psychological effects of the decision will stay with her.

While further ruminating on the reality of her loss, she talks about the feeling of mourning that accompanied her after her abortion. It was, for her, "un luto que no añoraba lo que nunca existió, pero que [le] exigía a gritos desprender[se] de una parte de [sí misma]" [a mourning that did not long for what never existed but that loudly demanded that she let go of a part of herself]. She continues, "Por primera vez en mi vida, la maternidad en todas sus formas—incluida la no maternidad—pasó a ocupar una parte central de mis preocupaciones y desvelos" [For the first time in my life, motherhood in all of its forms—including nonmotherhood—came to occupy a central part of my worries and sleeplessness].[61] The mothering decision to end her pregnancy created a need to investigate further the idea of maternity. The process of ending a pregnancy does not equal the end of the questioning of a woman's connection to her reproductive functions.

Maternofobia highlights the essential question of many women: If I'm not a mother, am I still a woman? By refusing to equate motherhood with being a woman, we unmask dualisms that date back to earlier times and continue to influence us today. Simon Williams and Gillian Bendelow, in their book *The Lived Body: Sociological Themes, Embodied Issues*, explain this construct as having been "mapped onto the gendered division of labour in which men, historically, have been allied with the mind, culture and the public realm of production, whilst women have been tied to their bodies, nature and the private sphere of domestic reproduction."[62] They explain that in the nineteenth and twentieth centuries, "menstruation and pregnancy were treated as 'abnormal' and as a 'sickness' rather than normal bodily functions. Within patriarchal medicine, women were seen as being 'controlled' by their uterus and ovaries, and doctors found reproductive 'disorders' behind almost every female complaint."[63] If we continue to equate women with mothers, we fall into the trap of associating women primarily with their biological status, whereas men continue to be associated with the mind instead of the body. In their study on infertility, the authors of "The Continuity and Discontinuity of the Embodied Self in Infertility" illustrate this concept when they explain that "whereas motherhood is regarded as a natural and instinctual role or ascribed status, fathering a child is experienced as an accomplishment and a source of pride."[64] Patriarchal society continues to force women into these categories by supporting pronatalist ideas of motherhood, whereas neoliberal rhetoric disguises this mandate as a personal choice. As women seem to have more choices, societal backlash increases to try to keep them in their place.[65] Lina Meruane warns that "a cada logro feminista ha seguido un retroceso, a cada golpe femenino un contragolpe social destinado a domar los impulsos centrífugos de la liberación" [every feminist achievement has been followed by a setback, every feminine blow has been followed by a social counterblow aimed at taming the centrifugal impulses of liberation].[66] Braidotti fears "that the dislocation of sexual differences, the new hiatus between reproduction and sexuality and the biotechnical appropriation of procreation, occurs precisely at the time in history when women have explicitly revindicated political control over their body and their sexuality."[67] These different theorists agree that women need to question their compliance with societal norms as they accept or reject the role of motherhood.

López Varela offers a unique perspective on the concept of structural infertility in her decision to terminate a pregnancy and not to become a mother, thus expanding the way we interpret infertility. Based on the economic and social aspects of her personal situation, she chooses to end an unexpected pregnancy. She faces the judgment of those around her, including the office staff at the clinic, and deals with the guilt of her decision and the mourning for what could have been. Her portrayal of not only her experience with abortion but those others shared with her opens a space for conversation about a previously taboo subject. She ends her book with a rumination of what it could be like to have a child, when and if the time is right. She states that she would like to tell her embryo, "Soy una mujer que trabaja, y tengo muchos otros compromisos y curiosidades; ya te dije que no te necesito. Pero, de todos modos, llevaré adelante tu gestación, te guste o no" [I am a woman who works, and I have many other commitments and curiosities; I already told you that I don't need you. But anyway, I will carry on with your gestation, like it or not].[68] Her open-ended conclusion reinforces just how hard it is to choose, especially when choices are governed by outside pressures. Multiple aspects of structural infertility—the societal constraints in Spain, the economic disparity between women and men, and the biological mandate—work against women freely making mothering choices.

While there has been a recent rise in the number of books published in Spain about mothers and motherhood (and perhaps about infertility and adoption), there are still few books that address nonmotherhood, the decision not to mother, or abortion. Laura Freixas, in her book of essays *El silencio de las madres* [The Silence of Mothers], points out this lack of women's voices in publishing, especially about pregnancy and abortion, stating,

> Cada año, puntualmente, la literatura española arroja su cosecha de novelas de la guerra civil, a cargo de autores que no la conocieron; mientras, también todos los años, más de cuatrocientas mil españolas dan a luz y más de cien mil abortan, pero de eso la literatura no dice una palabra.[69]
>
> [Every year, promptly, Spanish literature throws out its harvest of novels about the civil war, written by authors who never experienced it; meanwhile, also every year, more than four hundred thousand Spanish women give birth and more than one hundred thousand abort, but literature says nothing about this.]

Diana López Varela's book begins a new era of openness about women who make the choice to be a nonmother, notwithstanding the complicated concept of choice existing within a society that praises the freedom to choose while espousing the norm of motherhood.

Whereas previous chapters have all analyzed books where women who were unable to become pregnant naturally make choices to have families through alternative routes, such as egg donation or adoption, only López Varela's and Silvia Nanclares's narratives end with women choosing not to have children. While López Varela's work focuses on issues of structural infertility that inhibit her from having children, Nanclares's follows the fictional journey of her protagonist's failed interventions to attain a pregnancy and her choice not to pursue further medical treatments. In actuality, Nanclares did resort to egg donation to become pregnant, while López Varela still is child-free. As we have seen, both of these choices are fraught. In López Varela's case, she sees the judgment of others for her decision to end her pregnancy. Nanclares questions her decision to use an egg donor and wonders if she can consider herself a feminist after partaking in the systemic inequality that is part of assisted reproduction. All of these so-called choices are motivated by larger power structures that impact how women perceive themselves and their bodies and urge us to question the concept of choice in relationship to motherhood.

Conclusion

Many women in Spain now postpone having children for varied reasons, such as to secure their financial stability or to launch their careers, and that delay makes them less likely to become pregnant without medical intervention. Their resulting infertility is still considered a stigma in Spain and even points to a crisis in society that devalues women who do not produce offspring. Despite governmental efforts to provide fertility treatments or expand family leave, women still postpone childbearing. When women discover they cannot become pregnant, some of them face the commercialization of the fertility industry that takes advantage of and devalues women's bodies while profiting from their infertility. Women who make the choice not to become mothers are deprecated even more. The issue is complex, as most Spanish women still want to have children. While the authors of the *Informe España 2018* state that the number of people in Spain who choose not to have children is on the rise, at about 5 percent of the population, most Spaniards still retain the preference to have two children.[1] However, biological and structural infertility keep women from achieving that desire. The varied modes of writing included in this book—fiction, nonfiction, memoir, and autobiographical fiction—illustrate that women want to share their experiences. And these experiences have an audience—for instance, almost twenty-five million people follow Spanish TikToker Julia Menú García—revealing the various ways that women seek out information about infertility. The experience of infertility does not solely affect women, but motherhood is still closely tied to womanhood, and women who do not, cannot, or choose not to have children want to tell their stories.

In addition to the five authors studied here, there are many more who speak in various modes about their struggles with infertility, such as Menú, as well as both journalists and academics. Belén García Abia, who published her book about infertility, *El cielo oblicuo* [The Oblique Sky], in 2015, tells her reader in her article "Carta a una futura no madre" [Letter to a Future Nonmother], "Querida futura no-madre, quiero contarte que vas a sentirte impotente, culpable y sola. Resultarás incómoda. No sabrán si preguntarte, no sabrán qué decirte, no querrán hablar de los hijos delante de ti" [Dear future no-mother, I want to tell you that you are going to feel impotent, guilty, and alone. You will make people uncomfortable. They will not know whether to ask you, they will not know what to say to you, they will not want to talk about their children in front of you].[2] She explains that she and her partner decided not to seek intervention to get pregnant. If a baby should arrive, however, she says, "Yo estaría esperándolo, le recibiría con todo el amor que me era posible darle pero no iba a someterme a tratamiento alguno. Ya sabes que mi bebé nunca llegó" [I would be waiting, would receive (the child) with all of the love possible to give him, but I wasn't going to submit to a single treatment. And you already know that my baby never arrived].[3] She talks about mourning the child who never was and how her position as a nonmother causes discomfort to those around her. The sad tone of the letter emphasizes what she feels she has lost by not having a child while also calling out the lies that surround us, telling us "Todo es posible, nos repiten. Pero no es así. No todo lo es" [Everything is possible, they repeat to us. But it is not like that. Not everything is].[4] In her 2012 article in *The Atlantic*, Anne-Marie Slaughter also speaks to the lie that women can have it all. While Slaughter focuses on the social structures that impede women from achieving work-life balance, García Abia speaks more to the physical inability to have children, both of which impact women more profoundly than men, since motherhood is seen as equivalent to womanhood.

The connection between women and motherhood is intense. Common terms such as the *biological clock* or *baby fever* reinforce the concept that motherhood is the norm and nonmothers are deviant. Beatriz San Román also finds that "the underlying idea is that a woman is not complete (is not 'authentically a woman') without motherhood."[5] When women decide not to have children or must use fertility treatments to attain a pregnancy, they begin to question why: Why must they be judged for their choice? Why do they feel pressure to have children? Why does society not support their choices? Diana Oliver exhorts us to "desproblematizar la maternidad. Es algo natural, debe ser una elección, no un impedimento ni un sufrimiento" [deproblematize motherhood. It is something natural; it should be a choice, not an impediment or a suffering].[6] In her article on the transition to motherhood (while not yet a mother herself), Elissa Foster explores "the entrenched divisions of public and private life that frame and constrain women's identities and experiences as they anticipate motherhood" and argues that "silence and constraint are produced and reproduced through phallocentric binaries and the ideological, discursive, and functional separation of public (work) and private (family) life."[7] The public/private divide keeps the difficulties of motherhood in the realm of the private, whereas the avenue for change lies in removing motherhood and its corresponding care work from the private sector and seeing it represented and discussed in public. Only by demystifying and supporting motherhood can women freely choose whether to become mothers. And only by allowing women to make their own decisions without societal and political implications and pressures and negative economic consequences can motherhood be a choice.

Whatever the reasons may be for putting off the decision, delaying motherhood causes a higher chance of infertility. Chapter 2 of this work, "Infertility as Stigma," examines the idea of infertility as an illness, or as a disability, or as a curse. Viewed this way, the concept of motherhood as the norm continues to stand out. The diagnosis of infertility leads women to question their purpose. Indeed, in 2012, then–Spanish Minister of Justice Alberto Ruiz-Gallardón stated publicly that motherhood is what makes women authentically women.[8] (He was forced to resign after making this statement.) From a societal perspective, the equivalency between women and mothers still exists and still exerts social pressure on women to procreate. When explaining why infertility is recognized as a disease that is covered under Spain's system of socialized medicine, Federico Pérez Millán says that this illness "es la limitación de una función biológica esencial para la realización del plan de vida, y cuya frustración supone un importante menoscabo de la salud física y psicoemocional" [is the limitation of an essential biological function for the realization of a life plan whose frustration represents a significant impairment of physical and psychoemotional health].[9] By terming procreation an "essential biological function," Pérez Millán nods to the fact that without procreation, the human race ceases to exist and that women who do not have children are biologically less important—broken machines that cannot perform their duties.

On the one hand, we have the issue of women who would like to have children but cannot. On the other, we have women who could procreate but decide not to due to structural infertility. Both sets of women are the focus of this book as I expand the concept of fertility to address not only biological but structural aspects of infertility. However, even women who do choose to have children, through either sexual intercourse or fertility treatments, find that motherhood is not what they expected it to be. Diana Oliver, author of *Maternidades precarias* and the mother of two children, tells us of her difficulties balancing work and home life, paying her bills, and finding affordable housing. The authors included in this book who do become mothers also find that motherhood is harder than they thought. Samanta Villar's headlines from her interviews yell "La maternidad es un horror" [Motherhood is a horror] and "Mi vida es peor desde que tengo hijos" [My life is worse since I had children].[10] Laura Freixas discusses how difficult work-life balance is to achieve once she becomes a mother, saying, "Los horarios de sueño de la niña [. . .] no casaban con mi propio ritmo [del trabajo]" [The schedule of my daughter's sleep didn't work with my own rhythm of work].[11] Silvia Nanclares is very vocal about her perspectives on motherhood and care work, saying, "Vemos más claro que tantísimas mujeres no están siendo madres porque es imposible después cuidar" [We clearly see that many women are not becoming mothers because it's impossible afterward to take care (of children)].[12] These women who have children thanks to assisted reproductive technology still question why motherhood changes everything and why it has to be so hard. Societal understanding of motherhood, the lack of equality in care work, and the difficulty of maintaining a work-life balance all make the lived experience of motherhood complicated and, perhaps, unwanted.

In Spain, motherhood is in crisis. The crisis is multifaceted. One factor is the economic situation in Spain, with its lack of stable employment for young people and rising housing costs, which cause women to delay childbearing. Since the age of the mother is intrinsically linked to the ability to attain a pregnancy, more women struggle to get pregnant. Environmental factors also impact the ability to become pregnant, from dropping sperm count to low egg quality.[13] Another issue is the medical side of infertility. Spain's reputation as a hub for reproductive travel has caused immense growth in this category of medical specialization. A 2019 article in *El País* states that "el mercado potencial crece con más de siete millones de mujeres que retrasan la maternidad por circunstancias profesionales y personales cada año. En ese país [hay] alrededor de 480 clínicas, más de 100 bancos de esperma, un número desconocido de donantes de óvulos y 1.700 embriólogos" [the market potential grows with more than seven million women who delay motherhood for professional and personal circumstances each year. In this country (there are) around 480 clinics, more than 100 sperm banks, an unknown number of egg donors, and 1,700 embryologists].[14] Fertility treatments have become a multimillion-euro industry, with Spain outperforming all other countries in Europe. Fernández and Sevillano offer that the 285 private fertility clinics in Spain earned €467 million in 2018, with an expected yearly growth of 5 percent.[15] These statistics show how Spain dominates Europe in its number of fertility clinics and cycles performed each year. By promising women the possibility of pregnancy, these fertility companies market lifestyle choices and family-building concepts that, only several decades ago, didn't exist. Indeed, Fernández and Sevillano, when investigating advertising done by fertility clinics, cite an interview with an investigator who says she is worried about "el excesivo tono comercial de la información que las clínicas proporcionan. La mayoría de las comunicaciones no están basadas en fuentes científicas rigurosas, sino que se centran en conseguir más clientes" [the excessively commercial tone of the information given by clinics. The majority of the communications are not based on rigorous scientific sources; rather, they are centered on how to get more clients].[16] The commercialization of infertility underlines how industry quickly responds to a crisis in fertility, while economic and social policies delay making changes.

Yet another part of this crisis connects back to the economic situation. While young women wait to have children, they might also "donate" their eggs to attain both a sense of helping another woman have a child and the small sum of money they receive for their donation. Women who experience infertility, however, must be able to pay for egg donation out of pocket or find other ways to fulfill their desire for motherhood, such as adoption, which is also very expensive. The economic inequality illustrates what Shellee Colen calls "stratified reproduction."[17] This term aims to describe "the power relations by which some categories of people are empowered to nurture and reproduce while others are disempowered."[18] Some might argue that women *choose* to delay childbearing *choose* to donate eggs and that these choices are an example of women's free will. But Rosalind Petchesky argues that "women make their own reproductive choices, but they do not make them just as they please; they do not make them under conditions they create but under conditions and constraints they, as mere individuals, are powerless to change."[19] The misuse or misunderstanding of choice reminds us of Ana de Miguel's book *Neoliberalismo sexual*, about the myth of free will and her assertion that women's decisions are based on unequal systems of power that force women to make a choice when there is really no other option.[20] The broken economic system and the neoliberal understanding that we can achieve whatever we want if we work hard enough (and pay enough) for it, combined with systems of power that disenfranchise women, cause a breakdown in reproduction.

The purpose of this book is to analyze how various texts narrate infertility, exploring the societal impact of infertility, the commercialization of the fertility industry, and the stigma around childlessness, infertility, and fertility treatments. This analysis shows that motherhood is in crisis and offers the reconception of both fertility and motherhood as including more than two people. However, by including more than two people in reproduction, we support a system of inequality in reproduction, where some women procreate and others are paid to help. In *Women as Wombs: Reproductive Technologies and the Battle over Women's Freedom*, Janice Raymond offers that "at this historical point when feminists have de-essentialized motherhood—politicizing the natural definition of women as mothers and distinguishing between motherhood as experience and motherhood as institution—along come the reproductive medical fundamentalists to put mothering back into the sphere of women's natural destiny."[21] Raymond argues that reproductive medicine is violence against women, because "all these technologies, drugs, and procedures violate the integrity of a woman's body in ways that are dangerous, destructive, debilitating, and demeaning."[22] Her book challenges the idea that infertility is a disease that needs to be cured and instead asks us to question the mother/woman binary. I have shown here how imperative it is to question the biological mandate of motherhood while also exploring how we can adjust our perspectives on infertility and its medical treatments.

This book focuses exclusively on the perspective of white, European, heterosexual women. American feminist theorist Patricia Hill Collins offers that "existing feminist theories of motherhood have emerged in specific intellectual and political contexts."[23] Due to these contexts, motherhood theories are not "universal and objective"; instead, they reflect the context we embody. Hill Collins urges us to examine "motherhood and mother-as-subject from multiple perspectives" to recontextualize and diversify motherhood.[24] In this book, I have tried to include diverse perspectives when available, examining how women of color are mistreated or taken advantage of within the context of childcare and child creation, such as egg donation and adoption. Even as I acknowledge this as a limitation of this study, I nevertheless believe that the issue at hand, the infertility among women in Spain, deserves the critical eye that this book provides.

Each chapter focuses on a different aspect of infertility. Chapter 1, "Infertility as Business," examines the industry of infertility and how this industry markets its products to women through the analysis of *Quién quiere ser madre* by Silvia Nanclares. From apps to track fertility, to "natural" alternatives such as acupuncture and diet changes, to artificial insemination and in vitro fertilization, women can shop for their fertility needs. And easy financing allows them to incur debt in order to fulfill their desire for motherhood. While we could interpret these industries as helping women become mothers, the more nefarious interpretation reveals that the financial bottom line of these multinational medical companies is what drives decision-making, not altruistic desires to help women. By moving from medical necessity to purchasable outcomes, fertility clinics navigate a fine line. Medical treatments to aid fertility serve not those in need but those who can afford the upselling that happens in privatized medicine.

These same aspects of commercialization continue in chapter 2, "Infertility as Stigma," this time from the fictional perspective of a doctor who works in a clinic in *Tengo los óvulos contados* by Raquel Sánchez-Silva. This chapter, though, focuses on the stigma felt by women (and men) who access these fertility treatments. Most people believe they will have no problem having children. When they discover that they cannot achieve pregnancy through sexual intercourse, they do not want to admit to what they see as a failure. Both men and women who struggle with infertility see themselves as tainted or damaged. Applying the concept of stigma helps explore why people feel broken when they are diagnosed with infertility. The links between stigma and disability also arise in this chapter. In order to be diagnosed as infertile, a couple must have attempted to become pregnant without success for a year. Once the diagnosis is given, patients can seek treatment to overcome their disability. However, as both the first and subsequent chapters show, these treatments have limited success and high price tags. The patients struggle to deal with their own interpretations of themselves as stigmatized and then with the difficult choices about how to proceed. Infertility affects both the psychological and physical parts of the body, and it manifests as a lived stigma that creates a feeling of being less-than. Even when pregnancy is attained through fertility treatments, women still view their bodies as failures for not being able to do what they should naturally do.

Chapter 3, "Infertility as Crisis," focuses on the motherhood crisis, with a complicated possible solution about including more than one mother in the concept of mothering. From the idea of altruistic egg donation in Spain to the hiring of a nanny, this chapter takes into account how the system of motherhood takes advantage of young, economically precarious women to provide eggs and older, frequently immigrant women of color to fulfill the "mothering" duties of care work.[25] Samanta Villar plays with this concept in the title of her book, *Madre hay más que una*, suggesting an it-takes-a-village approach to not only child-rearing but also child creation through the use of donated gametes. Villar's question, simply put, is, Who is a mother? Is it the person with a genetic relationship to the child? Is it the person who undergoes the gestation of the child? Is it the person who performs the caretaking duties that come with raising a child? Is it the one who does all of these things? What if they only do some of these things? If other women provide services to fulfill some of these mothering responsibilities, are they also mothers to the child? Her rather simplistic answer is that "una madre es una mujer fuerte y templada que antepone el bienestar de su hijo al suyo propio siempre" [a mother is a strong, temperate woman who always puts her child's best interests before her own].[26] If we take this definition at face value, then each of the people described in the questions above could be a mother. The question of egg donation explored in this chapter, however, shows how the fertility industry tries to separate the concept of donation from that of motherhood to make both the donors and the recipients more comfortable. In marketing egg donation this way, the mother is the woman who gestates the baby, and the donor is a helpful outsider with no physical connection to the pregnancy or the subsequent child. Villar examines multiple aspects of infertility in her book, and there are still more avenues for exploration, such as same-sex family formation, the use of sperm donation, the perspective of the children born from donated gametes, or the loss of a pregnancy.

Laura Freixas's *A mí no me iba a pasar* narrates a different alternative to the inability to attain a pregnancy: adoption. Chapter 4 of this book, "Infertility as Classist," identifies Spain as one of the top countries that participates in international adoption. The complicated situation of adopting a child internationally appears in Freixas's narration of her personal experience of adopting her son from Russia. This chapter examines the binary opposition between international adoption as imperial kidnapping and humanitarian rescue. Freixas illustrates this push and pull when she talks about the feeling of superiority of "saving" this child from his difficult life in Russia and the guilt she experiences about "stealing" the child from his family and culture. Her story shows how adoptive parents can be both of these things, saviors and kidnappers, but she does rely on the idea of motherly love as the cure for all of the worries about adoption. Freixas refers to an unnamed short story by Carmen Laforet, using Laforet's expression "Una especie de borrachera de ternura" [A type of drunk love] to describe the affection she feels for her children.[27] Even for women like Freixas, who are not especially interested in becoming mothers, motherhood becomes a central part of their lives, and they discover that they always define themselves in the context of their children.

Maternofobia, the book analyzed in chapter 5, "Infertility as Choice," illustrates how structural infertility impacts young women in Spain. Diana López Varela narrates her decision to terminate a pregnancy based on an economic and social situation in which she feels unable to raise or care for a child while also exploring how society judges women who are not mothers. López Varela's book contains a sharp critique of both the Spanish medical system and the economic precarity that many young Spaniards face. Her narration teaches us that "mothering decisions" such as having an abortion are not freely made choices because patriarchal structures of power and traditional societal norms impact how women make these decisions. Societal pressures posit mothers as the norm and nonmothers as odd women who need to explain why they don't want children. Women, López Varela suggests, cannot choose not to be mothers without having a reason or explanation for this choice. The social pressure to fulfill the biological mandate of motherhood weighs heavily on women to conform. This pressure is what makes women who are infertile feel stigmatized in their own bodies for their inability to procreate. For López Varela, however, the "choice" not to become a mother is structural: The lack of housing, of contract jobs, and of long-term partners keep women from being able to become mothers as they might have imagined when they were younger. Her perspective on structural infertility adds yet another layer to how women deal with and interpret infertility in Spain.

Infertility is on the rise. According to one study, 90 percent of women between the ages of thirty and thirty-four who did not have children cited work and financial issues as the reason they did not, while that percentage was 85 percent for women aged thirty-five to thirty-nine.[28] Diana Oliver wonders when the appropriate time to have children is: "¿Cuando consiga un trabajo fijo? ¿Cuando alcancemos un nivel económico que nos saque del presentismo en el que estábamos instalados? ¿Cuando el precio de la vivienda estabilice? ¿Llegará ese momento?" [When you get a stable job? When you attain an economic level that takes us out of the presenteeism in which we are installed? When the price of housing stabilizes? Will that moment arrive?].[29] If women do wait until all of these prerequisites are met, will they then be able to have children? As Oliver says,

"Existe un desfase monstruoso entre el reloj biológico y el reloj social" [There is a monstrous lag between the biological clock and the social clock], which makes women easy targets for the commodification of their bodies.[30] She suggests that this "mercantilización de la reproducción generará e intensificará nuevas formas de explotación racial y de género" [commercialization of reproduction will generate and intensify new forms of racial and gender exploitation], as we have already seen in chapter 4, "Infertility as Classist," where international adoption takes advantage of the higher birth rates of non-Western nations.[31]

In middle-class Western societies, if women continue to wait to have children, or decide not to have children, what happens? In a 2019 article titled "The End of Babies" in *The New York Times*, Anna Louie Sussman tells us that, on the one hand, "declining fertility typically accompanies the spread of economic development, and it is not necessarily a bad thing. At its best, it reflects better educational and career opportunities for women, increasing acceptance of the choice to be child-free, and rising standards of living."[32] However, she explains, declining fertility also signals the failure

> of employers and governments to make parenting and work compatible; of our collective ability to solve the climate crisis so that children seem a rational prospect; of our increasingly unequal global economy. In these instances, having fewer children is less a choice than the poignant consequence of a set of unsavory circumstances.[33]

In her articulate positioning of why women and men around the world delay childbearing or choose not to have children, Sussman offers the possibility that "economic, social and environmental conditions function as a diffuse, barely perceptible contraceptive."[34] Sussman's article talks about fertility in not only the United States but also Denmark, a country that has one of the most extensive family leave policies in the world, at twelve months. Trent MacNamara, in his 2019 article in *The Atlantic*, offers two ways of approaching the declining birth rate. First, he says, we could celebrate it because it is better for the planet and reflects human freedom.[35] However, he warns, this does not address the issues that keep people who want to have children from having them. Instead, MacNamara gives the option of societal and political change: "Policies such as subsidized child care, state-mandated parental leave, and even direct cash payments can help make children more feasible."[36] Of course, some of these standards already exist at certain levels in Spain and other European countries where birth rates are falling.[37] So while his comments point more to a lack of support for U.S. women and families, they also show that these insufficient policies do not necessarily encourage women to have more children.

Clearly, then, fertility is an issue that affects nearly everyone at some point in their lives, be it through the discovery that they are not able to have children, their decision not to have children, their decision to end a pregnancy, their choice regarding how many children to have, or their decision to donate sperm or eggs. While many of these issues are echoed throughout other countries, especially in Europe, Spain's situation, as noted in the introduction, is unique because of the contrast between Franco-era fertility and norms for women and the twenty-first-century liberal society that exists today. The authors analyzed in this book show how several women, through their works of fiction or nonfiction, narrate their encounters with infertility. Through their works, we readers can explore and understand questions of infertility as they relate to our own lived experiences or to the experiences of others.

By writing about Spain's situation with infertility, these authors bring to the forefront questions about the position of women in society, about the structures that keep women from having children, and about the inequality, violence, and oppression still faced by women today. When more people understand why women cannot or decide not to have children, perhaps there can be more support for women's decisions and their effects. Spain's demographic position is mirrored in other countries in Europe. In Italy in 2016, the minister of health started a campaign to improve fertility rates and named September 22 "Fertility Day."[38] The campaign, which hoped to call attention to the low birth rate and encourage women to have children, faced a huge backlash, with many complaining that Italy needed to improve youth unemployment and labor precarity before asking young women to have children.[39] The Italian prime minister at the time, Matteo Renzi, admitted that marketing would not correct a situation that is caused by structural issues.[40] While Spain's situation is unique due to its historical, cultural, and religious connections to motherhood, similar factors reverberate throughout the world. Through the research presented in this book, I hope to expand the interpretation of infertility and motherhood and begin new conversations about how we as a society can support women's fertility choices, how we can fight for structural changes to equalize care work, and how we should question the medical interventions that are sold to us in order to procreate.

Notes

INTRODUCTION

All translations in this book are mine unless otherwise noted. Ellipses in brackets are my own.

1. Andrea Jiménez, "Julia Menú, la 'tiktoker' más seguida de España y que ha logrado quedarse embarazada tras 14 años: 'Compartir todo es lo mejor que he hecho,'" *El País*, 20 February 2023, https://elpais.com/mamas-papas/actualidad/2023-02-20/ (page no longer extant).

2. Jiménez, "Julia Menú."

3. Loretta Ross and Rickie Solinger, *Reproductive Justice: An Introduction* (University of California Press, 2017), 9, https://doi.org/10.1525/9780520963207.

4. Michelle Leve defines neoliberalism as "a political-economic ideology and practice that promotes individualism, consumerism, deregulation, and transferring state power and responsibility to the individual" and shifts "responsibility from the state to the individual." Leve, "Reproductive Bodies and Bits: Exploring Dilemmas of Egg Donation Under Neoliberalism," *Studies in Gender and Sexuality* 14 (2013): 279, 278. She further explains that assisted reproduction techniques "are then marketed as an individualized solution to a social problem" (278).

5. Margarete J. Sandelowski, "Failures of Volition: Female Agency and Infertility in Historical Perspective," *Signs* 15, no. 3 (1990): 477, https://www.jstor.org/stable/3174424.

6. Margarete J. Sandelowski, *With Child in Mind: Studies of the Personal Encounter with Infertility*, Studies in Health, Illness, and Caregiving (University of Pennsylvania Press, 2016), 10, https://doi.org/10.9783/9781512806779.

7. Pau Baizan, "The Policy Context of Fertility in Spain: Toward a Gender-Egalitarian Model?," in *Low Fertility, Institutions, and Their Policies: Variations Across Industrialized Countries*, ed. Ronald R. Rindfuss and Minja Kim (Springer Nature, 2016), 198.

8. Marina Bettaglio, "(Post)Feminist Maternal Chronicles and Their Discontents," *Letras femeninas* 41, no. 1 (2015): 228, https://doi.org/10.2307/44733780.

9. Bettaglio, "(Post)Feminist Maternal Chronicles," 228.

10. I define these terms in later chapters, but as an introduction to the concepts, *secondary infertility* is infertility after a successful pregnancy and *structural infertility* is infertility based on economic or social barriers. See Bruna Álvarez and Diana Marre, "Motherhood in Spain: From the 'Baby Boom' to 'Structural Infertility,'" *Medical Anthropology* 41, nos. 6–7 (2021): 718–731, https://doi.org/10.1080/01459740.2021.1961246.

11. For more information about the 8M movement in Spain, please see the website https://hacialahuelgafeminista.org/comision/.

12. "Encuesta de fecundidad: Año 2018," Instituto Nacional de Estadística, 9 April 2019, https://www.ine.es/dyngs/INEbase/es/operacion.htm?c=Estadistica_C&cid=1254736177006&menu=ultiDatos&idp=1254735573002.

13. Although Jurado does not explain how to promote fertility, a later quote from Toni Morillas, director of the Instituto de Mujeres [Institute of Women], offers these ideas: "Es necesaria la corresponsabilidad del Estado, del hombre, y también del ámbito laboral" [Co-responsibility of the state, of men, and of the workplace is necessary].

14. Jesús Rodríguez, "Un país sin hijos: Radiografía de la baja natalidad en España," *El País*, 16 April 2022, https://elpais.com/eps/2022-04-17/un-pais-sin-hijos-radiografia-de-la-baja-natalidad-de-espana.html.

15. Quoted in Rodríguez, "Un país sin hijos."

16. This term comes from Álvarez and Marre, "Motherhood in Spain."

17. For more information on Spain's Second Republic, please see Julio Gil Pecharromán, *Historia de la Segunda República española (1931–1936)* (Biblioteca Nueva, 2014). Esperanza Yllán Calderón's book *El franquismo* (Ediciones Akal, 2016) gives an excellent overview of Spain during Franco. Mary Nash's "Pronatalism and Motherhood in Franco's Spain," in *Maternity and Gender Policies: Women and the Rise of the European Welfare States, 1880s–1950s*, ed. Gisela Bock and Pat Thane (Routledge, 1991), speaks specifically about maternity in these times.

18. Pilar Folguera, "El franquismo: El retorno a las esfera privada (1939–1975)," in *Historia de las mujeres en España*, ed. Elisa Garrido (Editorial Síntesis, 1997), 528.

19. Aurora G. Morcillo, *The Seduction of Modern Spain: The Female Body and the Francoist Body Politic* (Bucknell University Press, 2010), 87.

20. Agencia Estatal Boletín Oficial del Estado, "Ley de bases creando el régimen obligatorio de subsidios familiares," *BOE*, no. 19 (19 July 1938): 272–275, https://www.boe.es/buscar/doc.php?id=BOE-A-1938-8202.

21. Pilar Folguera, "Relaciones privadas y cambio social: 1940–1970," in *Otras visiones de España*, ed. Pilar Folguera (Editorial Pablo Iglesias, 1993), 192.

22. Morcillo, *Seduction of Modern Spain*, 69.

23. Folguera, "Relaciones privadas," 196.

24. Folguera, "Relaciones privadas," 196.

25. Morcillo, *Seduction of Modern Spain*, 68.

26. Comisión Episcopal de Ortodoxia y Moralidad, *Normas de decencia cristiana* (Secretariado del Episcopado Español, 1959), 28.

27. Morcillo, *Seduction of Modern Spain*, 81.

28. Morcillo, *Seduction of Modern Spain*, 81.

29. Inbal Ofer, "Historical Models—Contemporary Identities: The Sección Femenina of the Spanish Falange and Its Redefinition of the Term 'Femininity,'" *Journal of Contemporary History* 40, no. 4 (2005): 664, https://doi.org/10.1177/0022009405056123.

30. Morcillo, *Seduction of Modern Spain*, 141.

31. Folguera, "El franquismo," 545.

32. Folguera, "Relaciones privadas," 200.

33. For more information about the impact of the Sección Femenina, please see Carmen Martín Gaite, *Los usos amorosos de la postguerra española*, 5th ed. (Anagrama, 1998).

34. Agencia Estatal Boletín Oficial del Estado, "Ley 56/1961, de 22 de julio, sobre derechos políticos profesionales y de trabajo de la mujer," *BOE*, no. 175 (24 July 1961): 11004–11005, https://www.boe.es/buscar/doc.php?id=BOE-A-1961-14132.

35. Agencia Estatal Boletín Oficial del Estado, "Ley 16/1976, de 8 de abril, de relaciones laborales," *BOE*, no. 96 (21 April 1976): 7894–7902, https://www.boe.es/buscar/doc.php?id=BOE-A-1976-8373.

36. Gudrun Sailer, "Women at Vatican II: Surprising Women, a Surprising Council!," *Vatican News*, 18 June 2019, https://www.vaticannews.va/en/vatican-city/news/2019-06/second-vatican-council-women-regina-heyder.html.

37. Manuel Ansede, "El tobogán de la natalidad en España," *El País*, 10 January 2015, https://www.elpais.com.

38. Morcillo, *Seduction of Modern Spain*, 172.

39. Morcillo, *Seduction of Modern Spain*, 172.

40. See Eugenio Bregolat, "Spain's Transition to Democracy," *SAIS Review* 19, no. 2 (1999): 149–155, https://doi.org/10.1353/sais.1999.0029, for more information about the Spanish transition.

41. Teresa Vilarós, *El mono del desencanto: Una crítica cultural de la transición española (1973–1993)* (Siglo XXI, 2018), 26.

42. Elena Vázquez, "Demografía y cambios culturales," in *Las representaciones de la maternidad: Debates teóricos y repercusiones sociales*, ed. C. Fernández-Montraveta et al. (Instituto Universitario de Estudios de la Mujer, 2000), 87.

43. "Total Fertility Rate in Europe in 2022, by Country," Statista, accessed 28 September 2022, https://www.statista.com/statistics/612074/fertility-rates-in-european-countries/.

44. Malta provides up to eighteen weeks paid leave, Italy offers twenty weeks, and Spain has just recently moved to twenty weeks. See "Maternity Benefit," Department of Social Security, Malta, accessed 16 June 2025, http://www.socialsecurity.gov.mt.

45. María Sosa Troya and Noor Mahtani, "La España de la maternidad tardía," *El País*, 14 December 2019, https://www.elpais.com.

46. Rita Abundancia, "¿Es tener hijos la gran transgresión de la mujer trabajadora en España?," *El País*, 30 October 2017, https://www.elpais.com.

47. Vilarós, *El mono del desencanto*, 26.

48. Vilarós, *El mono del desencanto*, 26.

49. Baizan, "Policy Context of Fertility," 202.

50. Josune Aguinaga Roustan, "Mujer y fecundidad," in *La mujer en la España actual ¿Evolución o involución?*, ed. Jacqueline Cruz and Barbara Zecchi (Icaria, 2004), 119.

51. Aguinaga Roustan, "Mujer y fecundidad," 119.

52. See Sebastián Royo, "The Causes and Legacy of the Great Recession in Spain," in *The Oxford Handbook of Spanish Politics*, ed. Diego Muro and Ignacio Lago (February 2020), https://doi.org/10.1093/oxfordhb/9780198826934.013.8.

53. Bregolat, "Spain's Transition to Democracy."

54. Vázquez, "Demografía y cambios culturales," 127.

55. Vázquez, "Demografía y cambios culturales," 129.

56. "Encuesta de condiciones de trabajo 2015," Instituto Nacional de Estadística, https://www.ine.es/jaxiT3/Datos.htm?t=26060 (page no longer extant).

57. Ana de Miguel, *Neoliberalismo sexual: El mito de la libre elección* (Cátedra, 2015), 31.

58. Marina Garcés, "Comprensión y reparación: Por una filosofía del cuidado y el daño," *Folia Humanística* 12 (2019): 4–5, https://doi.org/10.30860/0052.

59. Victoria Camps, *El tiempo de cuidados: Otra forma de estar en el mundo* (Arpa, 2021), 13.

60. Camps, *El tiempo de cuidados*, 12.

61. Sandra Ezquerra, "De la economía feminista a la democratización de los cuidados," *Viento sur* 158 (February 2018): 43.

62. Ezquerra, "De la economía feminista," 42.

63. Patricia Merino Murga, "La maternidad como cuidado: Guía hacia un futuro sostenible," *Viento sur* 156 (February 2018): 75.

64. Merino Murga, "La maternidad como cuidado," 75.

65. Patricia Merino Murga, *Maternidad, igualdad y fraternidad: Las madres como sujeto político en las sociedades poslaborales* (Clave Intelectual, 2017), 14.

66. Merino Murga, *Maternidad, igualdad y fraternidad*, 23–24.

67. "Gender Equality Index," European Institute for Gender Equality, accessed 16 December 2024, https://eige.europa.eu/gender-equality-index/game/ES/W.

68. Baizan, "Policy Context of Fertility," 199.

69. Baizan, "Policy Context of Fertility," 200.

70. Esther Vivas, *Mamá desobediente: Una mirada feminista a la maternidad* (Capitán Swing, 2019), 30.

71. Vivas, *Mamá desobediente*, 70.

72. Vivas, *Mamá desobediente*, 72.

73. Álvarez and Marre, "Motherhood in Spain," 719.

74. Noemí López Trujillo, *El vientre vacío* (Capitán Swing, 2019), 24.

75. López Trujillo, *El vientre vacío*, 24.

76. Noemí López Trujillo announced her pregnancy on Instagram (@nlopeztrujillo) on 29 January 2024 with a post that reads, "Hay algo aquí dentro creciendo que se siente como la supernova Casiopea A" [There is something here inside growing that feels like the supernova Cassiopeia A]. On 11 August, she posted a photo of herself and her child Ariel from the hospital.

77. López Trujillo, *El vientre vacío*, 31.

78. De Miguel, *Neoliberalismo sexual*, 10.

79. López Trujillo, *El vientre vacío*, 31.

80. Silvia Federici, "El cuerpo de la mujer es la última frontera del capitalismo," Feministas.org, 19 May 2014, https://www.feministas.org/silvia-federici-el-cuerpo-de-la.html.

81. Federici, "El cuerpo."

82. De Miguel, *Neoliberalismo sexual*, 24.

83. It is interesting to note that the United States of America is one of only seven countries in the world without national paid maternity leave. Therefore, from a U.S. perspective, any paid leave is generous. However, Spain had one of the lowest paid leave policies in Europe, with only Switzerland being lower, with fourteen paid weeks. See Claire Cain Miller, "The World 'Has Found a Way to Do This': The U.S. Lags on Paid Leave," *New York Times*, 25 October 2021.

84. Javier Martín Arroyo, "Hasta tres años de espera para poder ser madre," *El País*, 13 May 2019, https://elpais.com/sociedad/2019/05/12/actualidad/1557676986_761783.html.

85. "Insights into the Fertility Clinics & Infertility Services Industry in the US to 2025," Intrado: Global Newswire, 22 May 2020, https://www.globenewswire.com.

86. Martín Arroyo, "Hasta tres años."

87. Renwick McLean, "Spain Gives Approval to Gay Unions," *New York Times*, 1 July 2005, https://www.nytimes.com/2005/07/01/world/europe/spain-gives-approval-to-gay-unions.html.

88. Since this time, Spain's laws have caused changes in the European Union. In 2022, the Court of Justice of the European Union ruled that "if one EU country recognises the child's parental relationship, as Spain had done, then all EU countries should do the same, and so guarantee the child its freedom of movement across the region, which is a right of all EU citizens" (ILGA Europe, "Update: The Rights of Rainbow Families in the EU," 2022, https://www.ilga-europe.org/blog/update-the-rights-of-rainbow-families-in-the-eu/). Israel also guaranteed this right to its citizens in 2024 (George Avni, "Israeli Supreme Court Rules Country Must Allow Two Mothers on Child's Birth Certificate," *Washington Blade*, 22 March 2024). Patricia Esteban also mentions parental rights for homosexual parents in her article "El laberinto legal que sufren las parejas homosexuales para inscribir a sus hijos," *El País*, 8 April 2019.

89. Ana Somavilla, "Los últimos de la fe: Así ha perdido España un millón de jóvenes católicos en 20 años," *El Confidencial*, 10 September 2023, https://www.elconfidencial.com/espana/2023-09-10/ultimos-fe-asi-perdido-espana-millon-jovenes-catolicos-20-anos_3731573/.

90. Statistical Institute of Catalonia, "Live Births Outside Marriage," GenCat, accessed 2024, https://www.idescat.cat/indicadors/?id=ue&n=10088&lang=en.

91. Raquel Sánchez Silva, *Tengo los óvulos contados* (Planeta, 2017), 11.

CHAPTER 1 — INFERTILITY AS BUSINESS

1. Carmen Alborch, *Solas* (Planeta, 1999); Beatriz San Román, "Waiting Too Long to Mother: Involuntary Childlessness and Assisted Reproduction in Contemporary Spain," in *Waithood: Gender, Education, and Global Delays in Marriage and Childbearing*, ed. Marcia C. Inhorn and Nancy J. Smith-Hefner (Berghahn, 2021), 342, https://doi.org/10.1515/9781789209006-017.

2. The "mother as normal" concept dates back centuries but was revived more recently as part of the Franco regime, when "mandatory motherhood remained at the center of the Francoist regime's discourse on Spanish women's national identity" (Aurora G. Morcillo, *The Seduction of Modern Spain: The Female Body and the Francoist Body Politic* [Bucknell University Press, 2010], 138).

3. Valledelkas Editorial, "La maternidad según la autora Silvia Nanclares," *Valledelkas*, 23 March 2017.

4. Silvia Nanclares, "La infertilidad es una patología social a la que ha contribuido el Estado," *Pikara Online Magazine*, 2017.

5. Nanclares, "La infertilidad."

6. Olga Albarrán Caselles, *(Pro)creación: Escritura y maternidad en la España contemporánea* (Libertarias, 2022), 96.

7. María Reyes Ferrer, "Spain and Structural Infertility: Towards an Integrative Vision of Motherhood in the Novel *Quién quiere ser madre* by Silvia Nanclares," in *The Palgrave Handbook of Reproductive Justice and Literature*, ed. B. W. Capo and L. Lazzari (Palgrave, 2022), 385.

8. Nanclares, "La infertilidad."

9. For more information about Spain's state-sponsored system, see Verónica Ramírez and Inma Escobar, "Estos son los requisitos para acceder a la reproducción asistida en la sanidad pública," *La Sexta*, 2 January 2019, https://www.lasexta.com/noticias/economia/consumo/estos-son-requisitos-acceder-reproduccion-asistida-sanidad-publica_20190123 5c54102000cf2be7ee4853696.html.

10. Hans-Peter Kohler et al., "The Emergence of Lowest-Low Fertility in Europe in the 1990s," *Population and Development Review* 28, no. 4 (2002): 668.

11. "Movimiento natural de la población (nacimientos, defunciones y matrimonios): Indicadores demográficos básicos año 2015; Datos provisionales," Instituto Nacional de Estadística, 2016, https://www.ine.es/.

12. Diana Marre et al., "On Reproductive Work in Spain: Transnational Adoption, Egg Donation, Surrogacy," *Medical Anthropology* 37, no. 2 (2018): 160.

13. Marre et al., "On Reproductive Work," 160.

14. Marre et al., "On Reproductive Work," 160.

15. Sharon Hays, *The Cultural Contradictions of Motherhood* (Yale University Press, 1996), 21.

16. One study found that the imagined burdens of intensive mothering cause some women to postpone childbearing or decide not to become mothers (Kit Myers, "If I'm Going to Do It, I'm Going to Do It Right," *Gender and Society* 31, no. 6 [2017]: 777–803).

17. According to one study in Spain, 54 percent of women who live close to their mothers depend on their mothers for help caring for their children. Another study shows that 22 percent of grandparents take care of their grandchildren daily in Spain (Carolina Del Olmo, *¿Dónde está mi tribu? Maternidad y crianza en una sociedad individualista* [Clave Intelectual, 2013], 29).

18. Elixabete Imaz, *Convertirse en madre: Etnografía del tiempo de gestación* (Cátedra, 2010), 70.

19. Robin E. Jensen, *Infertility: Tracing the History of a Transformative Term* (Pennsylvania State University Press, 2016), 18.

20. Jensen, *Infertility*, 19.

21. Silvia Nanclares, *Quién quiere ser madre* (Alfaguara, 2017), 80.

22. Nanclares, *Quién quiere ser madre*, 80.

23. Nanclares, *Quién quiere ser madre*, 80.

24. Albarrán Caselles points out previous representations of infertility in literature from Spain, such as García Lorca's *Yerma* (1934), which she considers a "hipotexto" [hypertext] for *Quién quiere ser madre* (Albarrán Caselles, *(Pro)creación*, 99). Albarrán Caselles also mentions *Fortunata y Jacinta* (1887) by Benito Pérez Galdós as a pretext for female authored novels about infertility (99).

25. Kelly Oliver, "Motherhood, Sexuality, and Pregnant Embodiment: Twenty-Five Years of Gestation," *Hypatia* 25, no. 4 (2010): 765.

26. Gayle Letherby, "Challenging Dominant Discourses: Identity and Change and the Experience of 'Infertility' and 'Involuntary Childlessness,'" *Journal of Gender Studies* 11, no. 3 (2002): 285.

27. Belle Bogg's *The Art of Waiting: On Fertility, Medicine, and Motherhood* (Graywolf Press, 2016) tells us that wanting "biological children is coded into most of the world's major religions" (30).

28. Esther Vivas, *Mamá desobediente: Una mirada feminista a la maternidad* (Capitán Swing, 2019), 32.

29. Vivas, *Mamá desobediente*, 72.

30. Laura Hurd Clarke et al., "The Continuity and Discontinuity of the Embodied Self in Infertility," *Canadian Review of Sociology / Revue Canadienne de Sociologie* 43, no. 1 (2006): 96.

31. Hurd Clarke et al., "Continuity and Discontinuity," 97.

32. Hurd Clarke et al., "Continuity and Discontinuity," 99.

33. Hurd Clarke et al., "Continuity and Discontinuity," 109.

34. Hurd Clarke et al., "Continuity and Discontinuity," 104.

35. Hurd Clarke et al., "Continuity and Discontinuity," 103, 109.

36. Silvia Federici, *Caliban and the Witch* (Autonomedia, 2004), 89.

37. Nuria Varela, *Feminismo para principiantes*, rev. ed. (Ediciones B, 2019), 25.

38. Varela, *Feminismo para principiantes*, 25.

39. Federici, *Caliban and the Witch*, 89.

40. Peter Conrad, *The Medicalization of Society: On the Transformation of Human Conditions into Treatable Disorders* (Johns Hopkins University Press, 2007), 4.

41. Silvia Tubert, "La maternidad en el discurso de las nuevas tecnologías reproductivas," in *Las mujeres y los niños primero: Discursos de la maternidad*, ed. Ángeles de la Concha and Michelle Osbourne (Icaria, 2004), 121.

42. Jensen, *Infertility*, 2.

43. Jensen, *Infertility*, 6–7.

44. Jensen, *Infertility*, 7.

45. Federici, *Caliban and the Witch*, 138–140.

46. Helena Michie and Naomi R. Cahn, *Confinements: Fertility and Infertility in Contemporary Culture* (Rutgers University Press, 1997), 121.

47. Michie and Cahn present Gena Corea, in her book *The Mother Machine: Reproductive Technologies from Artificial Insemination to Artificial Wombs* (Perennial Library, 1985), as the main voice of this perspective (124).

48. Michie and Cahn, *Confinements*, 124.

49. Michie and Cahn, *Confinements*, 125.

50. Nanclares, *Quién quiere ser madre*, 107.

51. Nanclares, *Quién quiere ser madre*, 62.
52. Nanclares, *Quién quiere ser madre*, 72.
53. Nanclares, *Quién quiere ser madre*, 74.
54. Hurd Clarke et al., "Continuity and Discontinuity," 110.
55. Nanclares, *Quién quiere ser madre*, 119.
56. Hurd Clarke et al., "Continuity and Discontinuity," 110.
57. Nanclares, *Quién quiere ser madre*, 88.
58. Nanclares, *Quién quiere ser madre*, 107.
59. Nanclares, *Quién quiere ser madre*, 156.
60. Varela, *Feminismo para principiantes*, 341.
61. Emily Martin, "Medical Metaphors of Women's Bodies: Menstruation and Menopause," in *Writing on the Body: Female Embodiment and Feminist Theory*, ed. Katie Conboy et al. (Columbia University Press, 1997), 29–30.
62. Margarete J. Sandelowski, *With Child in Mind: Studies of the Personal Encounter with Infertility*, Studies in Health, Illness, and Caregiving (University of Pennsylvania Press, 2016), 11–12, https://doi.org/10.9783/9781512806779.
63. In 2017, the World Health Organization defined *infertility* as "a disease of the male or female reproductive system" ("Infertility," World Health Organization, accessed 16 June 2025, https://www.who.int/health-topics/infertility#tab=tab_1) However, many other health organizations do not recognize infertility as a disease, which allows insurance companies in the United States to deny coverage for treatments.
64. See Valerie R. Renegar and Kirsti K. Cole, "Evil Is Part of the Territory: Inventing the Stepmother in Self-Help Books," *Women's Studies in Communication* 42, no. 4 (2019): 511–533.
65. Nanclares, *Quién quiere ser madre*, 194.
66. Nanclares, *Quién quiere ser madre*, 204.
67. Nanclares, *Quién quiere ser madre*, 201, 211.
68. Nanclares, *Quién quiere ser madre*, 212.
69. Albarrán Caselles, *(Pro)creación*, 109.
70. K. Animashaun Ducre, "Race(ing) to the Baby Market: The Political Economy of Overcoming Infertility," in *The Motherhood Business: Consumption, Communication, and Privilege*, ed. Anne Teresa Demo et al. (University of Alabama Press, 2015), 52.
71. Nanclares, *Quién quiere ser madre*, 81.
72. Nanclares, *Quién quiere ser madre*, 77.
73. Nanclares, *Quién quiere ser madre*, 102.
74. Nanclares, *Quién quiere ser madre*, 74–75.
75. Nanclares, *Quién quiere ser madre*, 75. In a sad but fascinating connection to the overturn of *Roe v. Wade*, "many American women [. . .] have deleted period tracking apps from their cell phones, amid fears the data collected by the apps could be used against them in future criminal cases in states where abortion has become illegal" ("Why US Women Are Deleting Their Period Tracking Apps," *The Guardian*, 28 June 2022).
76. Charis M. Thompson, "Fertile Ground: Feminists Theorize Infertility," in *Infertility Around the Globe: New Thinking About Childlessness, Gender and Reproductive Technologies*, ed. Marcia C. Inhorn and Frank Van Balen (University of California Press, 2002), 58.
77. Ducre, "Race(ing)," 54.
78. Charlotte Kroløkke, "Eggs and Euros: A Feminist Perspective on Reproductive Travel from Denmark to Spain," *IJFAB: International Journal of Feminist Approaches to Bioethics* 7, no. 2 (2014): 150.
79. Nanclares, *Quién quiere ser madre*, 173.
80. Nanclares, *Quién quiere ser madre*, 139.
81. Nanclares, *Quién quiere ser madre*, 174.
82. Nanclares, *Quién quiere ser madre*, 174.
83. Nanclares, *Quién quiere ser madre*, 175.

84. Nanclares, *Quién quiere ser madre*, 108.

85. In March 2023, Ana Obregón, a famous television actress in Spain, announced the birth of her child. Obregón, who is sixty-eight, had used the sperm of her deceased son, an egg donor, and a surrogate to have this baby, who was born in the United States. She then adopted the child, who will have a U.S. passport. While Spain does recognize internationally adopted babies, surrogacy is illegal in Spain. Verónica Fumanal, president of Spain's Association of Political Communication (ACOP), said that Obregón "bought herself a granddaughter with sperm from her dead son" (Jack Guy, "Mother and Grandmother to the Same Baby: Spanish Actress Sparks Surrogacy Debate," CNN, 2023).

86. Noemí López Trujillo, *El vientre vacío* (Capitán Swing, 2019), 93.

87. Nanclares, "La infertilidad."

88. Nanclares, "La infertilidad."

89. Nanclares, *Quién quiere ser madre*, 144–150.

90. Nanclares, *Quién quiere ser madre*, 209.

91. Nanclares, *Quién quiere ser madre*, 180.

92. Tubert, "La maternidad," 125.

93. Nanclares, *Quién quiere ser madre*, 85.

94. Nanclares, *Quién quiere ser madre*, 95.

95. Nanclares, *Quién quiere ser madre*, 204.

96. Albarrán Caselles, *(Pro)creación*, 135.

97. Silvia Nanclares, "¿Soy una mala feminista si acepto la ovodonación? Claroscuros de una maternidad bajo el capitalismo reproductivo," *El Diario*, 17 July 2019, https://www.eldiario.es/nidos/claroscuros-maternidad-feminista-ovodonacion_1_1433839.html.

98. Nanclares, "¿Soy una mala feminista?"

99. Nanclares, "¿Soy una mala feminista?"

100. Nanclares, "¿Soy una mala feminista?"

CHAPTER 2 — INFERTILITY AS STIGMA

1. Raquel Sánchez-Silva, *Tengo los óvulos contados* (Planeta, 2017), 83.

2. Sánchez-Silva, *Tengo los óvulos contados*, 188.

3. Spain is tied with Ukraine and Macau at the eighth-lowest fertility rate worldwide, as shown in data from 2019. Please see "Total Fertility Rate 2021," World Population Review, accessed 20 December 2024, https://worldpopulationreview.com/country-rankings/total-fertility-rate.

4. Quote from the article by Juan Bedoya, "El 30% de las madres españolas tienen su primer hijo a partir de los 35 años," *El País*, 4 December 2018, https://elpais.com/sociedad/2018/12/04/actualidad/1543935531_127370.html.

5. From the article by Carmen Pérez-Lanzac, "Demasiado tarde para ser madre," *El País*, 8 February 2016, https://elpais.com/politica/2016/01/27/actualidad/1453904610_786378.html.

6. Quoted in Pérez-Lanzac, "Demasiado tarde."

7. "Raquel Sánchez-Silva," Planetadelibros, accessed 20 December 2024, https://www.planetadelibros.com/autor/raquel-sanchez-silva/000036784.

8. In an interview in 2015 in *ABC Estilo*, Sánchez-Silva states that her twins were born through assisted reproduction, but she does not specify what procedures. Seeing as Sánchez-Silva was forty-two when her children were born, there is a high likelihood that her children were born of egg donors, which I will examine more in depth in the next chapter.

9. Sánchez-Silva, *Tengo los óvulos contados*, 11.

10. Sánchez-Silva, *Tengo los óvulos contados*, 11.

11. Pérez-Lanzac, "Demasiado tarde."

12. Esther Vivas, *Mamá desobediente: Una mirada feminista a la maternidad* (Capitán Swing, 2019), 69.

13. Vivas, *Mamá desobediente*, 72.

14. Vivas, *Mamá desobediente*, 30.

15. Vivas, *Mamá desobediente*, 32.

16. Erving Goffman, *Stigma: Notes of the Management of Spoiled Identity* (Prentice Hall, 1963), 3.

17. Bruce G. Link and Jo C. Phelan, "Conceptualizing Stigma," *Annual Review of Sociology* 27 (2001): 377.

18. Elizabeth A. Sternke and Kathleen Abrahamson, "Perceptions of Women with Infertility on Stigma and Disability," *Sexuality and Disability* 33 (2015): 3–17.

19. Charlene E. Miall, "The Stigma of Involuntary Childlessness," *Social Problems* 33, no. 4 (1986): 270.

20. Miall, "Stigma of Involuntary Childlessness," 270.

21. Candida R. Moss and Joel S. Baden, *Reconceiving Infertility: Biblical Perspectives on Procreation and Childlessness* (Princeton University Press, 2015), 12.

22. Moss and Baden, *Reconceiving Infertility*, 14.

23. Moss and Baden, *Reconceiving Infertility*, 7.

24. Moss and Baden, *Reconceiving Infertility*, 9.

25. Moss and Baden, *Reconceiving Infertility*, 11.

26. World Health Organization (WHO), *Preamble to the Constitution of the World Health Organization* (WHO, 1946).

27. United Nations, "Article 1: Purpose," in *Convention on the Rights of Persons with Disabilities*, United Nations Department of Economic and Social Affairs Social Inclusion, 2008, https://www.un.org/development/desa/disabilities/convention-on-the-rights-of-persons-with-disabilities/article-1-purpose.html.

28. WHO, "Infertility Is a Global Public Health Issue," *Human Reproduction Programme*, accessed 20 December 2024, https://www.who.int/reproductivehealth/topics/infertility/perspective/en/ (page no longer extant).

29. Sánchez-Silva, *Tengo los óvulos contados*, 40.

30. Moss and Baden, *Reconceiving Infertility*, 4.

31. Sternke and Abrahamson, "Perceptions of Women," 4.

32. Sternke and Abrahamson, "Perceptions of Women," 6.

33. Sternke and Abrahamson, "Perceptions of Women," 13.

34. Óscar García Muñoz, adapt., "Ley General de derechos de las personas con discapacidad y de su inclusión social (en lectura fácil)," Ministerio de Sanidad, Servicios Sociales e Igualdad, December 2015, https://www.plenainclusion.org/sites/default/files/ley_general_de_derechos.pdf, 27.

35. Moss and Baden, *Reconceiving Infertility*, 4.

36. Sternke and Abrahamson, "Perceptions of Women," 13.

37. Sternke and Abrahamson, "Perceptions of Women," 4.

38. Sternke and Abrahamson, "Perceptions of Women," 5.

39. Sternke and Abrahamson, "Perceptions of Women," 11.

40. Sternke and Abrahamson, "Perceptions of Women," 5.

41. Sternke and Abrahamson, "Perceptions of Women," 5.

42. Sánchez-Silva, *Tengo los óvulos contados*, 73. According to the television program *Binario* on RTVE, the situation of sperm is dire: sperm quality declines by 2 percent annually, with statistics showing that sperm count has gone from 337.3 million per ejaculation in 1973 to 137.5 million thirty years later.

43. Randi Sylvest et al., "Low Semen Quality and Experiences of Masculinity and Family Building," *Acta Obstetrecia et Gynecologica Scandinavica* 97 (2018): 729.

44. Sylvest et al., "Low Semen Quality," 731.
45. Sylvest et al., "Low Semen Quality," 731.
46. Sánchez-Silva, *Tengo los óvulos contados*, 70.
47. Sánchez-Silva, *Tengo los óvulos contados*, 72.
48. Sternke and Abrahamson, "Perceptions of Women," 5.
49. Sánchez-Silva, *Tengo los óvulos contados*, 14.
50. Sternke and Abrahamson, "Perceptions of Women," 12.
51. Miall, "Stigma of Involuntary Childlessness," 268.
52. Sánchez-Silva, *Tengo los óvulos contados*, 14.
53. Sánchez-Silva, *Tengo los óvulos contados*, 14.
54. Sánchez-Silva, *Tengo los óvulos contados*, 80.
55. Sánchez-Silva, *Tengo los óvulos contados*, 80.
56. Sánchez-Silva, *Tengo los óvulos contados*, 81.
57. Linda M. Whiteford and Lois Gonzalez, "Stigma: The Hidden Burden of Infertility," *Social Science and Medicine* 40, no. 1 (1995): 27.
58. Sternke and Abrahamson, "Perceptions of Women," 6.
59. Sánchez-Silva, *Tengo los óvulos contados*, 61–62.
60. Sánchez-Silva, *Tengo los óvulos contados*, 62.
61. Sánchez-Silva, *Tengo los óvulos contados*, 62. This theme of women using online sources for help or information appears in all of the novels analyzed in this book, except for the autobiography by Laura Freixas. Nanclares both consumes and creates online information, while Villar and López Varela share their online research.
62. Sánchez-Silva, *Tengo los óvulos contados*, 189.
63. Sánchez-Silva, *Tengo los óvulos contados*, 189.
64. Whiteford and Gonzalez, "Stigma," 29.
65. Sternke and Abrahamson, "Perceptions of Women," 6.
66. Arjan Bos et al., "Stigma: Advances in Theory and Research," *Basic and Applied Social Psychology* 35, no. 1 (2013): 2.
67. Sánchez-Silva, *Tengo los óvulos contados*, 14.
68. Sánchez-Silva, *Tengo los óvulos contados*, 85.
69. Sánchez-Silva, *Tengo los óvulos contados*, 87.
70. In chapter 5, "Infertility as Choice," I delve further into the concept of childlessness as a result of structural infertility.
71. Miall, "Stigma of Involuntary Childlessness," 277. Quoting J. E. Veevers, "Voluntary Childlessness: A Review of Issues and Evidence," *Marriage and Family Review* 2, no. 2 (1979): 4–5.
72. Sánchez-Silva, *Tengo los óvulos contados*, 117.
73. Sánchez-Silva, *Tengo los óvulos contados*, 127–128.
74. Sánchez-Silva, *Tengo los óvulos contados*, 124.
75. Sánchez-Silva, *Tengo los óvulos contados*, 112.
76. Sánchez-Silva, *Tengo los óvulos contados*, 115.
77. Nicky Hudson et al., "'Public' Perceptions of Gamete Donation: A Research Review," *Public Understanding of Science* 18 (2009): 65.
78. Sánchez-Silva, *Tengo los óvulos contados*, 99–100.
79. Shanna Swan and Stacey Colino, *Count Down: How Our Modern World Is Threatening Sperm Counts, Altering Male and Female Reproductive Development, and Imperiling the Future of the Human Race* (Scribner, 2020), 7–8.
80. Swan and Colino, *Count Down*, 23.
81. Sternke and Abrahamson, "Perceptions of Women," 11.
82. Sánchez-Silva, *Tengo los óvulos contados*, 128.
83. Charis M. Thompson, "Fertile Ground: Feminists Theorize Infertility," in *Infertility Around the Globe: New Thinking About Childlessness, Gender and Reproductive Technologies*, ed. Marcia C. Inhorn and Frank Van Balen (University of California Press, 2002), 52.

84. Sternke and Abrahamson, "Perceptions of Women," 13.
85. Sánchez-Silva, *Tengo los óvulos contados*, 14.

CHAPTER 3 — INFERTILITY AS CRISIS

1. "Quién es Samanta Villar," *20 minutos*, 21 April 2021, https://www.20minutos.es/noticia/4667901/0/quien-es-samanta-villar.
2. The television series, which aired in 2016 on Cuatro, while not analyzed here, includes investigative journalism about the state of fertility throughout Europe as well as her own experience with infertility and the birth of her twins.
3. Samanta Villar, *Madre hay más que una: Un relato en primera persona sobre la aventura de la maternidad* (Planeta, 2018), 16.
4. Villar, *Madre hay más que una*, 26.
5. In *Sexografías* (Melusina, 2008), Gabriela Wiener includes a story called "Adiós, Ovocito, adiós," where she talks about her experience as an egg donor in Spain. According to Wiener, statistics state that 15 percent of donors are from Latin America, although she believes the number is higher (162). Since the eggs come from anonymous donors, Villar cannot include the voice of her donor or those of any other egg donors in her book.
6. EUR-Lex, "Charter of Fundamental Rights of the European Union," *Official Journal of the European Union* C 326 (26 October 2012): 391.
7. Agencia Estatal Boletín Oficial del Estado, "La ley española sobre las técnicas de reproducción humana asistida (Ley 14/2006)," *BOE*, no. 126 (27 May 2006), https://www.boe.es/eli/es/l/2006/05/26/14/con.
8. Natacha Salomé Lima et al., "Donantes de ovocitos: Análisis comparativo de dos muestras de Argentina y España sobre perfil de donantes, motivaciones y anonimato," *Política y sociedad* 56, no. 3 (2019): 605. Ovarian hyperstimulation syndrome (OHSS) generally occurs after egg retrieval and involves swelling of the ovaries, bloating, weight gain, and abdominal pain. Only 1 percent of egg donors suffer a severe form of OHSS. During egg retrieval, one in one thousand women have complications that can include hospitalization due to blood loss, damage to internal organs, and infection (University of California San Francisco, "FAQ: Common Questions for Egg Donors," USCF Health, 2023, https://www.ucsfhealth.org/en/education/faq-common-questions-for-egg-donors).
9. Guido Pennings et al., "Socio-Demographic and Fertility-Related Characteristics and Motivations of Oocyte Donors in Eleven European Countries," *Human Reproduction* 29, no. 5 (2014): 1083.
10. Lima et al., "Donantes de ovocitos," 605.
11. Charlotte Kroløkke, "Eggs and Euros: A Feminist Perspective on Reproductive Travel from Denmark to Spain," *IJFAB: International Journal of Feminist Approaches to Bioethics* 7, no. 2 (2014): 145.
12. Kroløkke, "Eggs and Euros," 144–145.
13. Pennings et al., "Socio-Demographic," 79–80.
14. Michelle Leve, "Reproductive Bodies and Bits: Exploring Dilemmas of Egg Donation Under Neoliberalism," *Studies in Gender and Sexuality* 14 (2013): 277.
15. Leve, "Reproductive Bodies and Bits," 280, writing about Gina Corea, *The Mother Machine: Reproductive Technologies from Artificial Insemination to Artificial Wombs* (Perennial Library, 1985).
16. Laura Mamo, "Fertility, Inc.: Consumption and Subjectification in U.S. Lesbian Reproductive Practices," in *Biomedicalization: Technoscience, Health, and Illness in the U.S.*, ed. A. E. Clarke et al. (Duke University Press, 2010), 176.
17. Ana María Rivas et al., "El anonimato y el altruismo en la donación de gametos: La producción de biocapital en la industria reproductiva," *Política y sociedad* 56, no. 3 (2019): 638.

18. Also see Bruna Álvarez and Diana Marre, "Motherhood in Spain: From the 'Baby Boom' to 'Structural Infertility,'" *Medical Anthropology* 41, nos. 6–7 (2021): 718–731, https://doi.org/10.1080/01459740.2021.1961246. In this work, the authors define structural infertility, the delay of motherhood in Spain due to, among other things, lack of job stability, lack of housing, lack of policies that support women and children, and the double shift (remunerated versus care work) of women.

19. Leve, "Reproductive Bodies and Bits," 281.

20. Susana Silva and Helena Machado, "Trust, Morality and Altruism in the Donation of Biological Material: The Case of Portugal," *New Genetics and Society* 28, no. 2 (June 2009): 107.

21. Rene Almeling, *Sex Cells* (University of California Press, 2011), 163.

22. Almeling, *Sex Cells*, 162.

23. Creating a child can include a sperm donor, an egg donor, and a surrogate, along with the people who will serve as the parents to the child born. Moreover, on 30 October 2023, the first baby gestated by two mothers was born in Mallorca, Spain, via a new technique called Invocell ("Nace en Mallorca el primer bebé gestado por dos mujeres," *El Mundo*, 3 November 2023, https://www.elmundo.es/baleares/2023/11/02/6543608fe4d4d804558b45a0.html).

24. "Why 50% of European Egg Donation Happens in Spain?," Surrogacy 365, 6 August 2018, https://www.surrogacy365.com/why-50-of-european-egg-donation-happens-in-spain/.

25. Lima et al., "Donantes de ovocitos," 607.

26. Sara Lafuente Funes, *Mercados reproductivos: Crisis, deseo y desigualdad* (Katakrak, 2021), 88.

27. Lafuente Funes, *Mercados reproductivos*, 117.

28. Lima et al., "Donantes de ovocitos," 614.

29. Priscila Rivera, "¿Por qué algunas mujeres donan sus óvulos? Altruismo, sacrificio y trabajo reproductivo," *Afin* 127 (May 2021): 12.

30. Rivas et al., "El anonimato," 637.

31. For more information about the international baby market, please see K. Animashaun Ducre, "Race(ing) to the Baby Market: The Political Economy of Overcoming Infertility," in *The Motherhood Business: Consumption, Communication, and Privilege*, ed. Anne Teresa Demo et al. (University of Alabama Press, 2015).

32. Rivas et al., "El anonimato," 637.

33. Rivas et al., "El anonimato," 637.

34. Villar, *Madre hay más que una*, 64–65.

35. Villar, *Madre hay más que una*, 26, 27.

36. Villar, *Madre hay más que una*, 32.

37. Villar, *Madre hay más que una*, 39.

38. Villar, *Madre hay más que una*, 27.

39. Villar, *Madre hay más que una*, 178.

40. Kroløkke, "Eggs and Euros," 152.

41. Kroløkke, "Eggs and Euros," 152.

42. Law 35/1988, chapter 3, article 10 says, "Será nulo de pleno derecho el contrato por el que se convenga la gestación, con o sin precio, a cargo de una mujer que renuncia a la filiación materna en favor del contratante o de un tercero" [The contract by which the gestation is agreed upon shall be null and void, with or without price, at the expense of a woman who renounces maternal filiation in favor of the contracting party or a third party], which suggests that the woman who gives birth is the legal mother ("Ley 35/1988, de 22 de noviembre, sobre técnicas de reproducción asistida," Agencia Estatal Boletín Oficial del Estado, accessed 16 June 2025, https://www.boe.es/buscar/doc.php?id=BOE-A-1988-27108).

43. Villar, *Madre hay más que una*, 42.

44. Rivera, "¿Por qué algunas mujeres?," 5.

45. Kroløkke, "Eggs and Euros," 155.

46. In her 2017 exhibition *Ficciones de la no-maternidad*, Mexican artist Paola Livas has created a work that deals with her experience donating eggs, saying it caused "una intensiva reflexión en torno a la maternidad, la no-maternidad, la identidad y lo materno" [an intense reflection about motherhood, nonmotherhood, identity, and the maternal] (Paolo Livas, "Ficciones de la no-maternidad," NoAutomático, 8 May 2017, http://noautomatico.blogspot.com/2017/05/ficciones-de-la-no-maternidad-paola.html).

47. Charlotte Kroløkke, "The Golden Egg: The Business of Making Mothers Through Egg Donation," in *The Motherhood Business: Consumption, Communication, and Privilege*, eds. Anne Teresa Demo et al. (University of Alabama Press, 2015), 31.

48. Villar, *Madre hay más que una*, 174.

49. Villar, *Madre hay más que una*, 174.

50. According to Noemí López Trujillo, "España tiene la mayor proporción de población joven de toda la UE que trabaja con contrato temporal (56,4%). Y un 64,2% de los jóvenes que trabaja a tiempo parcial lo hace de manera involuntaria: no hay oportunidad en el mercado laboral de hacerlo a tiempo completo" [Spain has the highest proportion of young population of the whole European Union who works on temporary contracts (56.4 percent). And 64.2 percent of young people who work part time do so involuntarily: There is no opportunity in the labor market to work full time] (*El vientre vacío* [Capitán Swing, 2019], 20).

51. In 2023, some adults born of donated gametes began to challenge the system of anonymous donation, asking for medical records to be shared. The president of the Sociedad Español de Fertilidad (SEF), Juanjo Espinós, argues that donors want to remain anonymous, saying, "Los donantes no tienen ningún interés en formar una familia y quieren preservar su derecho a la intimidad" [The donors do not have any interest in forming a family and want to preserve their right to privacy] (Begoña Gómez Urzaiz, "'No somos el sueño de nadie': Los hijos de la 'in vitro' reclaman el fin de las donaciones anónimas," *La Vanguardia*, 27 March 2023, https://www.lavanguardia.com/vivo/tendencias/20230327/8850981/sueno-personas-derechos.html).

52. Villar, *Madre hay más que una*, 173–174.

53. Villar, *Madre hay más que una*, 41.

54. Quote from Villar, *Madre hay más que una*, 178. Silvia Nanclares, as we saw, also reflects on egg donation and its relationship to her own feminism after writing her novel *Quién quiere ser madre* (Nanclares, "¿Soy una mala feminista si acepto la ovodonación? Claroscuros de una maternidad bajo el capitalismo reproductivo," *El Diario*, 17 July 2019, https://www.eldiario.es/nidos/claroscuros-maternidad-feminista-ovodonacion_1_1433839.html).

55. Villar, *Madre hay más que una*, 179.

56. Rivas et al., "El anonimato," 634.

57. Villar, *Madre hay más que una*, 59.

58. Rivas et al., "El anonimato," 636.

59. Rivas et al., "El anonimato," 636.

60. Rivera, "¿Por qué algunas mujeres?," 4–5.

61. In her article about egg donation in Romania, Michal Nahman explains how Romanian donors are popular due to their low price (donors, according to her article, received $200) and for their European background. See Nahman, "Nodes of Desire: Romanian Egg Sellers, 'Dignity' and Feminist Alliances in Transnational Ova Exchanges," *European Journal of Women's Studies* 15, no. 2 (2008): 65–82.

62. Villar, *Madre hay más que una*, 60.

63. Villar, *Madre hay más que una*, 91.

64. Villar, *Madre hay más que una*, 93.

65. Villar, *Madre hay más que una*, 96.

66. For more information about the health system in Spain and its process regarding assisted reproduction techniques, see Verónica Ramírez and Inma Escobar, "Estos son los

requisitos para acceder a la reproducción asistida en la sanidad pública," *La Sexta*, 2 January 2019, https://www.lasexta.com/noticias/economia/consumo/estos-son-requisitos-acceder-reproduccion-asistida-sanidad-publica_201901235c5410200cf2be7ee4853696.html.

67. Lafuente Funes, *Mercados reproductivos*, 36.

68. Lafuente Funes, *Mercados reproductivos*, 37, 36.

69. Orna Donath, *Regretting Motherhood: A Study* (North Atlantic Books, 2017), xix.

70. Villar, *Madre hay más que una*, 43. This theme of the demythification of motherhood in Spain can be found in books such as Carme Riera, *Tiempo de espera* (Lumen, 1996); and Olga Albarrán Caselles, *(Pro)creación: Escritura y maternidad en la España contemporánea* (Libertarias, 2022).

71. Villar, *Madre hay más que una*, 267.

72. Isabel García-Zarza, *Diario de una madre imperfecta* (Editorial Viceversa, 2010), quote from a booklet that came inside the paperback version of this book.

73. Donath, *Regretting Motherhood*, xvii.

74. Villar, *Madre hay más que una*, 239.

75. Inés Campillo and Sandra Ezquerra, "¿Qué hacer con los cuidados?," *Viento sur* 156 (February 2018): 39, https://dialnet.unirioja.es/ejemplar/479769.

76. Lafuente Funes, *Mercados reproductivos*, 30.

77. Lafuente Funes, *Mercados reproductivos*, 30.

78. Villar, *Madre hay más que una*, 268.

79. Villar, *Madre hay más que una*, 238.

80. Villar, *Madre hay más que una*, 238.

81. Villar, *Madre hay más que una*, 266.

82. Donath, *Regretting Motherhood*, xviii.

83. Villar, *Madre hay más que una*, 270.

84. "Samanta Villar: La maternidad es un horror," *20 minutos*, 11 March 2019, https://www.20minutos.es/noticia/3584931/0/villar-maternidad-es-un-horror/?autoref=true.

85. "Samanta Villar"; Lorena Ferro, "Samanta Villar: 'Mi vida es peor desde que tengo hijos,'" *La Vanguardia*, 11 March 2019, https://www.lavanguardia.com/vida/20190311/46914412106/entrevista-samanta-villar-carga-mental.html.

86. Ferro, "Samanta Villar."

87. Campillo and Ezquerra, "¿Qué hacer?," 43.

88. In 2015, the average age of women giving birth to their first child was 31.9 years, in comparison with the average in the European Union of 28.8 years ("Movimiento natural de la población [nacimientos, defunciones y matrimonios]: Indicadores demográficos básicos año 2015; Datos provisionales," Instituto Nacional de Estadística, 2016, https://www.ine.es/).

89. Javier Martín Arroyo, "Hasta tres años de espera para poder ser madre," *El País*, 13 May 2019, https://elpais.com/sociedad/2019/05/12/actualidad/1557676986_761783.html.

90. Lima et al., "Donantes de ovocitos," 606.

91. While this book does not address the issue of surrogacy in Spain, please see Katharine Aha et al., "Populism and Surrogacy in Spain," *Women's Studies* (2022): 1–21, https://doi.org/10.1080/00497878.2022.2147178, for an in-depth analysis of debates around surrogacy in Spain.

92. Esther Vivas, *Mamá desobediente* (Capitán Swing, 2019), 70.

93. Lafuente Funes, *Mercados reproductivos*, 192.

94. Lafuente Funes, *Mercados reproductivos*, 195.

95. Sandra Ezquerra, "De la economía feminista a la democratización de los cuidados," *Viento sur* 156 (February 2018): 40.

96. Villar, *Madre hay más que una*, 270.

97. Marina Bettaglio, "(Post)Feminist Maternal Chronicles and Their Discontents," *Letras femeninas* 41, no. 1 (2015): 233, https://doi.org/10.2307/44733780.

CHAPTER 4 — INFERTILITY AS CLASSIST

1. Benyam D. Mezmur, "From Angelina (to Madonna) to Zoe's Ark: What Are the 'A–Z' Lessons for Intercountry Adoptions in Africa?," *International Journal of Law, Policy and the Family* 23, no. 2 (2009): 127, https://doi.org/10.1093/lawfam/ebn013.

2. "Lazos de sangre," RTVE, 2022, https://www.rtve.es/television/20220803/rocio-jurado-hijos-rocio-carrasco-gloria-camila-jose-fernando-abortos-depresion/2393445.shtml.

3. "Así descubrió Isa Pantoja que era adoptada: 'Mi madre me dijo que mis padres estaban muertos,'" *20 minutos*, 9 December 2023, https://www.20minutos.es/television/isa-pantoja-como-descubrio-adoptada-madre-dijo-padres-muertos-5197377/.

4. Mezmur, "From Angelina (to Madonna)," 156.

5. Mezmur, "From Angelina (to Madonna)," 148.

6. Adoption as a literary subject, especially from the perspective of the adopted child, is rare. Asha Miró, in her book *La hija del Ganges* (Lumen, 2003), narrates her experience of discovering her roots in India after growing up as an adopted daughter in Barcelona. María Larrea, in *Los de Bilbao nacen donde quieren* (Alianza, 2023), recovers her family history hidden by illegal adoptions during the Franco regime.

7. "Biografía," Laurafreixas.com, accessed 23 November 2019, https://www.laurafreixas.com/freixasbio.htm.

8. Laura Freixas, *El silencio de las madres y otras reflexiones sobre las mujeres en la cultura* (Editorial UOC, 2015), 160.

9. Patricia Burgo Muñoz, "La cultura idealiza la maternidad pero al mismo tiempo no la valora," *El Diario*, 22 May 2015, https://www.eldiario.es/euskadi/euskadi/cultura-idealiza-maternidad-tiempo-valora_1_5863101.html.

10. Celeste López, "No quería ser maruja de lujo . . . pero lo fui," *Mujeres en Red: El periódico feminista*, 2019, https://www.mujeresenred.net/spip.php?article2350.

11. Genevieve Lloyd, "The Self as Fiction: Philosophy and Autobiography," *Philosophy and Literature* 10, no. 2 (1986): 170.

12. Lloyd, "Self as Fiction," 170.

13. Paul De Man, "Autobiography as De-Facement," *Modern Language Notes* 94, no. 5 (1979): 921.

14. De Man, "Autobiography as De-Facement," 922.

15. Jairo Marcos, *Rasgados: Un viaje a la adopción internacional España-China* (Noufront, 2010), 20.

16. Marcos, *Rasgados*, 20.

17. Peter Selman, "Intercountry Adoption of Children from Asia in the Twenty-First Century," *Children's Geographies* 13, no. 3 (2015): 313.

18. Teresa Castro Martín et al., "El desafío de la baja fecundidad en España," in *Informe España 2018*, ed. Agustín Blanco et al. (Universidad Pontificia Comillas, Cátedra J. M. Martín Patino, 2018), 167.

19. Castro Martín et al., "El desafío," 168.

20. Castro Martín et al., "El desafío," 168.

21. Jessaca B. Leinaweaver et al., "Homework and Transnational Adoption Screening in Spain: The Coproduction of Home and Family," *Journal of the Royal Anthropological Institute* 23 (2017): 566.

22. Castro Martín et al., "El desafío," 173.

23. Castro Martín et al., "El desafío," 173–174.

24. "España registra la tasa de natalidad más baja en 40 años," *El Confidencial*, 19 June 2018, https://www.elconfidencial.com/economia/2018-06-19/espana-natalidad-poblacion_1580932/.

25. "Movimiento natural de la población / indicadores demográficos básicos / tablas de mortalidad: Año 2022," Instituto Nacional de Estadística (INE), 2022, https://ine.es/prensa/mnp_2022.pdf.

26. "Home Page," American Society of Reproductive Medicine, accessed 14 June 2016, https://www.asrm.org/?vs=1.

27. Taina Sormunen et al., "Infertility-Related Communication and Coping Strategies Among Women Affected by Primary or Secondary Infertility," *Journal of Clinical Nursing* 27 (2018): 336, https://doi-org.southwesternu.idm.oclc.org/10.1111/jocn.13953.

28. Castro Martín et al., "El desafío," 176–177.

29. Castro Martín et al., "El desafío," 176.

30. Castro Martín et al., "El desafío," 178.

31. Ana Berástegui Pedro-Viejo et al., *Adopción internacional en la Comunidad de Madrid: Una guía para orientar y ayudar a las personas que estén pensando adoptar un niño en el extranjero* (Instituto Madrileño del Menor y la Familia, 2017), 57, http://www.madrid.org/bvirtual/BVCM014016.pdf.

32. Xulio Vásquez, "La adopción de una niña china cuesta 12.000 euros y si es de Rusia vale 30.000," *La voz de Galicia*, 13 May 2008, https://www.lavozdegalicia.es/noticia/vigo/2008/05/13/adopcion-nina-china-cuesta-12000-euros-rusia-vale-30000/0003_6813676.htm.

33. "Estadística del padrón continuo," INE, accessed 11 December 2019, https://www.ine.es/jaxiT3/Datos.htm?t=1380.

34. "Spain Youth Unemployment Rate," YCharts, accessed 22 November 2022, https://ycharts.com/indicators/spain_youth_unemployment_rate_lfs.

35. Beatriz San Román and Karen Rotabi, "Rescue, Red Tape, Child Abduction, Illicit Adoptions, and Discourse: Intercountry Adoption Attitudes in Spain," *International Social Work* 62, no. 1 (2019): 201. Nanclares tells us that couples spend around €7,000 per round of IVF with, as Villar stated earlier, only a 15 percent chance of success. That means adoption can be more affordable, since it guarantees a child at the end, while any ART only offers the chance of taking home a baby.

36. Judith Masson, "Intercountry Adoption: A Global Problem or a Global Solution?," *Journal of International Affairs* 55, no. 1 (2001): 143, http://www.jstor.org/stable/24357675.

37. Masson, "Intercountry Adoption," 143.

38. Masson, "Intercountry Adoption," 143.

39. Masson, "Intercountry Adoption," 144. For the actual text and information about the Hague Adoption Convention, see Hague Conference on Private International Law (HCCH), *Convention of 29 May 1993 on Protection of Children and Co-operation in Respect of Intercountry Adoption* (HCCH, 1993), https://www.hcch.net/en/instruments/conventions/specialised-sections/intercountry-adoption.

40. Jessaca B. Leinaweaver, *Adoptive Migration: Raising Latinos in Spain* (Duke University Press, 2013), 27, https://doi.org/10.1515/9780822377511.

41. Peter Selman, "The Global Decline of Intercountry Adoption: What Lies Ahead?," *Social Policy and Society* 11, no. 3 (2012): 384.

42. Selman, "Global Decline," 383.

43. Leinaweaver, *Adoptive Migration*, 28.

44. Lilia Khabibullina, "International Adoption in Russia: 'Market,' 'Children for Organs,' and 'Precious' or 'Bad' Genes," in *International Adoption: Global Inequalities and the Circulation of Children*, ed. Diane Marre and Laura Briggs (NYU Press, 2009), 197, https://doi.org/10.18574/nyu/9780814791011.003.0010.

45. Peter Selman, "Intercountry Adoption in the New Millennium: The 'Quiet Migration' Revisited," *Population Research and Policy Review* 21, no. 3 (2002): 222, https://www.jstor.org/stable/40230785.

46. Khabibullina, "International Adoption in Russia," 174; Karen Smith Rotabi and Nicole F. Bromfield, *From Intercountry Adoption to Global Surrogacy: A Human Rights History and New Fertility Frontiers* (Routledge, Taylor & Francis Group, 2017), 45.

47. Karen Dubinsky, *Babies Without Borders: Adoption and the Symbolic Child in a Globalizing World* (University of Toronto Press, 2010).

48. Dubinsky, *Babies Without Borders*, 3.

49. Dubinsky, *Babies Without Borders*, 20.

50. Patricia Sawin, "Listening to Stories, Negotiating Responsibility: Exploring the Ethics of International Adoption Through Narrative Analysis," in *Unsettling Assumptions: Tradition, Gender, Drag*, ed. Pauline Greenhill (Utah State University Press, 2014), 178.

51. Sawin, "Listening to Stories," 172.

52. Sawin, "Listening to Stories," 173–174.

53. Sawin, "Listening to Stories," 174.

54. Sung Hee Yook and Hosu Kim, "Decolonizing Adoption Narratives for Transnational Reproductive Justice," *CLCWeb: Comparative Literature and Culture* 20, no. 6 (2018): 2, http://docs.lib.purdue.edu/clcweb/vol20/iss6/8.

55. Kristen Cheney and Stephen Ucembe, "The Orphan Industrial Complex: The Charitable Commodification of Children and Its Consequences for Child Protection," in *Disadvantaged Childhoods and Humanitarian Intervention: Processes of Affective Commodification and Objectification*, ed. Kristen Cheney and Aviva Sinervo (Palgrave Studies on Children and Development, Springer International, 2019), 29, https://doi.org/10.1007/978-3-030-01623-4.

56. Cheney and Ucembe, "Orphan Industrial Complex," 47.

57. Cheney and Ucembe, "Orphan Industrial Complex," 40.

58. Kathryn E. Van Doore, "Paper Orphans: Exploring Child Trafficking for the Purpose of Orphanages," *International Journal of Children's Rights* 24, no. 2 (2016): 397, https://doi.org/10.1163/15718182-02402006.

59. Diana Marre, "Los silencios de la adopción en España," *Revista de Antropología Social* 18 (2009): 116.

60. Marre, "Los silencios," 116.

61. Laura Freixas, *A mí no me iba a pasar* (Penguin Random House, 2019), 108.

62. Freixas, *A mí no me iba a pasar*, 109.

63. Freixas, *A mí no me iba a pasar*, 112.

64. Freixas, *A mí no me iba a pasar*, 113.

65. Freixas, *A mí no me iba a pasar*, 114.

66. Sandra Ezquerra, "De la economía feminista a la democratización de los cuidados," *Viento sur* 156 (2018): 41.

67. Ezquerra, "De la economía feminista," 42.

68. Ezquerra, "De la economía feminista," 42.

69. The Real Decreto-ley 5/2023 [Royal Decree-Law 5/2023] expanded many rights for families in Spain. An upcoming change, what will be the 2024 Ley de familias [Law of Families], works to recognize, support, and protect the different types of families that exist in Spain, expanding the existing sixteen weeks of leave to twenty for both parents ("Así quedan los permisos con la nueva Ley de familias," *El Mundo*, 28 February 2024, https://www.elmundo.es/como/2024/02/28/65def71fe9cf4a721c8b4574.html).

70. Freixas, *A mí no me iba a pasar*, 179.

71. Freixas, *A mí no me iba a pasar*, 191.

72. Freixas, *A mí no me iba a pasar*, 192, 199.

73. Freixas, *A mí no me iba a pasar*, 200.

74. Silvia Tubert, "La maternidad en el discurso de las nuevas tecnologías reproductivas," in *Las mujeres y los niños primero: Discursos de la maternidad*, ed. Ángeles de la Concha and Michelle Osbourne (Icaria, 2004), 127.

75. Berástegui Pedro-Viejo et al., *Adopción internacional*, 18.

76. Berástegui Pedro-Viejo et al., *Adopción internacional*, 20.

77. Berástegui Pedro-Viejo et al., *Adopción internacional*, 20.

78. Berástegui Pedro-Viejo et al., *Adopción internacional*, 21.

79. Freixas, *A mí no me iba a pasar*, 212–213.

80. Freixas, *A mí no me iba a pasar*, 207.

81. Freixas, *A mí no me iba a pasar*, 207.
82. Freixas, *A mí no me iba a pasar*, 208.
83. Berástegui Pedro-Viejo et al., *Adopción internacional*, 20.
84. Freixas, *A mí no me iba a pasar*, 231.
85. Freixas, *A mí no me iba a pasar*, 232.
86. Freixas, *A mí no me iba a pasar*, 232.
87. Freixas, *A mí no me iba a pasar*, 232.
88. Freixas, *A mí no me iba a pasar*, 233.
89. Freixas, *A mí no me iba a pasar*, 235.
90. See Khabibullina, "International Adoption in Russia," which addresses multiple instances of U.S. families later refusing to accept (and trying to return) their Russian adopted child.
91. Freixas, *A mí no me iba a pasar*, 244–245.
92. Sawin, "Listening to Stories," 173.
93. Freixas, *A mí no me iba a pasar*, 238.
94. Freixas, *A mí no me iba a pasar*, 238–239.
95. Freixas, *A mí no me iba a pasar*, 239.
96. Freixas, *A mí no me iba a pasar*, 234.
97. Freixas, *A mí no me iba a pasar*, 248.
98. Freixas, *A mí no me iba a pasar*, 248–249.
99. Freixas, *A mí no me iba a pasar*, 256.
100. Freixas, *A mí no me iba a pasar*, 256.
101. Marta Bertran, "Being a Mother and Father in International Adoption in Spain: Towards the Child's Wellbeing," *Childhood* 20, no. 4 (2012): 511.
102. Bertran, "Being a Mother," 515.
103. Freixas, *A mí no me iba a pasar*, 258.
104. Cheney and Ucembe, "Orphan Industrial Complex," 29.
105. Sawin, "Listening to Stories," 172.
106. Sawin, "Listening to Stories," 177.
107. Freixas, *A mí no me iba a pasar*, 242.
108. Freixas, *A mí no me iba a pasar*, 242.
109. Sawin, "Listening to Stories," 181.
110. Sawin, "Listening to Stories," 187.
111. Laura Freixas, "Cuando recuerdo a aquel bebé . . . ," Instagram, 13 June 2022, https://www.instagram.com/p/CevA4IEjueR/?igshid=MDJmNzVkMjY=.
112. Freixas, *A mí no me iba a pasar*, 331–332.
113. Raquel Sánchez Silva, *Tengo los óvulos contados* (Planeta, 2017), 127.

CHAPTER 5 — INFERTILITY AS CHOICE

1. Bruna Álvarez and Diana Marre, "Motherhood in Spain: From the 'Baby Boom' to 'Structural Infertility,'" *Medical Anthropology* 41, nos. 6–7 (2021): 719, https://doi.org/10.1080/01459740.2021.1961246.
2. Álvarez and Marre, "Motherhood in Spain," 2.
3. David Harvey, *A Brief History of Neoliberalism* (Oxford University Press, 2007), 29.
4. Bruna Álvarez, "Reproductive Decision Making in Spain: Heterosexual Couples' Narratives About How They Chose to Have Children," *Journal of Family Issues* 39, no. 13 (2018): 3489.
5. Ana de Miguel, *Neoliberalismo sexual: El mito de la libre elección* (Cátedra, 2015), 339.
6. De Miguel, *Neoliberalismo sexual*, 320, 339.
7. Tejaswini Ganti, "Neoliberalism," *Annual Review of Anthropology* 43 (2014): 92.

8. Karen Weingarten, "Impossible Decisions: Abortion, Reproductive Technologies, and the Rhetoric of Choice," *Women's Studies* 41 (2012): 265.

9. Loretta Ross and Rickie Solinger, *Reproductive Justice: An Introduction* (University of California Press, 2017), 102.

10. De Miguel, *Neoliberalismo sexual*, 31.

11. María Reyes Ferrer, "Spain and Structural Infertility: Towards an Integrative Vision of Motherhood in the Novel *Quién quiere ser madre* by Silvia Nanclares," in *The Palgrave Handbook of Reproductive Justice and Literature*, ed. B. W. Capo and L. Lazzari (Palgrave, 2022), 382.

12. Helena Michie and Naomi R. Cahn, *Confinements: Fertility and Infertility in Contemporary Culture* (Rutgers University Press, 1997), 149–150.

13. Michie and Cahn, *Confinements*, 145.

14. Álvarez, "Reproductive Decision Making," 3492.

15. De Miguel, *Neoliberalismo sexual*, 339.

16. Michie and Cahn, *Confinements*, 72.

17. Carlota E. Ramírez, "Diana López Varela: 'Se creen que violar no es para tanto mientras no la maten,'" *Huffington Post*, 15 October 2016, https://www.huffingtonpost.es/2016/10/06/entrevista-a-diana_n_12376178.html.

18. Diana López Varela, "Sobre mí," accessed 4 May 2020, https://dianalopezvarela.com/bio (page no longer extant).

19. López Varela, "Sobre mí."

20. Diana López Varela, *Maternofobia: Retrato de una generación enfrentada a la maternidad* (Ediciones Península, 2019), 15.

21. López Varela, *Maternofobia*, 227.

22. Lorena Ferro, "Un aborto es la decisión más meditada que toma una mujer," *La Vanguardia*, 11 June 2019, https://www.lavanguardia.com/vida/20190611/462774349246/maternofobia-aborto-diana-lopez-varela.html.

23. López Varela, *Maternofobia*, 82.

24. López Varela, *Maternofobia*, 83.

25. For a brief moment during the Second Republic, in 1937, Catalonia legalized abortion under the then minister of health Federica Montseny. With the fall of the Second Republic, that right was removed, and abortion again became illegal. See Laura Granda Berridi and María Pilar García Álvarez, *El aborto, entre la legalidad y la bioética* (RCA Grupo Editor, 2018), 13.

26. Granda Berridi and García Álvarez, *El aborto*, 13.

27. Granda Berridi and García Álvarez, *El aborto*, 23.

28. Granda Berridi and García Álvarez, *El aborto*, 31.

29. Granda Berridi and García Álvarez, *El aborto*, 31.

30. Quoted in Granda Berridi and García Álvarez, *El aborto*, 31.

31. López Varela, *Maternofobia*, 124. In February 2024, the Spanish government passed a new Ley de familias [Law of Families] that allows for twenty weeks of leave for both parents, with the hope that this will address the inequity between men and women as caretakers ("El gobierno aprueba la Ley de familias," *Ondacero*, 27 February 2024, https://www.ondacero.es/noticias/sociedad/ley-familias-vuelve-consejo-ministros_2024022765dd9d264129260001dbaf1d.html).

32. López Varela, *Maternofobia*, 124. These quotes within the quote come from de Miguel, *Neoliberalismo sexual*, cited by López Varela.

33. Federico Pérez Millán, "La reproducción asistida en el medio sanitario público," in *Libro blanco sociosanitario: La infertilidad en España; Situación actual y perspectivas*, ed. Roberto Matorras Weinig (Imago Concept & Image Development, 2011), 155.

34. Silvia Tubert, "La maternidad en el discurso de las nuevas tecnologías reproductivas," in *Las mujeres y los niños primero: Discursos de la maternidad*, ed. Ángeles de la Concha and Raquel Osborne (Icaria, 2004), 118.

35. Donna J. Haraway, "A Cyborg Manifesto," in *Manifestly Haraway* (University of Minnesota Press, 2016), 65; Rosi Braidotti, *Nomadic Subjects: Embodiment and Sexual Difference in Contemporary Feminist Theory*, Gender and Culture (Columbia University Press, 1994), 227.
36. Alys Einion and Jen Rinaldi, *Bearing the Weight of the World: Exploring Maternal Embodiment* (Demeter Press, 2018), 11.
37. López Varela, *Maternofobia*, 39.
38. López Varela, *Maternofobia*, 39.
39. López Varela, *Maternofobia*, 43.
40. Joan Williams, "Gender Wars: Selfless Women in the Republic of Choice," *New York University Law Review* 66 (1991): 1564.
41. López Varela, *Maternofobia*, 17.
42. Lina Meruane, *Contra los hijos* (Penguin, 2014), 22.
43. López Varela, *Maternofobia*, 229.
44. López Varela, *Maternofobia*, 123–124.
45. López Varela, *Maternofobia*, 139.
46. Haraway, "Cyborg Manifesto," 24.
47. Haraway, "Cyborg Manifesto," 33.
48. Susan Bordo, *Unbearable Weight: Feminism, Western Culture, and the Body*, 10th anniversary ed. (University of California Press, 2003), 79.
49. Julia Hanigsberg, "Homologizing Pregnancy and Motherhood: A Consideration of Abortion," *Michigan Law Review* 94, no. 2 (1995): 373.
50. López Varela, *Maternofobia*, 45.
51. López Varela, *Maternofobia*, 77–78.
52. López Varela, *Maternofobia*, 53.
53. López Varela, *Maternofobia*, 54.
54. López Varela, *Maternofobia*, 54.
55. López Varela, *Maternofobia*, 51.
56. López Varela, *Maternofobia*, 51.
57. López Varela, *Maternofobia*, 43.
58. López Varela, *Maternofobia*, 75.
59. López Varela, *Maternofobia*, 223.
60. López Varela, *Maternofobia*, 75.
61. López Varela, *Maternofobia*, 223.
62. Simon J. Williams and Gillian Bendelow, *The Lived Body: Sociological Themes, Embodied Issues* (Routledge, 1998), 1.
63. Williams and Bendelow, *Lived Body*, 115.
64. Laura Hurd Clarke et al., "The Continuity and Discontinuity of the Embodied Self in Infertility," *Canadian Review of Sociology / Revue Canadienne de Sociologie* 43, no. 1 (2006): 107.
65. Susan Faludi's feminist classic *Backlash: The Undeclared War Against American Women*, 1st ed. (Crown, 1991) addresses the concept of backlash against women as they gain more visibility and power in U.S. society.
66. Meruane, *Contra los hijos*, 20.
67. Braidotti, *Nomadic Subjects*, 187.
68. López Varela, *Maternofobia*, 229, quoting Oriana Fallaci, *Carta a un niño que nunca nació*, trans. Atilio Pentimalli (Backlist, 2012).
69. Laura Freixas, *El silencio de las madres y otras reflexiones sobre las mujeres en la cultura* (Editorial UOC, 2015), 159.

CONCLUSION

1. Teresa Castro Martín et al., "El desafío de la baja fecundidad en España," in *Informe España 2018*, ed. Agustín Blanco et al. (Universidad Pontificia Comillas, Cátedra J. M. Martín Patino, 2018), 180, 166.

2. Belén García Abia, "Carta a una futura no madre," *El Diario*, 2018.

3. García Abia, "Carta."

4. García Abia, "Carta."

5. Beatriz San Román, "Waiting Too Long to Mother: Involuntary Childlessness and Assisted Reproduction in Contemporary Spain," in *Waithood: Gender, Education, and Global Delays in Marriage and Childbearing*, ed. Marcia Inhorn and Nancy J. Smith-Hefner (Berghahn, 2021), 340, https://doi.org/10.1515/9781789209006-017.

6. Diana Oliver, *Maternidades precarias* (Arpa, 2022), 188.

7. Elissa Foster, "Desiring Dialectical Discourse: A Feminist Ponders the Transition to Motherhood," *Women's Studies in Communication* 28, no. 1 (2005): 60.

8. Cited in San Román, "Waiting Too Long," 339.

9. Federico Pérez Millán, "La reproducción asistida en el medio sanitario público," in *Libro blanco sociosanitario: La infertilidad en España; Situación actual y perspectivas*, ed. Roberto Matorras Weinig (Imago Concept & Image Development, 2011), 147.

10. "Samanta Villar: La maternidad es un horror," *20 minutos*, 11 March 2019, https://www.20minutos.es/noticia/3584931/0/villar-maternidad-es-un-horror/?autoref=true; Lorena Ferro, "Samanta Villar: 'Mi vida es peor desde que tengo hijos,'" *La Vanguardia*, 11 March 2019, https://www.lavanguardia.com/vida/20190311/46914412106/entrevista-samanta-villar-carga-mental.html.

11. Laura Freixas, *A mí no me iba a pasar* (Penguin Random House, 2019), 154.

12. Mireia Salazar, "Silvia Nanclares: 'El deseo de ser madre es algo cambiante,'" Ayuntamiento de Rivas Vaciamadrid, 17 June 2020, https://www.rivasciudad.es/noticias/feminismos-mujeres-lgtbi/2020/06/17/silvia-nanclares-el-deseo-de-ser-madre-es-algo-cambiante/862600139653/.

13. In Shanna Swan and Stacey Colino, *Count Down: How Our Modern World Is Threatening Sperm Counts, Altering Male and Female Reproductive Development, and Imperiling the Future of the Human Race* (Scribner, 2020), the authors explain that the World Health Organization has changed the reference value for "normal" sperm count from 40 million/mL in 1970 to 20 million/mL in 1980 to 15 million/mL in 2010 (26).

14. María Fernández and Elena Sevillano, "El coste de ser madre a los 40 alumbra una millonaria industria de reproducción asistida," *El País*, 21 July 2019.

15. Fernández and Sevillano, "El coste."

16. María Fernández and Elena Sevillano, "'Tu bebé o te devolvemos el dinero' y otros controvertidos anuncios de las clínicas de reproducción," *El País*, 20 July 2019.

17. Shellee Colen, "Like a Mother to Them: Stratified Reproduction and West Indian Childcare Workers and Employers in New York," in *Conceiving the New World Order: The Global Politics of Reproduction*, ed. F. D. Ginsburg and R. Rapp (University of California Press, 1995), 78.

18. Faye Ginsburg and Rayna Rapp, eds., *Conceiving the New World Order: The Global Politics of Reproduction* (University of California Press, 1995), 3.

19. Rosalind Petchesky, *Abortion and Woman's Choice: The State, Sexuality and Reproductive Freedom* (Northeastern University Press, 1990), 11.

20. Ana de Miguel, *Neoliberalismo sexual: El mito de la libre elección* (Cátedra, 2015), 31.

21. Janice G. Raymond, *Women as Wombs: Reproductive Technologies and the Battle over Women's Freedom* (Harper, 1993), xix.

22. Raymond, *Women as Wombs*, viii.

23. Patricia Hill Collins, "Shifting the Center: Race, Class, and Feminist Theorizing About Motherhood," in *Mothering: Ideology, Experience, and Agency*, ed. Evelyn Nakano Glenn et al. (Routledge, 1994), 62.

24. Hill Collins, "Shifting the Center," 62.

25. Samanta Villar does not state the nationality of the woman who helps her care for her children, but statistically speaking, the majority of women who do childcare work in Spain are immigrants (Magdalena Díaz Gorfinkiel, "El mercado de trabajo de los cuidados y la creación de las cadenas globales de cuidado: ¿Cómo concilian las cuidadoras?," *Cuaderno de relaciones laborales* 26, no. 2 [2009]: 75).

26. Samanta Villar, *Madre hay más que una: Un relato en primera persona sobre la aventura de la maternidad* (Planeta, 2018), 192.

27. Freixas, *A mí no me iba a pasar*, 155.

28. Oliver, *Maternidades precarias*, 33.

29. Oliver, *Maternidades precarias*, 33.

30. Oliver, *Maternidades precarias*, 35.

31. Oliver, *Maternidades precarias*, 38.

32. Anna Louie Sussman, "The End of Babies," *New York Times*, 16 November 2019.

33. Sussman, "End of Babies."

34. Sussman, "End of Babies."

35. Trent MacNamara, "Liberal Societies Have Dangerously Low Birth Rates," *The Atlantic*, March 2019.

36. MacNamara, "Liberal Societies."

37. According to PETRA Maternidades Feministas, Spain needs to work to support mothers. They demand twelve months, not sixteen weeks, of maternity leave, with the option of transferring leave between parents, along with access to maternity leave for all workers, not just those who work full time on a permanent contract ("Petra maternidades feministas," accessed 28 May 2025, https://petramaternidadesfeministas.org/).

38. Castro Martín et al., "El desafío," 210.

39. Castro Martín et al., "El desafío," 210.

40. Castro Martín et al., "El desafío," 210.

Bibliography

20 minutos. "Así descubrió Isa Pantoja que era adoptada: 'Mi madre me dijo que mis padres estaban muertos.'" 9 December 2023. https://www.20minutos.es/television/isa-pantoja-como-descubrio-adoptada-madre-dijo-padres-muertos-5197377/.

20 minutos. "Quién es Samanta Villar." 21 April 2021. https://www.20minutos.es/noticia/4667901/0/quien-es-samanta-villar.

20 minutos. "Samanta Villar: La maternidad es un horror." 11 March 2019. https://www.20minutos.es/noticia/3584931/0/villar-maternidad-es-un-horror/?autoref=true.

Abundancia, Rita. "¿Es tener hijos la gran transgresión de la mujer trabajadora en España?" *El País*, 30 October 2017.

Agencia Estatal Boletín Oficial del Estado. "La ley española sobre técnicas de reproducción asistida (Ley 35/1988)." *BOE*, no. 282 (24 November 1988): 33373–33378. https://www.boe.es/eli/es/l/1988/11/22/35.

Agencia Estatal Boletín Oficial del Estado. "La ley española sobre las técnicas de reproducción humana asistida (Ley 14/2006)." *BOE*, no. 126 (27 May 2006). https://www.boe.es/eli/es/l/2006/05/26/14/con.

Agencia Estatal Boletín Oficial del Estado. "Ley de bases creando el régimen obligatorio de subsidios familiares." *BOE*, no. 19 (19 July 1938): 272–275. https://www.boe.es/buscar/doc.php?id=BOE-A-1938-8202.

Agencia Estatal Boletín Oficial del Estado. "Ley 16/1976, de 8 de abril, de relaciones laborales." *BOE*, no. 96 (21 April 1976): 7894–7902. https://www.boe.es/buscar/doc.php?id=BOE-A-1976-8373.

Agencia Estatal Boletín Oficial del Estado. "Ley 35/1988, de 22 de noviembre, sobre técnicas de reproducción asistida," Accessed 16 June 2025. https://www.boe.es/buscar/doc.php?id=BOE-A-1988-27108.

Agencia Estatal Boletín Oficial del Estado. "Ley 56/1961, de 22 de julio, sobre derechos políticos profesionales y de trabajo de la mujer." *BOE*, no. 175 (24 July 1961): 11004–11005. https://www.boe.es/buscar/doc.php?id=BOE-A-1961-14132.

Aguinaga Roustan, Josune. "Mujer y fecundidad." In *La mujer en la España actual ¿Evolución o involución?*, edited by Jacqueline Cruz and Barbara Zecchi, 117–132. Icaria, 2004.

Aha, Katharine, Catherine Heibel, and Catherine Bourland Ross. "Populism and Surrogacy in Spain." *Women's Studies* 52, no. 1 (2022): 1–21. https://doi.org/10.1080/00497878.2022.2147178.

Albarrán Caselles, Olga. *(Pro)creación: Escritura y maternidad en la España contemporánea*. Libertarias, 2022.

Alborch, Carmen. *Solas*. Planeta, 1999.

Almeling, Rene. *Sex Cells*. University of California Press, 2011.

Álvarez, Bruna. "Reproductive Decision Making in Spain: Heterosexual Couples' Narratives About How They Chose to Have Children." *Journal of Family Issues* 39, no. 13 (2018): 3487–3507.

Álvarez, Bruna, and Diana Marre. "Motherhood in Spain: From the 'Baby Boom' to 'Structural Infertility.'" *Medical Anthropology* 41, nos. 6–7 (2021): 718–731. https://doi.org/10.1080/01459740.2021.1961246.

American Society of Reproductive Medicine. "Home Page." Accessed 14 June 2016. https://www.asrm.org/?vs=1.

Ansede, Manuel. "El tobogán de la natalidad en España." *El País*, 10 January 2015. https://www.elpais.com.

Avni, George. "Israeli Supreme Court Rules Country Must Allow Two Mothers on Child's Birth Certificate." *Washington Blade*, 22 March 2024.

Baizan, Pau. "The Policy Context of Fertility in Spain: Toward a Gender-Egalitarian Model?" In *Low Fertility, Institutions, and Their Policies: Variations Across Industrialized Countries*, edited by Ronald R. Rindfuss and Minja Kim, 195–219. Springer Nature, 2016.

Bedoya, Juan. "El 30% de las madres españolas tienen su primer hijo a partir de los 35 años." *El País*, 4 December 2018. https://elpais.com/sociedad/2018/12/04/actualidad/1543935531_127370.html.

Berástegui Pedro-Viejo, Ana, Blanca Gómez Bengoechea, and Salomé Adroher Biosca. *Adopción internacional en la Comunidad de Madrid: Una guía para orientar y ayudar a las personas que estén pensando adoptar un niño en el extranjero*. Instituto Madrileño del Menor y la Familia, 2017. http://www.madrid.org/bvirtual/BVCM014016.pdf.

Bertran, Marta. "Being a Mother and Father in International Adoption in Spain: Towards the Child's Wellbeing." *Childhood* 20, no. 4 (2012): 507–520.

Bettaglio, Marina. "(Post)Feminist Maternal Chronicles and Their Discontents." *Letras femeninas* 41, no. 1 (2015): 228–245. https://doi.org/10.2307/44733780.

Bianci, Martín. "Raquel Sánchez Silva: 'No me siento menos mujer por haber necesitado la ciencia para ser madre.'" *ABC Estilo*, 18 December 2015. https://www.abc.es/estilo/gente/abci-raquel-sanchez-silva-no-siento-menos-mujer-haber-necesitado-ciencia-para-madre-201512182209_noticia.html.

Boggs, Belle. *The Art of Waiting: On Fertility, Medicine, and Motherhood*. Graywolf Press, 2016.

Bordo, Susan. *Unbearable Weight: Feminism, Western Culture, and the Body*. 10th anniversary ed. University of California Press, 2003.

Bos, Arjan E. R., John B. Pryor, Glenn D. Reeder, and Sarah E. Stutterheim. "Stigma: Advances in Theory and Research." *Basic and Applied Social Psychology* 35, no. 1 (2013): 1–9.

Braidotti, Rosi. *Nomadic Subjects: Embodiment and Sexual Difference in Contemporary Feminist Theory*. Gender and Culture. Columbia University Press, 1994.

Bregolat, Eugenio. "Spain's Transition to Democracy." *SAIS Review* 19, no. 2 (1999): 149–155. https://doi.org/10.1353/sais.1999.0029.

Burgo Muñoz, Patricia. "La cultura idealiza la maternidad pero al mismo tiempo no la valora." *El Diario*, 22 May 2015. https://www.eldiario.es/euskadi/euskadi/cultura-idealiza-maternidad-tiempo-valora_1_5863101.html.

Cain Miller, Claire. "The World 'Has Found a Way to Do This': The U.S. Lags on Paid Leave." *New York Times*, 25 October 2021.

Campillo, Inés, and Sandra Ezquerra. "¿Qué hacer con los cuidados?" *Viento sur* 156 (February 2018): 35–38. https://dialnet.unirioja.es/ejemplar/479769.

Camps, Victoria. *El tiempo de cuidados: Otra forma de estar en el mundo*. Arpa, 2021.

Castro Martín, Teresa, Teresa Martín García, Julia Cordero, and Marta Seiz. "El desafío de la baja fecundidad en España." In *Informe España 2018*, edited by Agustín Blanco, Antonio

Chueca, José Antonio López-Ruiz, and Sebastián Mora, 165–232. Universidad Pontificia Comillas, Cátedra J. M. Martín Patino, 2018.

Cheney, Kristen, and Stephen Ucembe. "The Orphan Industrial Complex: The Charitable Commodification of Children and Its Consequences for Child Protection." In *Disadvantaged Childhoods and Humanitarian Intervention: Processes of Affective Commodification and Objectification*, Palgrave Studies on Children and Development, edited by Kristen Cheney and Aviva Sinervo. Springer International, 2019. https://doi.org/10.1007/978-3-030-01623-4.

Colen, Shellee. "Like a Mother to Them: Stratified Reproduction and West Indian Childcare Workers and Employers in New York." In *Conceiving the New World Order: The Global Politics of Reproduction*, edited by F. D. Ginsburg and R. Rapp, 78–102. University of California Press, 1995.

Comisión 8M. "Comisión 8M." Accessed 14 January 2025. https://hacialahuelgafeminista.org/comision/.

Comisión Episcopal de Ortodoxia y Moralidad. *Normas de decencia cristiana*. Secretariado del Episcopado Español, 1959.

Conrad, Peter. *The Medicalization of Society: On the Transformation of Human Conditions into Treatable Disorders*. Johns Hopkins University Press, 2007.

Corea, Gena. *The Mother Machine: Reproductive Technologies from Artificial Insemination to Artificial Wombs*. Perennial Library, 1985.

Del Olmo, Carolina. *¿Dónde está mi tribu? Maternidad y crianza en una sociedad individualista*. Clave Intelectual, 2013.

De Man, Paul. "Autobiography as De-Facement." *Modern Language Notes* 94, no. 5 (1979): 919–930.

de Miguel, Ana. *Neoliberalismo sexual: El mito de la libre elección*. Cátedra, 2015.

Department of Social Security, Malta. "Maternity Benefit." Accessed 16 June 2025. http://www.socialsecurity.gov.mt.

Díaz Gorfinkiel, Magdalena. "El mercado de trabajo de los cuidados y la creación de las cadenas globales de cuidado: ¿Cómo concilian las cuidadoras?" *Cuaderno de relaciones laborales* 26, no. 2 (2009): 71–89.

Donath, Orna. *Regretting Motherhood: A Study*. North Atlantic Books, 2017.

Dubinsky, Karen. *Babies Without Borders: Adoption and the Symbolic Child in a Globalizing World*. University of Toronto Press, 2010.

Ducre, K. Animashaun. "Race(ing) to the Baby Market: The Political Economy of Overcoming Infertility." In *The Motherhood Business: Consumption, Communication, and Privilege*, edited by Anne Teresa Demo, Jennifer L. Borda, and Charlotte Kroløkke, 52–75. University of Alabama Press, 2015.

EFE. "Premios nacionales de natalidad." Accessed 14 January 2025. https://efs.efeservicios.com/en/foto/premios-nacionales-natalidad/8000716726.

Einion, Alys, and Jen Rinaldi. *Bearing the Weight of the World: Exploring Maternal Embodiment*. Demeter Press, 2018.

El Confidencial. "España registra la tasa de natalidad más baja en 40 años." 19 June 2018. https://www.elconfidencial.com/economia/2018-06-19/espana-natalidad-poblacion_1580932/.

El Mundo. "Así quedan los permisos con la nueva Ley de familias." 28 February 2024. https://www.elmundo.es/como/2024/02/28/65def71fe9cf4a721c8b4574.html.

El Mundo. "Nace en Mallorca el primer bebé gestado por dos mujeres." 3 November 2023. https://www.elmundo.es/baleares/2023/11/02/6543608fe4d4d804558b45a0.html.

Esteban, Patricia. "El laberinto legal que sufren las parejas homosexuales para inscribir a sus hijos." *El País*, 8 April 2019.

EUR-Lex. "Charter of Fundamental Rights of the European Union." *Official Journal of the European Union* C 326 (26 October 2012): 391–407. http://data.europa.eu/eli/treaty/char_2012/oj.

European Institute for Gender Equality. "Gender Equality Index." Accessed 16 December 2024. https://eige.europa.eu/gender-equality-index/game/ES/W.

European Society of Human Reproduction and Embryology. "Assisted Reproductive Technology in Europe, 2012: Results Generated from European Registers by ESHRE." *Human Reproduction* 31, no. 8 (2016): 1638–1652. https://doi.org/10.1093/humrep/dew151.

European Union. "Charter of Fundamental Rights of the European Union." *Official Journal of the European Union* C 326/391 (26 October 2012). https://www.europarl.europa.eu/charter/pdf/text_en.pdf.

Ezquerra, Sandra. "De la economía feminista a la democratización de los cuidados." *Viento sur* 156 (2018): 39–47.

Fallaci, Oriana. *Carta a un niño que nunca nació*. Translated by Atilio Pentimalli. Backlist, 2012.

Faludi, Susan. *Backlash: The Undeclared War Against American Women*. 1st ed. Crown, 1991.

Federici, Silvia. *Caliban and the Witch*. Autonomedia, 2004.

Federici, Silvia. "El cuerpo de la mujer es la última frontera del capitalismo." Feministas.org, 19 May 2014. https://www.feministas.org/silvia-federici-el-cuerpo-de-la.html.

Fernández, María, and Elena Sevillano. "El coste de ser madre a los 40 alumbra una millonaria industria de reproducción asistida." *El País*, 21 July 2019.

Fernández, María, and Elena Sevillano. "'Tu bebé o te devolvemos el dinero' y otros controvertidos anuncios de las clínicas de reproducción." *El País*, 20 July 2019.

Ferro, Lorena. "Samanta Villar: 'Mi vida es peor desde que tengo hijos.'" *La Vanguardia*, 11 March 2019. https://www.lavanguardia.com/vida/20190311/46914412106/entrevista-samanta-villar-carga-mental.html.

Ferro, Lorena. "Un aborto es la decisión más meditada que toma una mujer." *La Vanguardia*, 11 June 2019. https://www.lavanguardia.com/vida/20190611/462774349246/maternofobia-aborto-diana-lopez-varela.html.

Folguera, Pilar. "El franquismo: El retorno a las esfera privada (1939–1975)." In *Historia de las mujeres en España*, edited by Elisa Garrido González, 527–548. Síntesis, 1997.

Folguera, Pilar. "Relaciones privadas y cambio social: 1940–1970." In *Otras visiones de España*, edited by Pilar Folguera, 187–211. Editorial Pablo Iglesias, 1993.

Foster, Elissa. "Desiring Dialectical Discourse: A Feminist Ponders the Transition to Motherhood." *Women's Studies in Communication* 28, no. 1 (2005): 57–83.

Freixas, Laura. *A mí no me iba a pasar*. Penguin Random House, 2019.

Freixas, Laura. "Cuando recuerdo a aquel bebé . . ." Instagram, 13 June 2022. https://www.instagram.com/p/CevA4IEjueR/?igshid=MDJmNzVkMjY=.

Freixas, Laura. *El silencio de las madres y otras reflexiones sobre las mujeres en la cultura*. Editorial UOC, 2015.

Ganti, Tejaswini. "Neoliberalism." *Annual Review of Anthropology* 43 (2014): 89–104.

Garcés, Marina. "Comprensión y reparación: Por una filosofía del cuidado y el daño." *Folia Humanística* 12 (2019): 1–19. https://doi.org/10.30860/0052.

García Abia, Belén. "Carta a una futura no madre." *El Diario*, 2018.

García Abia, Belén. *El cielo oblicuo*. Errata Naturae, 2015.

García Muñoz, Óscar, adapt. "Ley General de derechos de las personas con discapacidad y de su inclusión social (en lectura fácil)." Ministerio de Sanidad, Servicios Sociales e Igualdad, December 2015. https://www.plenainclusion.org/sites/default/files/ley_general_de_derechos.pdf.

García-Zarza, Isabel. *Diario de una madre imperfecta*. Editorial Viceversa, 2010.

Gil Pecharromán, Julio. *Historia de la Segunda República española (1931–1936)*. Biblioteca Nueva, 2014.

Ginsburg, Faye, and Rayna Rapp, eds. *Conceiving the New World Order: The Global Politics of Reproduction*. University of California Press, 1995.

Goffman, Erving. *Stigma: Notes of the Management of Spoiled Identity*. Prentice Hall, 1963.

Gómez Urzaiz, Begoña. "'No somos el sueño de nadie': Los hijos de la 'in vitro' reclaman el fin de las donaciones anónimas." *La Vanguardia*, 27 March 2023. https://www.lavanguardia.com/vivo/tendencias/20230327/8850981/sueno-personas-derechos.html.

Granda Berridi, Laura, and María Pilar García Álvarez. *El aborto, entre la legalidad y la bioética*. RCA Grupo Editor, 2018.

The Guardian. "Why US Women Are Deleting Their Period Tracking Apps." 28 June 2022.

Guy, Jack. "Mother and Grandmother to the Same Baby: Spanish Actress Sparks Surrogacy Debate." CNN, 6 April 2023.

Hague Conference on Private International Law. *Convention of 29 May 1993 on Protection of Children and Co-operation in Respect of Intercountry Adoption*. HCCH, 1993. https://www.hcch.net/en/instruments/conventions/specialised-sections/intercountry-adoption.

Hanigsberg, Julia. "Homologizing Pregnancy and Motherhood: A Consideration of Abortion." *Michigan Law Review* 94, no. 2 (1995): 371–418.

Haraway, Donna J. "A Cyborg Manifesto." In *Manifestly Haraway*. University of Minnesota Press, 2016.

Harvey, David. *A Brief History of Neoliberalism*. Oxford University Press, 2007.

Hays, Sharon. *The Cultural Contradictions of Motherhood*. Yale University Press, 1996.

Hill Collins, Patricia. "Shifting the Center: Race, Class, and Feminist Theorizing About Motherhood." In *Mothering: Ideology, Experience, and Agency*, edited by Evelyn Nakano Glenn, Grace Chang, and Linda Rennie. Routledge, 1994.

Hudson, Nicky, Lorraine Culley, Frances Rapport, Mark Johnson, and Aditya Bharadwaj. "'Public' Perceptions of Gamete Donation: A Research Review." *Public Understanding of Science* 18 (2009): 61–77.

Hurd Clarke, Laura, Anne Martin-Matthews, and Ralph Matthews. "The Continuity and Discontinuity of the Embodied Self in Infertility." *Canadian Review of Sociology / Revue Canadienne de Sociologie* 43, no. 1 (2006): 95–113.

ILGA Europe. "Update: The Rights of Rainbow Families in the EU." 28 July 2022. https://www.ilga-europe.org/blog/update-the-rights-of-rainbow-families-in-the-eu/.

Imaz, Elixabete. *Convertirse en madre: Etnografía del tiempo de gestación*. Cátedra, 2010.

Instituto Nacional de Estadística. "Encuesta de condiciones de trabajo 2015." https://www.ine.es/jaxiT3/Datos.htm?t=26060. Page no longer extant.

Instituto Nacional de Estadística. "Encuesta de fecundidad: Año 2018." 9 April 2019. https://www.ine.es/dyngs/INEbase/es/operacion.htm?c=Estadistica_C&cid=1254736177006&menu=ultiDatos&idp=1254735573002.

Instituto Nacional de Estadística. "Estadística del padrón continuo." Accessed 11 December 2019. https://www.ine.es/jaxiT3/Datos.htm?t=1380.

Instituto Nacional de Estadística. "Movimiento natural de la población / indicadores demográficos básicos / tablas de mortalidad: Año 2022." 22 November 2023. https://ine.es/prensa/mnp_2022.pdf.

Instituto Nacional de Estadística. "Movimiento natural de la población (nacimientos, defunciones y matrimonios): Indicadores demográficos básicos año 2015; Datos provisionales." 2016. https://www.ine.es/.

International Federation of Obstetrics and Gynecology. "FIGO: The Global Voice for Women's Health." Accessed 5 June 2020. https://www.figo.org/.

Intrado: Globe Newswire. "Insights into the Fertility Clinics & Infertility Services Industry in the US to 2025." 22 May 2020. https://www.globenewswire.com/news-release/2020/05/22/2037520/0/en/Insights-into-the-Fertility-Clinics-Infertility-Services-Industry-in-the-US-to-2025-Featuring-Allan-Guttmacher-Institute-California-Cryobank-Cryos-International-Among-Others.html.

Jefatura del Estado. "Ley 35/2007." *BOE*, no. 275 (2007): 46987–46991.

Jensen, Robin E. *Infertility: Tracing the History of a Transformative Term*. Pennsylvania State University Press, 2016.

Jiménez, Andrea. "Julia Menú, la 'tiktoker' más seguida de España y que ha logrado quedarse embarazada tras 14 años: 'Compartir todo es lo mejor que he hecho.'" 20 February 2023. https://elpais.com/mamas-papas/actualidad/2023-02-20/. Page no longer extant.

Khabibullina, Lilia. "International Adoption in Russia: 'Market,' 'Children for Organs,' and 'Precious' or 'Bad' Genes." In *International Adoption: Global Inequalities and the Circulation of Children*, edited by Diane Marre and Laura Briggs. NYU Press, 2009. https://doi.org/10.18574/nyu/9780814791011.003.0010.

Kohler, Hans-Peter, Francesco C. Billari, and José Antonio Ortega. "The Emergence of Lowest-Low Fertility in Europe in the 1990s." *Population and Development Review* 28, no. 4 (2002): 641–680.

Kroløkke, Charlotte. "Eggs and Euros: A Feminist Perspective on Reproductive Travel from Denmark to Spain." *IJFAB: International Journal of Feminist Approaches to Bioethics* 7, no. 2 (2014): 144–163.

Kroløkke, Charlotte. "The Golden Egg: The Business of Making Mothers Through Egg Donation." In *The Motherhood Business: Consumption, Communication, and Privilege*, edited by Anne Teresa Demo, Jennifer L. Borda, and Charlotte Kroløkke. University of Alabama Press, 2015.

Lafuente Funes, Sara. *Mercados reproductivos: Crisis, deseo y desigualdad*. Katakrak, 2021.

Larrea, María. *Los de Bilbao nacen donde quieren*. Alianza, 2023.

Laurafreixas.com. "Biografía." Accessed 23 November 2019. https://www.laurafreixas.com/freixasbio.htm.

LDcultura. "Entrevista a Raquel Sánchez Silva por 'Tengo los óvulos contados.'" YouTube, 11 February 2016. https://youtu.be/8JkniynrB6g.

Legazpe, Nuria, and María A. Davia. "Women's Employment and Childcare Choices in Spain Through the Great Recession." *Feminist Economics* 25, no. 2 (2019): 173–198.

Leinaweaver, Jessaca B. *Adoptive Migration: Raising Latinos in Spain*. Duke University Press, 2013. https://doi.org/10.1515/9780822377511.

Leinaweaver, Jessaca B., Diana Marre, and Susan Frekko. "Homework and Transnational Adoption Screening in Spain: The Coproduction of Home and Family." *Journal of the Royal Anthropological Institute* 23 (2017): 562–579.

Letherby, Gayle. "Challenging Dominant Discourses: Identity and Change and the Experience of 'Infertility' and 'Involuntary Childlessness.'" *Journal of Gender Studies* 11, no. 3 (2002): 277–288.

Leve, Michelle. "Reproductive Bodies and Bits: Exploring Dilemmas of Egg Donation Under Neoliberalism." *Studies in Gender and Sexuality* 14 (2013): 277–288.

Ley, Marta. "España, tercer país del mundo que más adopta." *El Mundo*, 22 January 2015. https://www.elmundo.es/blogs/elmundo/mas-datos/2015/01/22/espana-tercer-pais-del-mundo-que-mas.html.

Lima, Natacha Salomé, Consuelo Álvarez Plaza, and Carla Cubillos Vega. "Donantes de ovocitos: Análisis comparativo de dos muestras de Argentina y España sobre perfil de donantes, motivaciones y anonimato." *Política y sociedad* 56, no. 3 (2019): 603–622.

Link, Bruce G., and Jo C. Phelan. "Conceptualizing Stigma." *Annual Review of Sociology* 27 (2001): 363–385.

Livas, Paolo. "Ficciones de la no-maternidad." NoAutomático, 8 May 2017. http://noautomatico.blogspot.com/2017/05/ficciones-de-la-no-maternidad-paola.html.

Lloyd, Genevieve. "The Self as Fiction: Philosophy and Autobiography." *Philosophy and Literature* 10, no. 2 (1986): 168–185.

López, Celeste. "No quería ser maruja de lujo . . . pero lo fui." *Mujeres en Red: El periódico feminista*, June 2019. https://www.mujeresenred.net/spip.php?article2350.

López Trujillo, Noemí. *El vientre vacío*. Capitán Swing, 2019.

López Trujillo, Noemí. "Has apurado mi cuerpo hasta el último día." Instagram, 11 August 2024. https://www.instagram.com/p/C-iooSIKHUO/.

López Trujillo, Noemí. "Hay algo aquí dentro creciendo que se siente como la supernova Casiopea A." Instagram, 29 January 2024. https://www.instagram.com/p/C2r_OOyqdkY/.

López Varela, Diana. *Maternofobia: Retrato de una generación enfrentada a la maternidad.* Ediciones Península, 2019.

López Varela, Diana. *No es país para coños.* Ediciones Península, 2016.

López Varela, Diana. "Sobre mí." Accessed 4 May 2020. https://dianalopezvarela.com/bio. Page no longer extant.

López Varela, Diana. "Suspenso en religión." *Galiciaé, o Diario galego*, 2016. https://www.galiciae.com/blog/author/diana-lopez-varela.

MacNamara, Trent. "Liberal Societies Have Dangerously Low Birth Rates." *The Atlantic*, March 2019.

Mamo, Laura. "Fertility, Inc.: Consumption and Subjectification in U.S. Lesbian Reproductive Practices." In *Biomedicalization: Technoscience, Health, and Illness in the U.S.*, edited by A. E. Clarke, L. Mamo, J. R. Fosket, J. R. Fishman, and J. K. Shim, 82–98. Duke University Press, 2010.

Marcos, Jairo. *Rasgados: Un viaje a la adopción internacional España-China.* Noufront, 2010.

Marre, Diana. "Los silencios de la adopción en España." *Revista de Antropología Social* 18 (2009): 97–126.

Marre, Diana, Beatriz San Román, and Diana Guerra. "On Reproductive Work in Spain: Transnational Adoption, Egg Donation, Surrogacy." *Medical Anthropology* 37, no. 2 (2018): 158–173.

Martin, Emily. "Medical Metaphors of Women's Bodies: Menstruation and Menopause." In *Writing on the Body: Female Embodiment and Feminist Theory*, edited by Katie Conboy, Nadia Medina, and Sarah Stanbury. Columbia University Press, 1997.

Martín Arroyo, Javier. "Hasta tres años de espera para poder ser madre." *El País*, 13 May 2019. https://elpais.com/sociedad/2019/05/12/actualidad/1557676986_761783.html.

Martín Gaite, Carmen. *Los usos amorosos de la postguerra española.* 5th ed. Anagrama, 1998.

Mascarenhas, Maya, Seth Flaxman, Ties Boerma, Sheryl Vanderpoel, and Gretchen Stevens. "National, Regional, and Global Trends in Infertility Prevalence Since 1990: A Systematic Analysis of 277 Health Surveys." *PLoS Med* 9, no. 12 (2012).

Masson, Judith. "Intercountry Adoption: A Global Problem or a Global Solution?" *Journal of International Affairs* 55, no. 1 (2001): 141–166. http://www.jstor.org/stable/24357675.

McLean, Renwick. "Spain Gives Approval to Gay Unions." *New York Times*, 1 July 2005. https://www.nytimes.com/2005/07/01/world/europe/spain-gives-approval-to-gay-unions.html.

Merino Murga, Patricia. "La maternidad como cuidado: Guía hacia un futuro sostenible." *Viento sur* 156 (February 2018): 69–77.

Merino Murga, Patricia. *Maternidad, igualdad y fraternidad: Las madres como sujeto político en las sociedades poslaborales.* Clave Intelectual, 2017.

Meruane, Lina. *Contra los hijos.* Penguin, 2014.

Mezmur, Benyam D. "From Angelina (to Madonna) to Zoe's Ark: What Are the 'A–Z' Lessons for Intercountry Adoptions in Africa?" *International Journal of Law, Policy and the Family* 23, no. 2 (2009): 145–173. https://doi.org/10.1093/lawfam/ebn013.

Miall, Charlene E. "The Stigma of Involuntary Childlessness." *Social Problems* 33, no. 4 (1986): 268–282.

Michie, Helena, and Naomi R. Cahn. *Confinements: Fertility and Infertility in Contemporary Culture.* Rutgers University Press, 1997.

Miró, Asha. *La hija del Ganges.* Lumen, 2003.

Morcillo, Aurora G. *The Seduction of Modern Spain: The Female Body and the Francoist Body Politic.* Bucknell University Press, 2010.

Moreno Rosset, Carmen. *Infertilidad.* Síntesis, 2010.

Moss, Candida R., and Joel S. Baden. *Reconceiving Infertility: Biblical Perspectives on Procreation and Childlessness.* Princeton University Press, 2015.

Myers, Kit. "If I'm Going to Do It, I'm Going to Do It Right." *Gender and Society* 31, no. 6 (2017): 777–803.

Nahman, Michal. "Nodes of Desire: Romanian Egg Sellers, 'Dignity' and Feminist Alliances in Transnational Ova Exchanges." *European Journal of Women's Studies* 15, no. 2 (2008): 65–82.

Nanclares, Silvia. "La infertilidad es una patología social a la que ha contribuido el Estado." *Pikara Online Magazine*, 29 March 2017.

Nanclares, Silvia. *Quién quiere ser madre*. Alfaguara, 2017.

Nanclares, Silvia. "¿Soy una mala feminista si acepto la ovodonación? Claroscuros de una maternidad bajo el capitalismo reproductivo." *El Diario*, 17 July 2019. https://www.eldiario.es/nidos/claroscuros-maternidad-feminista-ovodonacion_1_1433839.html.

Nash, Mary. "Pronatalism and Motherhood in Franco's Spain." In *Maternity and Gender Policies: Women and the Rise of the European Welfare States, 1880s–1950s*, edited by Gisela Bock and Pat Thane, 160–177. Routledge, 1991.

Ofer, Inbal. "Historical Models—Contemporary Identities: The Sección Femenina of the Spanish Falange and Its Redefinition of the Term 'Femininity.'" *Journal of Contemporary History* 40, no. 4 (2005): 663–674.

Oliver, Diana. *Maternidades precarias*. Arpa, 2022.

Oliver, Kelly. "Motherhood, Sexuality, and Pregnant Embodiment: Twenty-Five Years of Gestation." *Hypatia* 25, no. 4 (2010): 760–777.

Ondacero. "El gobierno aprueba la Ley de familias." 27 February 2024. https://www.ondacero.es/noticias/sociedad/ley-familias-vuelve-consejo-ministros_2024022765dd9d264129260001dbafid.html.

Organización Nacional de Trasplantes. *Actividad de donación y trasplante España 2019*. Organización Nacional de Trasplantes, 2019.

Pennings, Guido. "Central Role of Altruism in the Recruitment of Gamete Donors." *Monash Bioethics Review* 33 (2015): 78–88.

Pennings, Guido, J. de Mouzon, F. Shenfield, A. P. Ferraretti, T. Mardesic, A. Ruiz, and V. Goossens. "Socio-Demographic and Fertility-Related Characteristics and Motivations of Oocyte Donors in Eleven European Countries." *Human Reproduction* 29, no. 5 (2014): 1076–1089.

Pérez-Lanzac, Carmen. "Demasiado tarde para ser madre." *El País*, 8 February 2016. https://elpais.com/politica/2016/01/27/actualidad/1453904610_786378.html.

Pérez Millán, Federico. "La reproducción asistida en el medio sanitario público." In *Libro blanco sociosanitario: La infertilidad en España; Situación actual y perspectivas*, edited by Roberto Matorras Weinig. Imago Concept & Image Development, 2011.

Petchesky, Rosalind. *Abortion and Woman's Choice: The State, Sexuality and Reproductive Freedom*. Northeastern University Press, 1990.

"Petra maternidades feministas." Accessed 28 May 2025. https://petramaternidadesfeministas.org/.

Planetadelibros. "Raquel Sánchez-Silva." Accessed 20 December 2024. https://www.planetadelibros.com/autor/raquel-sanchez-silva/000036784.

Ramírez, Carlota E. "Diana López Varela: 'Se creen que violar no es para tanto mientras no la maten.'" *Huffington Post*, 15 October 2016. https://www.huffingtonpost.es/2016/10/06/entrevista-a-diana_n_12376178.html.

Ramírez, Verónica, and Inma Escobar. "Estos son los requisitos para acceder a la reproducción asistida en la sanidad pública." *La Sexta*, 2 January 2019. https://www.lasexta.com/noticias/economia/consumo/estos-son-requisitos-acceder-reproduccion-asistida-sanidad-publica_201901235c5410200cf2be7ee4853696.html.

Raymond, Janice G. *Women as Wombs: Reproductive Technologies and the Battle over Women's Freedom*. Harper, 1993.

Renegar, Valerie R., and Kirsti K. Cole. "Evil Is Part of the Territory: Inventing the Stepmother in Self-Help Books." *Women's Studies in Communication* 42, no. 4 (2019): 511–533.

Renegar, Valerie R., and Kirsti K. Cole, eds. *Refiguring Motherhood Beyond Biology*. Routledge, 2023. https://library.oapen.org/handle/20.500.12657/61732.

Reyes Ferrer, María. "Spain and Structural Infertility: Towards an Integrative Vision of Motherhood in the Novel *Quién quiere ser madre* by Silvia Nanclares." In *The Palgrave Handbook of Reproductive Justice and Literature*, edited by B. W. Capo and L. Lazzari, 381–399. Palgrave Macmillan, 2022.

Riera, Carme. *Tiempo de espera*. Lumen, 1996.

Rivas, Ana María, Fernando Lores, and María Isabel Jociles. "El anonimato y el altruismo en la donación de gametos: La producción de biocapital en la industria reproductiva." *Política y sociedad* 56, no. 3 (2019): 623–644.

Rivera, Priscila. "¿Por qué algunas mujeres donan sus óvulos? Altruismo, sacrificio y trabajo reproductivo." *Afin* 127 (May 2021): 1–16.

Rodríguez, Jesús. "Un país sin hijos: Radiografía de la baja natalidad en España." *El País*, 16 April 2022. https://elpais.com/eps/2022-04-17/un-pais-sin-hijos-radiografia-de-la-baja-natalidad-de-espana.html.

Ross, Loretta, and Rickie Solinger. *Reproductive Justice: An Introduction*. University of California Press, 2017.

Royo, Sebastián. "The Causes and Legacy of the Great Recession in Spain." In *The Oxford Handbook of Spanish Politics*, edited by Diego Muro and Ignacio Lago. Oxford Handbooks, 2020. https://doi.org/10.1093/oxfordhb/9780198826934.013.8.

RTVE. "Binario: Capítulo 2, 'Nacidos bajo la boina.'" 7 June 2018. https://www.rtve.es/playz/binario/semen-capitulo-2/.

RTVE. "Lazos de sangre." 3 August 2022. https://www.rtve.es/television/20220803/rocio-jurado-hijos-rocio-carrasco-gloria-camila-jose-fernando-abortos-depresion/2393445.shtml.

Sailer, Gudrun. "Women at Vatican II: Surprising Women, a Surprising Council!" *Vatican News*, 18 June 2019. https://www.vaticannews.va/en/vatican-city/news/2019-06/second-vatican-council-women-regina-heyder.html.

Salazar, Mireia. "Silvia Nanclares: 'El deseo de ser madre es algo cambiante.'" Ayuntamiento de Rivas Vaciamadrid, 17 June 2020. https://www.rivasciudad.es/noticias/feminismos-mujeres-lgtbi/2020/06/17/silvia-nanclares-el-deseo-de-ser-madre-es-algo-cambiante/862600139653/.

Sánchez Silva, Raquel. *Tengo los óvulos contados*. Planeta, 2017.

Sandelowski, Margarete J. "Failures of Volition: Female Agency and Infertility in Historical Perspective." *Signs* 15, no. 3 (1990): 475–499. https://www.jstor.org/stable/3174424.

Sandelowski, Margarete J. *With Child in Mind: Studies of the Personal Encounter with Infertility*. Studies in Health, Illness, and Caregiving. University of Pennsylvania Press, 2016. https://doi.org/10.9783/9781512806779.

San Román, Beatriz. "Waiting Too Long to Mother: Involuntary Childlessness and Assisted Reproduction in Contemporary Spain." In *Waithood: Gender, Education, and Global Delays in Marriage and Childbearing*, edited by Marcia C. Inhorn and Nancy J. Smith-Hefner, 339–361. Berghahn, 2021. https://doi.org/10.1515/9781789209006-017.

San Román, Beatriz, and Karen Rotabi. "Rescue, Red Tape, Child Abduction, Illicit Adoptions, and Discourse: Intercountry Adoption Attitudes in Spain." *International Social Work* 62, no. 1 (2019): 198–211.

Sawin, Patricia. "Listening to Stories, Negotiating Responsibility: Exploring the Ethics of International Adoption Through Narrative Analysis." In *Unsettling Assumptions: Tradition, Gender, Drag*, edited by Pauline Greenhill, 172–190. Utah State University Press, 2014.

Selman, Peter. "The Global Decline of Intercountry Adoption: What Lies Ahead?" *Social Policy and Society* 11, no. 3 (2012): 381–397.

Selman, Peter. "Intercountry Adoption in the New Millennium: The 'Quiet Migration' Revisited." *Population Research and Policy Review* 21, no. 3 (2002): 205–225. https://www.jstor.org/stable/40230785.

Selman, Peter. "Intercountry Adoption of Children from Asia in the Twenty-First Century." *Children's Geographies* 13, no. 3 (2015): 312–327.

Silva, Susana, and Helena Machado. "Trust, Morality and Altruism in the Donation of Biological Material: The Case of Portugal." *New Genetics and Society* 28, no. 2 (June 2009): 103–118.

Slaughter, Anne-Marie. "Why Women Still Can't Have It All." *The Atlantic*, July 2012.

Smith Rotabi, Karen, and Nicole F. Bromfield. *From Intercountry Adoption to Global Surrogacy: A Human Rights History and New Fertility Frontiers.* Routledge, Taylor & Francis Group, 2017.

Sociedad Española de Fertilidad. *Informe estadístico de técnicas de reproducción asistida 2015.* Registro Nacional de Actividad 2015—Registro SEF, 2015. https://www.registrosef.com/public/docs/sef2015_IAFIVm.pdf.

Somavilla, Ana. "Los últimos de la fe: Así ha perdido España un millón de jóvenes católicos en 20 años." *El Confidencial*, 10 September 2023. https://www.elconfidencial.com/espana/2023-09-10/ultimos-fe-asi-perdido-espana-millon-jovenes-catolicos-20-anos_3731573/.

Sormunen, Taina, Arthur Aanesen, Bjöörn Fossum, Klas Karlgren, and Margareta Westerbotn. "Infertility-Related Communication and Coping Strategies Among Women Affected by Primary or Secondary Infertility." *Journal of Clinical Nursing* 27 (2018): 335–344. https://doi-org.southwesternu.idm.oclc.org/10.1111/jocn.13953.

Sosa Troya, María, and Noor Mahtani. "La España de la maternidad tardía." *El País*, 14 December 2019. https://www.elpais.com.

Statista. "Total Fertility Rate in Europe in 2022, by Country." Accessed 28 September 2022. https://www.statista.com/statistics/612074/fertility-rates-in-european-countries/.

Statistical Institute of Catalonia. "Live Births Outside Marriage." GenCat. Accessed 2 December 2024. https://www.idescat.cat/indicadors/?id=ue&n=10088&lang=en.

Sternke, Elizabeth A., and Kathleen Abrahamson. "Perceptions of Women with Infertility on Stigma and Disability." *Sexuality and Disability* 33 (2015): 3–17.

Surrogacy 365. "Why 50% of European Egg Donation Happens in Spain?" 6 August 2018. https://www.surrogacy365.com/why-50-of-european-egg-donation-happens-in-spain/.

Sussman, Anna Louie. "The End of Babies." *New York Times*, 16 November 2019.

Swan, Shanna, and Stacey Colino. *Count Down: How Our Modern World Is Threatening Sperm Counts, Altering Male and Female Reproductive Development, and Imperiling the Future of the Human Race.* Scribner, 2020.

Sylvest, Randi, Anders Nyboe Andersen, Lone Schmidt, Anna-Karina Ahlbom Ulrich, Tine Brink Henriksen, Bjørn A. Kjaer, and Marianne Skovsager Andersen. "Low Semen Quality and Experiences of Masculinity and Family Building." *Acta Obstetrecia et Gynecologica Scandinavica* 97 (2018): 727–733.

Thompson, Charis M. "Fertile Ground: Feminists Theorize Infertility." In *Infertility Around the Globe: New Thinking About Childlessness, Gender and Reproductive Technologies*, edited by Marcia C. Inhorn and Frank Van Balen, 52–78. University of California Press, 2002.

Tubert, Silvia. "La maternidad en el discurso de las nuevas tecnologías reproductivas." In *Las mujeres y los niños primero: Discursos de la maternidad*, edited by Ángeles de la Concha and Michelle Osbourne, 111–138. Icaria, 2004.

United Nations. "Article 1: Purpose." In *Convention on the Rights of Persons with Disabilities.* United Nations Department of Economic and Social Affairs Social Inclusion, 2008. https://www.un.org/development/desa/disabilities/convention-on-the-rights-of-persons-with-disabilities/article-1-purpose.html.

University of California San Francisco. "FAQ: Common Questions for Egg Donors." USCF Health, 2023. https://www.ucsfhealth.org/en/education/faq-common-questions-for-egg-donors.

Valledelkas Editorial. "La maternidad según la autora Silvia Nanclares." *Valledelkas*, 23 March 2017.

Van Doore, Kathryn E. "Paper Orphans: Exploring Child Trafficking for the Purpose of Orphanages." *International Journal of Children's Rights* 24, no. 2 (2016): 378–407. https://doi.org/10.1163/15718182-02402006.

Varela, Nuria. *Feminismo para principiantes*. Revised ed. Ediciones B, 2019.

Vásquez, Xulio. "La adopción de una niña china cuesta 12.000 euros y si es de Rusia vale 30.000." *La voz de Galicia*, 13 May 2008. https://www.lavozdegalicia.es/noticia/vigo/2008/05/13/adopcion-nina-china-cuesta-12000-euros-rusia-vale-30000/0003_6813676.htm.

Vázquez, Elena. "Demografía y cambios culturales." In *Las representaciones de la maternidad: Debates teóricos y repercusiones sociales*, edited by C. Fernández-Montraveta, P. Monreal Requena, A. Moreno Hernández, and P. Soto Rodríguez, 87–94. Instituto Universitario de Estudios de la Mujer, 2000.

Veevers, J. E. "Voluntary Childlessness: A Review of Issues and Evidence." *Marriage and Family Review* 2, no. 2 (1979): 1–26.

Vilarós, Teresa. *El mono del desencanto: Una crítica cultural de la transición española (1973–1993)*. Siglo XXI, 2018.

Villar, Samanta. *La carga mental femenina: O por qué las mujeres continúan al mando del hogar a coste cero*. Planeta, 2019.

Villar, Samanta. *Madre hay más que una: Un relato en primera persona sobre la aventura de la maternidad*. Planeta, 2018.

Vivas, Esther. *Mamá desobediente: Una mirada feminista a la maternidad*. Capitán Swing, 2019.

Weingarten, Karen. "Impossible Decisions: Abortion, Reproductive Technologies, and the Rhetoric of Choice." *Women's Studies* 41 (2012): 263–281.

Whiteford, Linda M., and Lois Gonzalez. "Stigma: The Hidden Burden of Infertility." *Social Science and Medicine* 40, no. 1 (1995): 27–36.

Wiener, Gabriela. "Adiós, Ovocito, adiós." In *Sexografías*, 159–166. Melusina, 2008.

Williams, Joan. "Gender Wars: Selfless Women in the Republic of Choice." *New York University Law Review* 66 (1991): 1559–1634.

Williams, Simon J., and Gillian Bendelow. *The Lived Body: Sociological Themes, Embodied Issues*. Routledge, 1998.

World Health Organization. "Infertility." Accessed 16 June 2025. https://www.who.int/health-topics/infertility#tab=tab_1.

World Health Organization. "Infertility Is a Global Public Health Issue." *Human Reproduction Programme*. Accessed 20 December 2024. https://www.who.int/reproductivehealth/topics/infertility/perspective/en/. Page no longer extant.

World Health Organization. *Preamble to the Constitution of the World Health Organization*. WHO, 1946.

World Population Review. "Total Fertility Rate 2021." Accessed 20 December 2024. https://worldpopulationreview.com/country-rankings/total-fertility-rate.

YCharts. "Spain Youth Unemployment Rate." Accessed 22 November 2022. https://ycharts.com/indicators/spain_youth_unemployment_rate_lfs.

Yllán Calderón, Esperanza. *El franquismo*. Ediciones Akal, 2016.

Yook, Sung Hee, and Hosu Kim. "Decolonizing Adoption Narratives for Transnational Reproductive Justice." *CLCWeb: Comparative Literature and Culture* 20, no. 6 (2018). http://docs.lib.purdue.edu/clcweb/vol20/iss6/8.

Index

Note: Photos, Figures are indicated by italicized page references.

About the Author

CATHERINE (KATY) BOURLAND ROSS is a professor of Spanish at Southwestern University in Georgetown, Texas. Her research focuses on contemporary Spanish literature and culture, with a particular emphasis on the representation of women as mothers. She has published over twenty academic articles and book chapters in this field. Her monograph *The Changing Face of Motherhood in Spain: The Social Construction of Maternity in the Works of Lucía Etxebarria* (Bucknell University Press) examines evolving perspectives on motherhood in contemporary Spanish literature.